To all adventurous OGs

For Joshua
with best wishes
from Catherine

David Benew

Henry Haversham Godwin-Austen 1834–1923

Spirit of Adventure

'In the footsteps of Godwin-Austen'

An Anthology of Mountain and Wilderness Tales

Edited by
Catherine Moorehead
&
David Dunmur

Moyhill Publishing

First Published in 2011 by Moyhill Publishing.

A CIP catalogue record for this book is available
from the British Library.

ISBN 978-1-905597-28-4

Designed & typeset by *Moyhill* Publishing.

Printed in UK.

The papers used in this book were produced in an
environmentally friendly way from sustainable forests.

Front cover: K2, viewed along the Godwin-Austen Glacier from
near Concordia. Photo courtesy of Rupert Dix.

Moyhill Publishing,
Suite 471, 6 Slington House,
Rankine Rd., Basingstoke, RG24 8PH, UK.
Order online at *www.moyhill.com*

Contents

Contents

Introduction

This book is inspired by one of the great Victorian mountaineers, Henry Haversham Godwin-Austen (1834–1923), and by a group of adventurers who share his urge for discovery and, more prosaically, his childhood roots. Godwin-Austen was a soldier, mountaineer, explorer and scientist. We know of his exploits largely through the erudite journals of the Royal Geographical Society (RGS) and the Natural History Museum, South Kensington. Godwin-Austen was not a great communicator with the public at large: consequently he is not well-known. He led, for the most part, an isolated and very self-contained life, but achieved everlasting fame as the first explorer of the second highest mountain on Earth, K2 (formerly Mt Godwin-Austen, where the access glacier still bears his name), a peak that presents, even to the modern climber, one of the severest mountaineering challenges anywhere.

An accident of history provides another reminder of Godwin-Austen, and that is his family's enduring legacy to one of Britain's ancient schools, another RGS, the Royal Grammar School, Guildford. John Austen and his son George were generous sixteenth century benefactors of the school, and connections between the Austen family (they changed their name by Special Licence from Queen Victoria to Godwin-Austen in 1854) remain to this day. Our inspirational H H Godwin-Austen was a pupil of the RGS during the mid-1840s, before going to Sandhurst where he learnt soldiering and surveying. He progressed from Guildford schoolboy to legendary explorer and scientist through a process of self-discovery and self-testing in some of the most difficult environments on the planet. This volume records some of Godwin-Austen's exploits, and those of other Guildford 'schoolboys', in their quest for fulfilment through exploration and adventure.

The RGS Guildford has a tradition of independence and adventure which is reflected in this anthology of writing from former Guildfordians and others associated with the school. In the mould of Godwin-Austen, the contributors to this volume have followed a path of self-discovery through adventure. Unlike Godwin-Austen, however, they have an urge to tell their tales. The stories record not only the highest levels of achievement in mountaineering, but also give inspiring accounts of more modest expeditions or excursions. The resulting collection contains stirring tales from all round the World. The stories come from non-heroic climbers, mountaineers, and others seeking to challenge themselves in a variety of environments. The result is, hopefully, a book of discovery for both readers and authors.

The Editors
Catherine Moorehead was brought up near the Cairngorms. She has been an English teacher at the RGS since 2001. She shares with Godwin-Austen a passion for adventure in high and remote places. An accomplished mountaineer, she has an enviable record of ascents (first and other), mainly in very obscure corners of Central Asia, and is a Compleat (*sic*) Munroist. She also has a desire to share this passion and expertise with others, particularly through school and other expeditions, and by writing about them.

David Dunmur is a recently retired academic whose lifetime involvement with mountains began during his schooldays at the RGS. He has climbed in most areas of the British Isles, the Alps and the Pyrenees. Treks in the Himalayas have brought him close to, if not onto, the summits of the highest peaks, and, like his co-editor, mountaineering has provided a parallel life outside the constraints of career and family.

The Contributors
The articles in the *Anthology* have been invited from Guildfordians who have followed in the footsteps of Godwin-Austen. The stories have come from military men, teachers, men of business, doctors and others, united through their love of mountains and linked through a Guildford connection. For the most part they are amateurs indulging their passion amidst busy lives. Their stories are not part of a career of mountain adventures, but are vivid accounts of particular and individual exploits. Collectively, they provide a kaleidoscope of experiences illustrating personal challenges and discoveries.

Acknowledgements

David Dunmur and Catherine Moorehead would like to thank several people at the RGS: the Headmaster for permission to access the School website, Jenny Hipwell, Development Director, and Jenny Rothwell, Foundation Administrator, for their help and encouragement. Oscar Lawson, Head of ICT, has, as ever, given freely of his tireless and expert assistance in preparing the text for publication. Both Editors would like to thank the late Michael Hetherington's sister, Mrs Mary MacLachlan, and his niece, Libby Mornement, for their kind assistance and loan of material relevant to the article on the modern retracing of Hannibal's route over the Alps. The Editors would like to thank Cicerone Press and Bart Jordans for permission to reproduce our modified version of their map (p.117), the original of which is in Cicerone's excellent *Trekking in Bhutan.* We would also like to thank David Cronin of Moyhill Publishing for his enthusiastic involvement with the project, and for his expert advice and guidance during the production of this volume. Above all, the Editors would like to thank the contributors whose enthusiasm and commitment has kept the project going through so many months, and immense thanks of course are due to our investors, without whom this book would never have come to press.

Catherine Moorehead would very much like to thank Robin and Kate, Richard and Sally and Jonathan and Mary Godwin-Austen for their generous hospitality and their most helpful access to Haversham Godwin-Austen's invaluable private papers. She would also like to thank Jerry Lovatt, Honorary Librarian and former Vice-President of the Alpine Club and Peter Mallalieu[1], Keeper of Pictures at the Alpine Club, for their advice and support, as well as Simon Watson and Pamela MacGregor, for their encouragement and critical acumen.

David Dunmur is indebted to his son Alan Dunmur, Mark Briggs and Jerry Lloyd for their leadership and skill on a memorable mountain adventure *(Rescue on the Ben)*, and additionally to Jerry for permission to use his photographs.

---

1. Not least in the excellent new edition of *The Artists of the Alpine Club* by Peter Mallalieu. Published jointly by the Alpine Club and the Ernest Press, 2007 and 2009. Copies obtainable from the Alpine Club, 55 Charlotte Road, LONDON EC2A 3QF.

Gareth Stewart would like to thank his brother, Alex, on whose original quite a lot of the article on the ascent of Mount Vinson is based.

James Slater is keen that the role played by his former RGS teachers, Justin Usher, Gavin Kerr and Steve Yetman, is given due recognition. This sentiment is echoed by Keith Browning: he would like to record his appreciation of the Scout leaders who gave so much of their time outside school hours while he was at the RGS and stimulated his interest in the hills.

David Benest would like to mention his appreciation of mountaineer, mountain rescuer and navigator extraordinary, Peter Cliff. As a UIAGM ski-instructor, it was Peter who gave David his initial interest in ski-mountaineering which led eventually to David's article on the *Haute Route*.

Miriam Manook would very much like to commemorate the memory of the popular Norfolk priest, industrial chaplain, politician and climate campaigner, the Rev Canon Hereward Cooke, who died in his sleep on December 15, 2009, while in Copenhagen (having cycled there!) for the United Nations Climate Change Conference. He took a tireless interest in trying to unravel the mystery of the bones and artefacts discovered at Musk Ox Col, high in Kazakhstan, in 1998.

Bruno Marques enjoyed the 2008 RGS OGs' Bhutan Expedition, which is where the *Anthology* project took root, so much that he wants to say thank you to Chambula Dorji in Bhutan and mountaineering legend Dr Barney Rosedale for making it happen in such an enjoyable way.

PIONEERS PAST AND PRESENT

Pioneers Past and Present:
Introduction

The Royal Grammar School Guildford is one of those schools which seems to produce a lot of mountaineers and adventurers. The spirit of adventure has largely been created and nurtured there by various school clubs and institutions such as the Scouts, the RumDoodle Society and the CCF. (In the case of Haversham Godwin-Austen and Algernon Durand, their 'adventure training' was completed at Sandhurst, and thereby makes a notable connection with the vigorous and diverse role played by the modern CCF.)

The organisations mentioned above have given the creative exploratory impetus to any number of individuals and their friends who, thereafter, have made their ways to the highest and wildest parts of our planet – or indeed of the United Kingdom. It does, for example, take someone with a pretty remarkable training, willpower and imagination, like Haversham Godwin-Austen, very soon after mountaineering began as a recognised sport in the mid-nineteenth century, to become the first explorer of the innermost recesses of the Karakoram, several years before the Matterhorn was climbed. Or to become, like Algernon Durand, the first British agent to encounter, then subdue, the fierce tribal societies in the most distant fastnesses of the North-West Frontier. And as the article on the 'adventure' revival after the school went private in 1977 makes clear, the opportunities provided since that date, indeed from a little time before it, have led to OGs testing their mettle in Antarctica, the highest Himalayas, the Andes, the very depths of Central Asia and any number of other distant and difficult places.

This section on the Pioneers, then, describes the kind of taste for adventure created by two exemplary Victorians and shows how the institutional links which gave them the training and the courage to venture so far from 'leafy Surrey' were taken up again in the modern period with such lively effect.

In the case of Godwin-Austen, a good part of the material has come from obscure corners of the archives of the Royal Geographical Society, the Natural History Museum and the British Library, but the bulk of it derives from his own letters and memoirs and other pieces of family memorabilia still in private hands: they form the basis of a forthcoming biography of the man who was effectively K2's discoverer.

Durand's story has by and large been synthesised from his own words in his account of the amazing Hunza Campaign (which he masterminded), now on the internet in its entirety, and from the enthralling account by *The Times'* correspondent, E F Knight, in *Where Three Empires Meet*, as well as some ancillary sources relating to the military history of that period and the travels of Sir Francis Younghusband described in Patrick French's admirable biography.

With this belief in letting people speak for themselves, the history of the Modern period has been compiled from interviews with these longstanding RGS human institutions, known as sources of inspiration to many of the contributors and doubtless to many others: Dick Seymour and Dai Cowx, with Steve Yetman, who arrived at the RGS in 2001, not far behind.

It is appropriate enough that the idea for this *Anthology* arose during the OGs' expedition to Bhutan in 2008. Conversations high in the Bhutanese hills revealed that a link could be made between the extraordinary adventurousness and courage of these Victorian pioneers and the spectacular character and variety of innovative expeditions carried out in the post-1977 period. While the Pioneers in this section largely tell a story created from a careful selection of their own words, in the five sections thereafter, the contributors describe their adventures directly: danger, daring, quirkiness, resoluteness, humour and perhaps best of all, a curiosity to see what new places and people are like, are all there. Combined, they provide a fitting continuity to the process begun by Godwin-Austen and Durand and make a memorable testimony to the school where the ideas and the qualities of character needed to carry them out were formed.

The Adventurous Spirit of Haversham Godwin-Austen

by Catherine Moorehead

It is August 1861, and a freezing night high in the Karakoram, on the mighty Baltoro Glacier. A lone European, with sixty-six 'coolies' to help him, is the first adventurer to follow one of the greatest rivers of ice on the planet. Such is its size, however, that they cannot readily reach the lateral moraines for an earthy (if bouldery) sleeping-place.

This icy wilderness has marked the European surveyor's imagination deeply,

> *...I struck diagonally across the glacier towards the left bank, through as extraordinary a scene as the imagination could picture; it was the desolation of desolation.*

Isolated, at a height of about 5000m, he and his companions are obliged to sleep out on the ice,

> *This night on the glacier was dreaded by us all; for in the evening the wind from the east sprung up again, and the cold became intense. The ice was much exposed...At sunset, every puddle and lake in the glacier began to film over with ice, which in the morning was more than an inch in thickness. The wind blew all night, getting stronger towards morning; and I pitied the poor coolies with only the rough, sharp stones to lie on, and separate them from the ice. The Balti, who carry only one rug, huddled together two or three under the same covering. Mahomed told me next morning that he heard them saying, 'Would that the Sahib felt it as cold as this! He would soon go back!' Few, if any, got any sleep; and all were right glad when the sun rose over the peaks ahead.*

> *Following up the ridge* (the spur of Masherbrum), *another 1000 feet of elevation was gained, when a distant bit of rock and snow could be seen just peering above the nearer snow-line. After another sharp push up to a point where it was impossible to mount further, there no longer remained a doubt about it. There, with not a particle of cloud to hide it, stood the great Peak K2, on the watershed of Asia!*

There is a near-Biblical quality to the awestruck nature of his description. His artist's eye, for this is no ordinary adventurer, takes in the scene,

> *Peak K2, the highest on this side...appeared of an airy blue tint, surrounded by the yellower peak, K1 (Masherbrum), K3, and others, all over 24,000ft in height. Other minor peaks, by hundreds, thrust up their heads – some snow-capped, some rounded, some bare and angular, running up as sharp as needles.*

But even this remarkable first serious explorer of the Karakoram, the greatest mountain range on Earth, found the going hard at times. He tells us that it was,

> *immense work – that of weeks, months, and years...; the altitudes climbed, the long, wearing descents...the days and nights spent taking observations from the many hundreds of trigonometrical stations....; and the large number of men who share in the work, from the officers in charge to the native signalers.*

On many occasions, he refers to various kinds of physically painful progress,

> *The most western peak of all, being a slaty rock, was very difficult and dangerous of ascent, on account of the loose stones which keep constantly falling; the weight of the foot often causing whole yards of surface to give way at a time.*

One does not have to go further than Snowdonia to recognise such difficulties. And there were others...

... Indeed, as anyone who has adventured through mountain areas will know, water, as much as rock, provides a great source of danger, particularly during river crossings. Our hero ran into trouble when crossing the Indus,

> *The men expected that we should reach the opposite bank near a large rock; but though they exerted themselves to the utmost, we soon saw that this was quite impossible, and we were swept past it some 50 yards distant, and went down the river at a mad pace, causing that curious feeling of excitement which a sense of some coming danger always produces; nor were we long kept in suspense. The raft-men behaved with great coolness, and steered safely close to the edge of a bank of boulders...we passed also some ugly waves beneath the cliff on the other side....Nothing could be seen ahead but curling waves and foam, with great black rocks here and there: into*

the midst of this our raft glided. Mahomed and the manjis[1] repeated the Kulmah or Mahomedan Creed in a rapid whisper, as we were carried over the crests and down again into the troughs between the curling waves. At one time I did not expect that we should come out of them; for whilst in the trough a great wave broke right over our frail craft, and completely buried us....For a moment we came to the surface, the manji shouted, "Ya, Ali, hold tight!"...When at last we came out upon the smooth water below, and looked back up the rapid we had just come down, every one breathed freely again, and the "Thank God" of each was never more sincerely uttered.

Reflecting under his blanket on top of hundreds of feet of ice, Godwin-Austen recalled the earlier dangers he had experienced on the glaciers. This can hardly be surprising since, as the sole European in one of the greatest mountain amphitheatres anywhere, he must have had a remarkable mental capacity indeed to be able to cope with it all. The physical dangers, however, came mainly from crevasses, for example on the Chiring Glacier on the way up to the Mustagh Pass. On his Second Baltistan Expedition, in 1861, he failed, in terrible weather, by 500 feet and a few hundred horizontal metres to cross it,

For the first three miles the crevasses were broad and deep in places only, and we could avoid them by making detours. They soon became more numerous, and were ugly things to look into, much more so to cross – going down into darkness between walls garnished with magnificent green icicles from 6 to 20 feet long, and of proportionate thickness, looking like rows of great teeth ready to devour one.

Thinking a little further back, when making his way towards the Mustagh with a view to opening up a new trade – and military? – route to Central Asia, Godwin-Austen experienced another nasty moment,

Whilst lying in my tent, after finishing up my work, I heard an unusual rumbling sound, and on going out I found all the men were wondering what it could be. After a few more seconds of suspense, some Balti coolies, who were cutting brushwood higher up the ravine, shouted out that the stream was coming down, and in a few seconds more we saw a black mass coming out of a lateral ravine from the right, and moving rapidly over the broad slope

---

1. Manji, or (Anglicised) Munshi: a native Indian secretary and, here, probably, an interpreter.

of boulders which formed the bed of the valley. Before the black stream reached us, it divided into two, and we saw that it consisted of a mass of stones and thick mud, about 30 yards in breadth, and about 15 feet deep. The servants by the side of the little rill near the tents had just time to escape before it came down upon their fires. It was a most wonderful sight: a great moving mass of stones and rock, some of great size, measuring 10 feet by 6, all traveling along together like peas shot out of a bag, rumbling and tumbling, one over the other, and causing the ground to shake....I was almost bewildered by the spectacle.

Sometimes, of course, it was just simply the weather which made life hard for him. On the Eden Mission, a clumsy political attempt to take Bhutan under the Imperial wing in February 1864, he got caught out on high ground,

Captain Godwin-Austen remained behind (the main party) with his small Survey party, and bivouacked under a rock for three days and nights on the Tegong La, at 12,200 feet, in the hope of getting a clear day for observation from so elevated a point. Unfortunately he and his party were driven from their shelter by a tremendous snow storm which caused the loss of two lives and nearly all the baggage.

During cold spells, though, Godwin-Austen's devotion to his surveying became all the more committed,

...the plane-table was set up, and as much as could be seen cut in at once. I got into a snug corner out of the wind, and then the day was spent in sundry rushes to the plane-table, whenever, on looking round, some peak would show out from amongst the heavy clouds which hung about. Many such days as these – days of long, dreary hours – have to be passed among the Himalayas. Our altitude was 16,919 feet.

On his way back to the plains, Godwin-Austen had the misfortune to encounter a man-made hazard, originally intended to get the better of some tricky cliffs – a hazard which anyone who has tackled the *via ferrata* will recognize,

We reached another bad part of the road...consisting of a series of ladders placed against the nearly perpendicular face of the cliffs; but

the ladders were more dangerously placed, and some of them very rickety. This route should not be attempted by any one liable to get dizzy on looking down from great heights. The ladders often rested only against pieces of wood driven into cracks in the rocks, and on looking through the rungs as you go up, the view presented is that of a great river rushing along like a foaming torrent, at the base of vertical cliffs, which descend 300 feet sheer beneath one's feet.

To combat these miseries and dangers, and many others, Godwin-Austen drew on his extraordinary physical reserves. Compared to many of his native assistants, he seemed to move up peaks very briskly, despite thin air and rough surfaces,

The first part of the way was good walking, but as soon as we got on the talus of angular rocks it became very laborious, several of the men became ill with bad headaches and lay down, and we did not reach the highest possible point until 3pm. This I found was 18,352 feet.

And as the following extract from his Journal makes clear, while on the Changchenmo uplands on the Tibet – Ladakh border, his daily physical exertions were of the most extraordinary kind,

July 23rd: Ascended Mata H.S. 20,607ft. – 24th Red Knob 17,000 – 26th to near Peak P 18,000 – 27th crossed Pangpo La 17,000 – 29th Peak 16,500 – 30th Recrossed Pangpo La 17,000 – August 6th Kato H.S. 19,000 – 8th Lachilunglango 16,630 – 11th Marang La 17,000 – 15th Sy.Pk. (?) 19,500; – 18th Surichan La 18,000 – 21st Lankar H.S. 19,273 Shingrugo 17,208.

Perhaps the greatest modern physical anxiety in high mountains concerns the body's ability to acclimatize, and thereby avoid pulmonary, then cerebral oedema. Godwin-Austen hardly gives this a thought. Unlike us, with our 'climb high, sleep low' tactics, our oxygen tanks and our pills, Godwin-Austen scarcely even pauses to consider such matters. When he does, he is rather dismissive about it all. For example, when approaching the Nushik La, further west in the Karakoram, from where, at close to 6000m, he obtains the first-ever Western view of the vast Hispar Glacier, he writes,

Several of the (native) men felt the height, and had to remain behind from sickness and headache. I scarcely felt it; and I think that the state of the stomach has a great deal to do with these sensations.

One other great curiosity about these expeditions is how so much was achieved, and so many hazards and so much danger were avoided without any technical equipment. To the end of his long life – he was eighty-nine when he died – Godwin-Austen maintained that to use artificial equipment was 'conduct unbecoming' to a 'worthy' mountaineer. He was horrified to hear of pitons, oxygen and, worst of all, crampons, and emphatically said so in an interview with the great Oxford geographer and mountaineering historian, Kenneth Mason, a few months before his death. (This did not deter Mason in 1955 from describing Godwin-Austen in *Abode of Snow*, his greatest work, as 'probably the greatest mountaineer of his day'.) On Godwin-Austen's major expeditions, one or two mentions are made of 'step-cutting', though with what it is not clear – certainly not the kind of ice-axe that Whymper, say, was using at this time. He does mention taking several 'ropes' until we find that while crossing a crevassed glacier, he gets around to tying them together (they were otherwise used for river-crossings), only to find that their total length is '162 feet', hardly adequate for a party of sixty-seven.

Much of Godwin-Austen's reputation as a fearless mountain pioneer is founded on his great expeditions through Kashmir and the Karakoram between 1857 and 1865, and on the Burma-Assam borders from 1865 to 1877. During these years, Haversham – as the family call him – surveyed Kashmir (1860) as far as the great twin 7000m peaks of Nun and Kun in Zanskar, where he also identified Brahmah Peak, near Kishtwar, a much sought-after climbing area for post-War British climbers (particularly in the 1960s and '70s); he conducted the first survey of the Vale of Kashmir; he undertook two expeditions (1860 and '61) which explored the Great Glaciers and passes of the Karakoram and obtained the first close-up sight of K2, from about 20,000ft on Masherbrum; he led an expedition to the Changchenmo district on the borders of Ladakh (1862), followed by an expedition to the wonderful bird-sanctuary of Tso Moriri, then to Lake Pangong in Western Tibet (1863); he concluded his work with two expeditions to Bhutan (1864 and '65), and all this around a year's exile in England after being beaten senseless by 'enraged Sepoys' during the Indian Mutiny! (His achievements, given the appalling surfaces and vast distances, were all the more remarkable as he had broken his thigh in a riding accident in Calcutta on the way out to Burma in 1852.)

Given this awesome reputation, then, we may well ask ourselves, 'What makes a great explorer?' The starting point is probably the range and

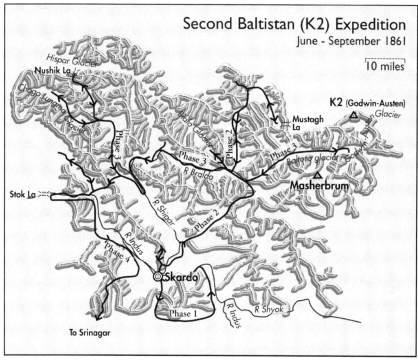

Map of the 1861 explorations of Baltistan. Four phases of the expedition are marked on the figure.(Redrawn by Mike Caunt, graphic designer, from an original map by Godwin-Austen.)

nature of the area he or she explores. Most adventurers stick, intensively, to one type of terrain: Lt-Col Percy Fawcett (1867–1925 or thereabouts) spent almost all of his time in the South American jungle until he disappeared on his last big expedition; David Livingstone (1813–73) wandered through the Dark Continent's rainforest intent on exploring with a missionary's zeal; Sir Ernest Shackleton (1874–1922), one of the great Antarctic explorers, culminating in his extraordinary escape from the ice, with all his crew, between 1914 and 1917) and Captain Scott (b.1868), until his death while leading the second expedition to reach the South Pole, in March 1912) stayed (and strayed) through the Antarctic ice-wastes. (By a curious connection, Scott spent his last night in England at Godwin-Austen's house at Nore, near Godalming.) Captain Cook (1728–79), who covered vast areas of ocean, never went very far inland. Only two great explorers can compare in this respect with Haversham Godwin-Austen (1834–1923). Sven Hedin's (1865–1952) vast expeditions lumbered through

11

the blistering sands of the Taklamakan Desert and the icy plateaux of what he called the Trans-Himalaya; Bill Tilman (1898–1977) made some very high Himalayan first ascents eg Nanda Devi, (26,660ft) at that time (1936) the highest peak wholly within the British Empire, and explored the alpine deserts of Central Asia with his fellow back-of-an-envelope expeditioner, Eric Shipton (1907–77); then he went off to sail through the wild seascapes around Patagonia (before disappearing on one such voyage). Both men added significantly to our knowledge of more than one major type of terrain. In this, they are joined by Godwin-Austen, whose 'work on the Great Glaciers' as he called it, was achieved before the Matterhorn was climbed – but who went on to spend six years as the first European to explore the pestilential jungles of Northern Burma and Assam. Moreover, he explored little-known Kashmir and Bhutan, and pushed some way into Western Tibet, at a time when entry to it was strictly forbidden to foreigners.

It is, however, not just a question of type and vastness of area covered. A great explorer needs the ability to observe the detail and diversity of his chosen country and to make his findings known; indeed, many distinguished explorers, such as Captain Cook or Sir Francis Younghusband (1863–1942), a fellow Central Asian mountaineer-explorer, have begun their professional careers with a surveyor's training. In the quality of his description, Godwin-Austen again ranks with Hedin and Tilman, and in some respects surpasses them: his maps are extraordinarily appealing, both in physical accuracy, and aesthetically; his collection of freshwater molluscs, now at the Natural History Museum, South Kensington, forms the basis of all modern science in the subject; his ornithological collection forms the core of both the British Museum and National Museum of India collections; his geological specimens are more than substantial; he wrote several books, at least two of which are definitive studies, and a great many letters on subjects as diverse as an earthquake in the Andaman Islands or the composition of the Mount Everest 1921 Reconnaissance Expedition. And if Hedin has his photographs, Godwin-Austen had his art. In Burma, on the North-West Frontier, in Kashmir and the Karakoram, Godwin-Austen sketched and painted as he went: he produced several dozen magnificent watercolours, not yet, bar one, on public view, ranging from the Shwedagon Pagoda in Prome, Burma, to the Khyber Pass, to K2 itself, the mountain which informally acquired his name for about eighty years (and which still has its 'Godwin-Austen' southern access glacier). As well as the watercolours, he left about seven hundred sketches and drawings on military, technological, ethnological and Natural History subjects. *(See Plate 1)*

Godwin-Austen was awarded the Founder's Gold Medal of the Royal Geographical Society (as well as Fellowships of the British Association and the Royal Society). In this, he contrasts well with Hedin, whose later inclination towards Fascism rightly lost him his British honours. If we consider his mountaineering, his science and his art, is there not then a case for describing this Surrey scientist, soldier and landowner (and RGS schoolboy) as our greatest explorer?

The problem in confirming this title is that Godwin-Austen was no populist. Virtually everything he wrote, apart perhaps from his letters to the *Surrey Advertiser*, was destined for a scholarly audience or reader-ship. He wrote, for example, many a scientific paper on the nature and distribution of land-snails in obscure parts of India, to be heard by an audience of no more than a dozen (although more widely read in the natural history community of scholars once published). His papers for the Royal Geographical Society reached a much smaller audience than they would now. That Godwin-Austen is one of our greatest explorers is beyond doubt, but his lack of interest in popularising his findings has severely stunted the growth of his reputation. Indeed, Godwin-Austen's final trial was, for an explorer-scholar who was proud of his scholarship, more of a mental problem than a physical one: lack of recognition – although only for reasons of scholarly and professional integrity, not for vanity.

Haversham remained a modest man throughout his life. Any great distinction he achieved was recorded unemotionally and coolly, with an admirable lack of interest in self-promotion. In a famous letter written some time after the event, his professional spleen is, however, directed at his superior officer, Colonel Montgomerie, who has taken the credit for all the hard fieldwork put in by Haversham,

> *...and I do sincerely ask that Sir H M Rawlinson will never again ask Col. Montgomerie to draw up the Summary of Indian Survey work. I am quite disgusted with Montgomerie for his unfairness.*

In later years, Godwin-Austen mellowed and recognized Montgomerie's achievements. He was equally happy with the suggestion that K2 be named 'Mount Waugh' in honour of the Surveyor-General at the time of its discovery, in the Everest fashion (after Sir George Everest), rather than 'Mount Godwin-Austen'.

We have looked at the various difficulties and dangers which beset our hero. What, then, were the compensations? They were certainly not financial: Godwin-Austen is reported as having been the only officer in the Indian Survey to have lost money through being consistently underpaid.

Haversham's largest reward was the views, which he comes back to time and again,

> *this...(river)...takes its rise near the famous peak of Nanga-Purbet (Nanga Parbat) (or the Naked Mountain), which, rising in grandeur to an altitude of 26,000 feet, presents from the Kajnag... one of the most magnificent and imposing views to be seen...*

Time and again, Haversham comes back to the view. His adjectives do not greatly vary, but that sameness perhaps reflects the stunned sense of awe he felt every time he looked out from a summit. Which mountaineer has not experienced something of the following?

> *The sun setting behind the line of snowy peaks...lit all up with a beautiful pink tint; whilst the rocks of the moraines, red, yellow and green, heightened in colour by the wet, sparkled in the sunlight.*

Aesthetic pleasure, then, is a major part of Godwin-Austen's motive for staying in the mountains. There are, however, sub-plots. He has a great eye for the local people and the way they live. The combination of local human detail and exact reproduction of landscape combine in his magnificent watercolours, still, regrettably, not yet on public display. As he approached the Mustagh Pass, for example, he comes across some Balti traders returning from their new home at Yarkand, in Chinese Turkestan,

> *...we were surprised by the sudden appearance of four men from Yarkand, who turned out to be Baltis of Shigar...I soon got into conversation, and learned from them a good deal about the country they had come from. The poor fellows had suffered a good deal while traversing the mountain portion from the robber tribes. These men wore the sheep-skin cap and long-skirted coat of stout leather boots or pubboos completed their somewhat stout appearance, and showed that emigration had been advantageous.*

This description, however, is not just a naïve account of one traveller meeting others in a remote spot; it also has a political aspect. Haversham is there not just to survey but to survey the frontier between British India and the spheres of Russian and Chinese influence, his own little part in the Great Game. Nor is it just a question of spheres of influence: the Mustagh Pass is a possible trade route: can the British make more money by setting up trade agreements with Chinese Turkestan? Given that it was Godwin-Austen who produced the first reliable map of the Chumbi Valley in Sikkim, and given that it was by this ancient trade-route that Younghusband carved his rather brutal military way through to Lhasa in 1904, with incalculable consequences for the wretched history of modern Tibet; and given that it was by this route that the British pre-war Everest expeditions all set out, then perhaps Godwin-Austen's part in the Great Game was not so very small after all.

This is confirmed by his rather crisp and dismissive assessment of the military prospects dependant on a successful crossing of the Mustagh Pass; his is the thrilling work of a spy,

My great object had been to get a march along the glacier...and determine the ridges on the northern side. This is quite feasible, and with a small guard the survey might be carried into the Yarkund country for a considerable distance, as, from all the accounts I heard of the tribes, their numbers cannot be great, nor their matchlocks much to be dreaded.

Godwin-Austen's skill in the way he dealt with the natives, apart from his facility for observation, was extended to diplomatic niceties. These were called upon during his second expedition to Tibet, the object of which was the exploration of the desolate area around Lake Pangong, in the far west of that forbidden country. Unfortunately for the locals, any Tibetan in a position of authority who permitted Westerners to pass through their local jurisdiction was likely to lose his head. Illicit Western journeys were usually officially punished by expulsion, although the death-threat was never far off. When trying to reach Rudok, the chief town of the Pangong area, Haversham encountered the local defence force,

Three men came out to meet us and turned out very mild individuals... Their dogs, of the large Tibetan breed, were much more noisy and furious at the intrusion of strangers...These Champahas informed me that one of their number was...about to give the news of our arrival... and have it sent on to Rudok. I instantly set my Bhut Moonshie down to write a letter to the governor of the place requesting that he would raise no difficulty to my paying a visit to the place, and see (sic) its monasteries....

...On the third day (of waiting for an answer), *the Zimskang of Rudok rode in with some twenty followers, and pitched his tents on the other bank of the little stream, and came over at once to see me. He was a...short, stout, jovial fellow and brought a letter from the Governor of Rudok, and a white scarf, together with a present of two damuns (bricks) of tea, and some sheep and goats for my men....It was not in his power to give me leave to visit Rudok, as he had strict orders from his superiors in Lhassa(sic) to prevent foreigners crossing the frontier, and that it would eventually be known if he permitted it.... Having received orders not to bring on any collision with the Chinese officials, I had to give up the idea of seeing Rudok; but I held out for one more march towards the place, and gained my point, but not before showing some anger at their absurd wishes.*

After the second Tibet expedition, Haversham was drafted across to Burma, where he began six seasons of unspeakable toil and danger in the malarial jungles of the area bordering Assam. One of his best assistants was killed by the Naga headhunters, a tribe who to this day retain a sceptical wariness of foreigners. His work here was just as dangerous as in the Karakoram, and just as laborious, though of course it lacks the grandeur and colour of description which Haversham could allow himself in the mountains.

Finally, Godwin-Austen's perceptions extended to climate change. He was an assiduous early observer of temperature change,

I have often been struck by the indications of considerable amounts of change of temperature within what we may call our own times. The proofs of this...consist in the enormous terminal moraines which in so many places abut on the larger rivers, down to which point glaciers must once have descended, and which in some cases must have rivaled in length the present ones of the Mustakh Range. Other evidence...is to be seen in the long furrows cut out of the solid rock as if with a chisel wielded by a gigantic hand...Many passes which were used, even in the time of Raja Ahmed, Shah of Skardo, are now closed. The road to Yarkund over the Baltoro Glacier which before his time was known as the Mustakh, has by the increase of the ice become quite impracticable...The Juserpo La can now be crossed only on foot; whereas in former times ponies could be taken over it.... Certain large glaciers have advanced, such as that at Arundu, of which the old men assured me that in their young days the terminal cliff was 1½ miles distant from the village...It is now only 400 yards. A like increase has taken place at Punmah...

Even so lately as twelve years since, the people of Shigar were enabled to get two crops off their fields. Thus the first crop (barley), was followed as soon as cut by a second (kunguni) which ripened by the end of autumn. Since that time it will not come to maturity, so that after the barley the fields now lie fallow, and the kunguni now has to be sown earlier in the season.

He was also perceptive enough to see that this great mountain fastness would one day be accessible to tourists. 'Tourist', of course, is a relative term, but could certainly apply to the thousands of trekkers who scramble along the riverbanks, over the moraines and along the glaciers, from the Indus at Skardu, even as far as Concordia where the Godwin-Austen glacier leads the eye straight to the mighty pyramid of K2.

The whole of the road to Arundu is excellent traveling. This adds greatly to the inducements which this valley (the Indus and its tribu-taries) offers to visitors, and it is well worth visiting by all such as may reach Skardu.

Skardu, of course, now has its own airport.

With such an invitation from Godwin-Austen, who qualifies as a very highly spirited adventurer and indeed one of our greatest explorers, it is unsurprising that so many have followed in his physical and metaphorical footsteps. It is fitting that he begins this collection of adventure narratives by those connected with the RGS Guildford and it is equally likely that he will provide the same basis for inspiration for a great many generations to come.

Algernon Durand Rides Out from Gilgit

by Catherine Moorehead

The following describes some of the experiences of the first British Agent at Gilgit (1889–1894), North-West Frontier Provinces, Pakistan, leader of the British Army Hunza Expedition and Military Secretary to the Viceroy of India, 1894–99, Col Algernon 'Algy' Durand CB, CIE, (OG).

Algernon Durand was a different sort of pioneer from Godwin-Austen, although both are connected by underlying similarities. Like Godwin-Austen, Durand was sent, as a soldier, to the North-West Frontier. Where Godwin-Austen succeeded in exploring some of the greatest mountain landscapes and topographical features on the planet, Durand passed through them on military expeditions as a warrior: not only was he the first Political Officer in the newly acquired British Territory of Gilgit, but he masterminded one of the most spectacular military adventures of the British Raj, the capture of the remote, clifftop fortress of Mayun, in Hunza. For Godwin-Austen, there was the intrigue of great lands to survey and new routes, such as the Mustagh Pass, to cross, in order to establish new trading partners. For Durand, there was the intrigue of the Great Game, his particular part being to define the extreme northerly border of India in order to curtail supposed Russian influence: the soldier's pleasure of thwarting or containing the Enemy.

Like many of the great travellers and explorers during Britain's imperial period in the nineteenth and early twentieth centuries, such as Robert Falcon Scott, Francis Younghusband or Percy Harrison Fawcett, or, latterly, Lord Hunt or Sir Chris Bonington, Algernon Durand's achievements are attributable, apart from particularities of his character, to his military training, background and situation.

Not much was known about Gilgit, where the British Political Officer was to be based, when Durand first led his military mission there in 1889. A hundred years later, much the same was true: I was told, by a reliable source, following a very successful expedition to the Chinese Pamirs by way of the Khunjerab Pass, that just after my return, there had been clashes between Shias and Sunnis that had resulted in about two thousand deaths, a bloodbath unreported in the outside world (admittedly before the days of email and 'rolling' news stations). *(See Plate 2)*

The following extracts, throughout this chapter, are taken from Durand's

1899 work, *The Making of a Frontier,* his description of his time as the British Political Agent in Gilgit, with jurisdiction of a sort over the Indus Valley to the South past Chilas, and the remote Chitral area. He also describes his campaign against the Mir or Thum of Hunza, in 1891 and the spectacular siege, then capture, of the Mir's stronghold at Karimabad.

Like a good soldier remaining cool under fire, Durand described the difficulties of the wild and, from a European point of view, untrodden road to Gilgit with detachment, where the main emotions were a rather conventional wonderment mixed with mild homesickness, and an excitement at being somewhere effectively unexplored, *(See Plate 3)*

> *The road out of the Gurais valley is either by the Kamri Pass or the Burzil. We chose the former, as by it the distance to Astor is about a march shorter. The road over the Kamri leaves the valley at the village of Bangla, goes straight up the side of the hill, and crosses the ridge at an altitude of over thirteen thousand feet. The ascent is very severe, but on the other side the descent is gentle. We camped on both sides of the pass just below snow level in most delicious air, like Northumberland in clear autumn...*

Sometimes, Durand takes more care to describe the nature of the area he is passing through,

> *The character of the mountains now began to change completely. Below eight thousand feet hardly a tree is to be seen, except where irrigation fertilises the lands of a village. Steep bare hillsides, streaked with reds and ochres, but generally grey and pale sandy yellow, covered where anything will grow with wormwood scrub, plunge down thousands of feet into the valleys, which are only wide enough at the bottom to admit the passage of the chafing stream. If you happen fortunately to be about the altitude of eight to twelve thousand feet, where the rain falls, you will march through forest and grass lands. Above that, again, run bare rock-strewn hillsides, the last vegetation being always the dwarf juniper, and from thirteen to fourteen thousand feet is the line of eternal snow.*

It is not just the occasional lyrical account of the changing colours of the countryside, however, which attracts Durand's eye, but the challenges and problems which he encounters along the way,

> *...The march was the worst on the whole road. Running along the*

*last spur between the Indus and the Astor river the path struck the
watershed at the height of ten thousand feet, and then dropped down
the Hattu Pir six thousand feet in about five miles to Shaitan Nara,
the "devil's bridge", until the Maharaja piously renamed it. It is
impossible to exaggerate the vileness of this portion of the road: it
plunged down over a thousand feet of tumbled rock, in steps from
six inches to two feet deep; then for a mile it ran ankle-deep in
loose sand filled with sharp-edged stones; it crossed shingle slopes
which gave at every step; it passed by a shelf six inches wide across
the face of a precipice; in fact it concentrated into those five miles
every horror which it would be possible to conceive of a road in
the worst nightmare, the whole six thousand feet was strewn with
the carcasses of expended baggage animals, and in more than one
place did we find a heap of human bones.*

The whole business of water and bridges, indeed, exercised Durand
a great deal. Bridges, unsurprisingly, gave him considerable pause for
thought, although, as we see in the following extract, he goes to the length
of reassuring himself, first by a fairly detailed technical description that
safe passage is possible, rather like a modern bad flyer reassuring himself
by reading about an aeroplane's technical capacity and accident record
before boarding,

*On this occasion we elected to try the rope bridge for the first time.
The bridge is made of ropes of twisted birch twigs, each rope being
about the thickness of a man's arm. Three of these make the footway,
bound together here and there by withes; the hand-rails are similar
ropes, the footway and hand-rails being fastened together by light
one-inch ropes at every six feet or so. All three sets of ropes pass
over one piece of timber set across uprights on each bank, and they
are anchored as a rule to another baulk of timber buried in loose
stone masonry. Advantage is taken of a high rock or bit of cliff for
a take-off; the nearer both ends of the bridge are to being at the
same level the better, but this is not essential, and one end may be
twenty feet higher than the other. (See Plate 4)*

But his technical self-persuasion gives way to the first anxieties creeping in,

*Even with the take-off at each end on a level, the bridge sags very
much in the centre; if there is much variation in the level the pitch*

*at one end is necessarily much steeper than at the other, and at either end there is a very decided slope. This is trying for a tall man, for the nearer to the anchorages the shallower the **V** made by the ropes, and in order to get hold of the side-ropes you must stoop forward very much, which is apt to be unpleasant when you necessarily look down and see, sixty feet below you, hard rocks. Once you get above the water all feeling of discomfort passes off, and in the hot weather it is pleasant to stand leaning your back against the side-rope, swaying in the wind, and facing the cold air which rushes down above the centre of these ice-fed torrents. In order to prevent the side-ropes getting close together they are kept apart by sticks inserted at every few yards, over which you have to step. This is rather an acrobatic performance, as in the middle of the bridge the side ropes are two-and-a-half to three feet above the foot rope, but you soon get used to it.*

Like a good explorer, having described particular bridges and experiences, he then moves on to general comments before the melodramatic conclusion,

Every one crosses these bridges, old women, children, men carrying any loads, alive or dead. Some dogs negotiate them quite easily, but many get frightened and lie down, half way and have to be picked up. We had one pariah, who followed us from Kashmir, drowned, alas! three years afterwards in the Indus, who always tried to walk over the rope bridge, and invariably fell into the water when half way over. He did not try the Shaitan Nara: nothing that fell into that boiling torrent could come out alive.

It is partly the danger, partly the horror of the awful consequences of neglect, but perhaps most striking of all is Durand's willingness to submit himself to being overawed by the fearsome power of Nature,

The great flood in 1841...was caused by a gigantic landslip, probably following an earthquake. The whole hillside facing the Indus, just above the Lechur nullah, from a height of about four thousand feet above the river, was precipitated into the valley below, impinging on the opposite bank, and bringing down on that side a secondary hill-fall. The course of the river was completely arrested by a huge dam thousands of feet thick and some hundreds high; the water must have risen at the dam to fully a thousand feet above its present level. Whatever may have been the ordinary level then, the Bunji plain was converted into a lake, and the Gilgit river, which runs into the Indus six miles above Bunji, was dammed up for thirty miles to just below the present fort of Gilgit. The tradition is that the dam held for months, and that, when it began to cut, the river completed its work in one day, and swept down in a solid wall of water carrying all before it. All down the Indus valley to the plains the people were of course prepared for the rush, and though miles of cultivated land were ruined, one does not hear of much loss of life. But where the river begins to open out into the plains of India near Attock, a great disaster occurred. A portion of the Sikh army was encamped practically in the river-bed, and the flood caught it and swept it away. In the picturesque native description it is said: "As an old woman with a wet cloth sweeps away an army of ants, so the river swept away the army of the Maharaja".

Heavy rain is another source of the frightening scale of natural disasters in this area,

Rain rarely falls below an altitude of eight thousand feet in these parts, and the streams as a rule can cope with the drainage from the hills. But in the spring, when the heavy melt of snow commences, and when consequently the hills above that level are for days together clothed in mist and drenched with rain; or in summer when, after ten days of brilliant weather, a three days' storm rages and the fountains of heaven are opened on the higher hills, the streams cannot drain the hillsides sufficiently quickly. They become heavy with mud, loosened boulders crash into them and are swept down, the main ravine becomes more and more choked as the tributary streams pour in, and at last in a solid mass forty, fifty, sixty feet deep, it pours its stream of mud, out of the hills into the river valley, the stream at once expanding as it leaves the embrace of the enclosing cliffs. In this way every (alluvial) fan has been formed, the stream which made it cutting its way through its own fan to reach the river. The mud flow of which we saw the traces was a mere baby; it had only covered rocks ten feet high in the stream bed, and made a miniature fan where it debouched, but its force was attested by the huge boulders it had moved. These

*mud flows come down with terrible rapidity and irresistible force,
and with no further warning than a tremble of the ground like an
earthquake and a grinding roar, followed immediately by the wall
of mud and rock: man or beast caught in a ravine by them is lost.
The peculiar formation so common in the Hindu-Kush by which
a stream, with a catchment area "perhaps thirty to fifty miles
round", cuts its way into the main river through a gorge fifty feet
wide, with walls several hundred feet in height, is what makes
these mud flows possible and so dangerous. No one who had not
had his attention drawn to them would believe in their action.
When making the road down to Chilas in 1893 I found a bridge
being built over a ravine apparently in a perfectly safe situation
about thirty feet above the bed. The engineer in charge would not
believe that it could be unsafe till I showed him on the cliffs not
fifty yards from the bridge traces of a mud flow, which I knew was
only a year or so old, some thirty feet higher than his bridge site.*

It is not, however, all disaster when contemplating the forces of Nature.
Even in stormy conditions, Durand sometimes exercises his more lyrical
side,

*It was far colder than when we had last been on the Chamarkand;
the snow in a light sprinkling was on the pass, and covered the
mountains in all directions down to twelve thousand feet. Frost had
taken a firm hold of ground and stream, and the banks of the latter
were hung with icicles. The road down ran through a broad open
valley, that carried one back to the moorland at home on an autumn
day. Clouds hung over the hills, dropping shifting curtains of snow
and sleet, the distant mountains stood out dark blue and purple
with snow-covered tops, the nearer showed grey dashed here and
there with bright colouring from the grasses in their autumn tints.*

Indeed, Durand is not slow to appreciate views. Many are described if
not in thrilling then at least appreciative and quite evocative detail,

*We moved up to a camp about eleven thousand feet high, from which
we had the most superb views. We were on a spur of Nanga Parbat,
the watershed between the Indus and Astor river, and surrounded
by a complete ring of snow-peaks, the average height of which is
about twenty thousand feet. The view from the crest, a couple of*

23

thousand feet above our camp, is one of the finest I should think in the world, certainly one of the finest in the Hindu-Kush. In a gorge nine thousand feet below, at your very feet, runs the Indus, giving that depth and proportion which is so often lacking in a mountain view; to the south, solitary, sublime, rises in one sweep from the spot on which you stand the mighty mass of Nanga Parbat, thirteen thousand feet of snow-field and glacier; to the east, magnificent peaks succeed each other till they join the main chain of the Hindu-Kush, which stretches in an unbroken line before you; while to the west the Hindu Raj towers over the Indus, backed by the snows of Chitral and of the Pathan Kohistan.

The descriptive terms are rather banal, but the analytical conclusion is correct. Sometimes, Durand cannot contain his sense of the sublime nor maybe a sense of being part of a larger historical drama, and he moves from topographical effusion to historical flights of fancy, although his conclusion is somewhat Gilbertian,

We reached the top of the Dorah, fourteen thousand eight hundred feet in height, without difficulty, riding practically to the top of the pass. We had a lovely day, the air was perfect, and the view from the top is fine. Immediately below you the ground drops very suddenly to the Hauz-i-Dorah, Lake Dufferin as it was christened by Lockhart's party, but the lake itself is out of sight. We stayed a short time at the top, looking out over the Badakshan mountains towards that mysterious Central Asia which attracts by the glamour of its past history, by the veil which shrouds its future. Balkh, Bokhara, Samarkhand, what visions come trooping as their names arise! The armies of Alexander, the hordes of Gengis Khan and Timur go glittering by; dynasties and civilisations rise and fall like the waves of the sea; peace and prosperity again and again go down under the iron hoof of the conqueror; for centuries past death and decay have ruled in the silent heart of Asia. Are we now looking on the re-awakening? Shall the land again blossom like the rose, and proud cities rise on the ruins of the old under semi-European sway, and greater emperors than the Great Khan rule through centuries of generally lasting peace a greater and united empire? Let us hope so. But who that knows her methods can dare to prophesy that Russian rule will necessarily prove better for the people than Mahomedan?

Sometimes, however, a more empirical reality returns, and the view of the surroundings becomes more matter-of-fact, bordering on the irritable,

We found Skardu possessed of an odious climate, consisting of considerable heat in the daytime, and of a gale of wind at night, which carried clouds of fine sand down the valley. It is said to be always windy here, and consequently very cold in winter.

One of the joys of reading Durand's book, however, is his ability to describe common ground. Durand was no mountaineer. He was largely satisfied with the enjoyment of playing politics and military adventuring in an unexplored (by Westerners) area. He is, however, game to try something, where necessary, which comes close to a mountaineering experience, albeit a rather comical one,

Next morning, after a very nasty shave of being brained by a falling stone, we discovered a way down, which involved one of the worst pieces of rock-climbing I ever came across. For about fifty feet the only foothold was a line of depressions a couple of inches deep, the only hold for the hands was well above one's head, and that was the smooth round cornice of a water-worn rock round which the fingers could bend, but which gave no grip; thirty feet below steamed the boiling sulphur water. It was nearly too much for me, but the knowledge that breakfast was within half a mile, that to go back meant several hours' work, carried the day. Even then I could not have crossed without help, but my shikari, who was like a monkey, got on to the cornice above me, and dropped me the end of his turban, with the assistance of which I got over all right, the shikari[2] moving along the ledge above...

And there must be many mountaineers who have experienced the situation and emotions Durand describes as follows,

...One way or another we all had exciting times...I have a nightmare recollection of one snow slope, which dropped a couple of thousand feet below one and ended in ghastly precipices, which we had to cross...The slightest slip meant death, and we had no ropes or ice axes, nothing but one small alpenstock with which to dig out steps in the frozen snow. Providence protects the ignorant mountaineer.

2. Shikari: native big game hunter; the Indian equivalent of a ghillie.

25

Unsurprisingly, therefore, Durand's main concern throughout his travels is the state of the path. Time and again he assesses the quality of the way ahead,

> *The further I went down the Indus valley the less I liked it. I could only get the mules down two marches, and even then I lost a couple down precipices. The road was awful, even for the Hindu-Kush; it ran along the face of precipices a thousand feet above the river, plunged down into great ravines with perpendicular conglomerate sides hundreds of feet high...*

On the way to Chitral, similar observations are made, although this time Durand dwells on the details,

> *We found the country we marched through to Gakuch, the last fort in Punyal, wilder than anything we had yet seen. For the most part the road runs through a narrow valley just wide enough to give room for a roaring torrent sixty to eighty yards across, with an average fall of forty feet to the mile, the valley here and there opening out and showing alluvial fans and patches of cultivation. The two most marked features of the road for a hundred miles from Gilgit, and practically throughout the Hindu-Kush, are shingle slopes and the "parris". Thousands of feet above you are the mountain tops, shattered by frost and sun into the most fantastic outlines, from whose rugged summits fall masses of rock. Below any precipice you consequently see the shingle slope in existence; these slopes sometimes running up thousands of feet at a steep unbroken angle, almost universally of thirty degrees. The sizes of the stones forming the slope vary with the character of the rock and the length of the fall. You may pass through the foot of a slope by a path running over and amongst a heap of gigantic fragments weighing many tons each, or you may ride across a slope of fine slaty shingle which gives at every step, but wherever you cross a slope you generally find all the stones at that point very much the same size. Whenever there is heavy rain, or snow begins to melt in the spring, rock avalanches come down, and I have lain at nights for hours listening to the thundering roar of great fragments plunging down from thousands of feet above one's camp. In the day-time you have to keep a sharp look-out. There are many places well-known as extremely danger-ous, in crossing which it is prudent not to loiter. I have never seen*

26

a man killed, but I have seen a man's leg broken a few yards in front of me by a falling stone, and have witnessed very narrow escapes. There was one particularly nasty stone shoot at Shaitan Nara, where stones fell all day long, the smaller whizzing by like a bullet, and the larger cannonading down in flying leaps, the last of which frequently carried them nearly across the Astor River.

Much of the commentary, as one might expect from a military tactician, is taken up with assessing the path from the point of view of a military column,

We passed out of the plain by a razor-backed pass, about fifteen thousand feet high, the last part of the ascent of which, in greasy mud and soft snow, was very trying for baggage animals. The descent to the Skardu plain is by a steep ravine which drops eight thousand feet in a couple of short marches. It was a funnel down which a raging wind poured at night, making a halt there hideous. The march down was very bad, the stream had to be crossed perpetually, each time getting heavier and more dangerous. We had to make a chain of men across it once or twice, and to pass the animals over above the men. Even then we had an excitement, one man being swept away and only extricated fifty yards down stream, half-drowned, and rather knocked about…

But there is one unexpected theme to this book. On page after page, Durand betrays his Northumbrian and Surrey background through an appreciation of flowers and trees. One is tempted to think that they were a perfect antidote to the horrors experienced on the precipices and the storms; but they also, for Durand, complete his sense of what is fitting in a good mountain prospect,

Our first camp was at an altitude of over nine thousand feet in a glade in the pine forest, the turf covered with blue forget-me-nots. The march up was lovely, through one succession of copses of jasmine and scented wild rose, the latter of all colours from white to dark red. The following morning we continued our march, the road winding up through pine forest till the rounded tops of the watershed were reached. We halted for an hour at the top, surrounded by a wilderness of flowers, blue gentian, anemones, acres of white and yellow blossoms bordering the wreaths of snow, masses of small pink alpine flowers, wild rhubarb and sorrel in profusion, and patches of dwarf juniper, for we were well above the pine and birches. The views from here are lovely – to the left, steep pine-clad slopes descend into the famed Lolab valley, behind, stretched out thousands of feet below, lie the valley of Kashmir and the blue sheet of the Woollar Lake, backed by the snowy range of the Pir Panjal; to the right stand the great square peak and snowfields of Haramukh; in front, a hundred miles away, towers Nanga Parbat, from which on both hands as far as the eye can reach tossed ranges patched with snow fill up the picture.

It is fitting to conclude Durand's response to his surroundings (which also includes many pages of politics, military exercises, battles and observations of social customs such as different regional dresses or the playing of goat's-head polo, *buzkashi*) with a short extract which shows the mountaineer in him – someone who loves the mountains but who sees them in the context of the benign and malign forces of Nature,

...and towering above all was the mass of Nanga Parbat. I loitered on the top of the pass for some time drinking in the glorious scene, and then plunged down over sloping snow-beds covering the glaciers, so as to get clear before the sun softened the crust. Once off the snow the path was bad: first descending the terminal face of the moraine, then running for many miles over lateral moraines and shingle slopes till we got to grass; after this it wound through thickets of myrtle and masses of forget-me-not of every colour, ranging from heaven's loveliest blue through pink to white.

If only to link the world of Godwin-Austen and Durand with that of the modern RGS, however, some account must be made of Durand's military exploits. His aim was to block the alleged but actually non-existent advance of the Russian Imperial forces through the Karakoram. To do this, British foreign policy required the subjugation of the infamous Mir of Hunza who had apparently intercepted and hindered communications between British India and Chinese Central Asia. The Mir had also given rather rough passage to the military adventurer-explorer, and later eccentric mystic, Francis Younghusband, with whom Durand became a longstanding friend, for example becoming a founding member of the Central Asian Society, on Younghusband's invitation, in the early twentieth century.

Durand's plan was first to capture the outlying fortress of Nilt. He was, unfortunately, shot in the groin early in the campaign, but did not relinquish his command. While he had to spend much time recuperating in Gilgit, he would occasionally be carried to his front line in a litter. The capture of Nilt is described matter-of-factly.

Aylmer laid his gun cotton, lit the fuse and stepped back under the wall; the fuse did not burn, and he had to return, cut it, and relight it. It was a desperate venture, for the defenders now knew what was going on, and were firing through loopholes in the gate itself. But the second time the explosion succeeded, and the gate was blown open. The little party dashed in, and were at once engaged in a furious hand-to-hand fight in the tunnel through the wall behind the gate. It was then that Boisragon, who was commanding the Gurkhas, found that he had only half-a-dozen men with him; his bugler had picked up a rifle and was in the thick of the fight, and he himself never thought of sounding the "advance," which would have told us the place was ours. There was nothing to be done but to go back under a hot cross fire and fetch up more men. Badcock, his junior officer, volunteered to go, but Boisragon insisted on going himself. The little party, too weak to push on, held their own grimly, repelling gallant and repeated attacks, till their reinforcements arrived and the fort was stormed. Badcock was severely wounded, and Aylmer desperately hurt, hit in three places. The struggle lasted twenty minutes.

His wound prevented him from being present at the capture of the Mir's stronghold of Mayun, the gateway to Hunza, but it was the scene of the most remarkable bravery and tactical daring,

There remained but the third course – to find a way up the cliffs opposite Nilt and to deliver a direct assault. Night after night reconnaissances were pushed up the great ravine leading to the glaciers of Rakapushi, and the opposing cliff was explored. The enemy's posts ran right up to the glaciers, and the cliffs became more forbidding the farther our men pushed their researches. Finally, with the necessity came the man. A little Dogra sepoy called Nagdu one night succeeded in climbing twelve hundred feet up the cliff, and found a practicable path, and preparations were made for the final assault.

As the assault was mounted, Durand was obliged to remain, frustrated, in Gilgit, anxiously awaiting dispatches. He summarises the successful action thus,

> *Suffice it to say that Manners-Smith led a little body of Kashmir troops up a cliff a thousand feet in height, under cover of a tremendous fire from our side of the ravine, that the attacking column was not discovered until more than half of the ascent was completed, that in consequence it escaped the danger of an avalanche of stones hurled down from the sungahs covering the path, and that these sungahs once taken the enemy's line was pierced, his opposition ceased, and the campaign was over. Within two days we had occupied Nagar, the Hunza Chief and Uzr Khan fled northwards across the frontier, the Hunza people made submission without striking a blow, and our plans were crowned with success.*

He might have added that three Victoria Crosses and several Orders of Merit were won in this action, one of the bravest in the history of the Empire. The whole campaign is described with magnificent accuracy by *The Times'* correspondent, E F Knight, in *Where Three Empires Meet*.

Both the local, Surrey boy, Godwin-Austen, and the Northumbrian, Durand (whose brother, Mortimer, was the Foreign Secretary of the Raj), used their RGS education and Sandhurst military training for contrasting purposes, one peaceful, as a scientist-explorer-surveyor, the other more political and warlike as a representative of the Raj who played his vigorous part in the Great Game. Happily, the RGS seems in modern times to have erred on the side of peace, science and exploration, yet with quite a lot of derring-do thrown into the mix, as the following chapter, which deals with those who from the 1970s onwards pioneered new kinds of mountaineering and rekindled the flame of adventure, tells us.

The Modern Pioneers
by Catherine Moorehead

B efore the RGS went private in 1977, the 'Adventure Activities' baton
seems to have been passed on from the memorable and gentlemanly
Deputy Head and Head of Classics, Jack Lauder, to Dick Seymour, who
arrived in 1972 and whose leadership of Scouts' expeditions was reinforced shortly after by the super-active energy of fellow-geographer Dai
Cowx in 1984. While the '80s and '90s became largely the fiefdom of the
Scouts, and although the Scouts remain highly active and adventurous,
new directions since about 2003 have been followed by the CCF and the
RumDoodle Society.

Things really took off in 1973 after Dick Seymour obtained his Surrey-
funded MLC from Plas-y-Brenin. The certificate itself was created as a
positive reaction to the 1971 Lochan Buidhe Disaster in the Cairngorms
(see *A Blizz on MacDhui*), where poor supervision of badly-equipped
teenagers was largely to blame for the avoidable loss of five young lives
and their inexperienced leader. Dai Cowx gained his ML in the mid-80s
and went on to acquire MIA experience shortly after. These two leaders,
still remembered by many of those who have contributed to this book,
such as those supermen who have climbed above 8000m: Mike Norris in
his magnificent *Cho Oyu Unsupported*, or Rupert Dix, who describes an
amazing attempt on *Gasherbrum II*, were therefore well placed to introduce
many young people to the pleasures of mountaineering, an influence still
widely recognised and deeply appreciated.

During these last two decades of the twentieth century, the Scouts
visited more and more adventurous areas. From basic training in the Lakes,
they moved on to Scotland, including a particularly active ten days of
glorious weather in the Cuillin, knocking off umpteen tops, not least
Sgurr Alasdair (993m) by the Great Stone Chute, Dick Seymour's earliest
memorable expedition. Dai led expeditions which alternated between
Chamonix and the Dolomites. Ice-climbing, glacier-walking, rock-climbing
and exploration, as well as exciting times on the Dolomites' *Via Ferrata*
(see James Slater's article for a later version of this most hair-raising of
mountain experiences) were enjoyed, and Iceland (see Colin Carmichael's
Scouting for Girls? for an earlier version) also figured largely.

Where did the funding come from? Early expeditions were unsubsidised:

sponsorship was at that time not a possibility (and the Scouts did not receive central funds from the Scout Organisation). Apart from parental contributions and fundraising (led by the indefatigable Judy Bartlett), much of the money came from that time-honoured form of financial extraction, 'car-parking', a genteel form of banditry involving asking those motorists desperate to park their cars in central Guildford – a particularly lucrative activity in the hell-for-leather run-up to the materialist orgy which is Guildford in the weeks before Christmas – for a 'donation' in return for the privilege of using the School car-park.

Diversification in the Scouts' activities took place as these two decades passed. Perhaps the climax was the highly adventurous trip to Colorado in 2000. On the menu was white-water rafting, exploring canyons, rock-climbing and, by using special out-of-reach bags, avoiding the predatory bears on the campsite!

By 2004, a strong and enthusiastic CCF leadership was, however, beginning to make its mark. Jez Ross led adventure training camps and challenging outings such as the Ten Tors, and one of the first trips abroad, to Germany. Justin Usher followed, with glacier-walking and ice-climbing in the Pitztal area of the Tyrol. Gavin Kerr organised a trip to the Dolomites (see James Slater's article) which developed an enduring love-fear relation-ship, begun by Dai Cowx, with the Dolomites' *Via Ferrata*. The Pitztal became a firm favourite: later expeditions, under the new CCF contingent commander, Steve Yetman, involved rafting, mountain biking, sailing, canyoning and other forms of outdoor torture which have been the highlight of many boys' school careers and given them a lifelong interest.

On Gavin Kerr's last trip, and Steve Yetman's first, in 2007, the CCF turned up the risk factor by going to Sonthofen in the most mountainous part of southern Germany – but in winter. Ski-ing, snowshoeing, and survival skills such as snowholing were all on offer. Most unusually, a *Fackeltour*[3] took place, a snowshoeing cross-country tour with only torches for guidance. In the summer, now under Steve Yetman's leadership, the CCF returned to Pitztal and at New Year in their next season headed for the Hählekopf (2058m) in the Kleinwalsertal area on the Austro-German border, based at the Schwarzwasser Hut. There, a biathlon was initiated, involving such esoteric sports as rifle-shooting with laser-targeted rifles and cross-country racing using skating skis.

The most recent trip of this kind was situated, again, among Germany's

---

3. From German, *Fackel*, a torch or firebrand.

highest mountains. With an ex-Everester mountain guide, a party traversed, at New Year, the various wide, open glaciers surrounding the Wildspitze (3774m). There are similar plans for the future.

The Noughties were indeed an important period for the extension of adventure activities at the RGS. In 2003, the School Tibet Expedition spent more than seven weeks travelling via Kathmandu to Lhasa then Shigatse, Tibet's second city. A four-day overland drive westwards took the sixteen-strong party to Mount Kailas (unclimbed: 6714m) where the fifty-two kilometre circumambulation was followed past its high point of 5660m on the Drölma La. (See *A Shortish Walk Round Mount Kailas*.) The well-acclimatised party returned half-way to Lhasa then headed north onto the Tibetan Plateau, where a Base Camp was established. How many school trips have spent three weeks above 5000m?

During that period, three first ascents, from just over 6000m to almost 6300m, were accomplished, as well as a number of lesser summits around 5500m. The mental trial involved is described in Alex Way's *The Hidden Summit*.

Following these ascents, the expedition crossed the Tsangpo-Brahmaputra and after three exciting days reached Everest (Tibet) Base Camp, from where several treks up the Rongbuk (now Rongphu) Glacier to about 5800m were enjoyed in generally superb weather. The expedition returned to Kathmandu and home via the fearsome Kodari Gorges and the 'Friendship' Highway.

At a cost of over £120,000 and a duration of fifty-two days, this was one of the most massive expeditions ever to leave a British school. The excitement it generated led to the formation of the RumDoodle Society. (See the School website.) The name derives from W E Bowman's comic novel, *The Ascent of Rum Doodle, 40,000½ feet,* appropriately enough, as Bowman had lived in Guildford for twenty-eight years. This Society is dedicated to twice-yearly expeditions to the harder areas of Scotland. All expeditions end with a fine dinner in a notable local hotel or restaurant. Memorable recent trips have taken in Ben Starav (1078m), Ben MacDhui (1309m) via the Goat Track in Coire an t-Sneachdha, The Saddle (1010m) in Kintail, and many other Mighty Munros. The latest trip was a multiple ascent of the Holy Grail, the Inaccessible Pinnacle (986m), in the Cuillin.

Reflecting on these thirty years or so of adventures, what have the various leaders got to say? Of course there have been easily-recalled moments of danger: passing (silently!) under a crumbling spike of rock on Tryfan; a horrendous, scary thunderstorm on Snowdon; an Alpine near-disaster when someone slipped from a ridge and headed for rocks, a *Bergschrund*[4] and oblivion, only prevented by a highly purposeful ice-axe brake; some 'interesting' scree-running where pupils had significantly outpaced the rocks they were running down; a helicopter evacuation on Rydal Fell in the Lakes; a white-out on Cairngorm. In more comic vein, a recollection surfaces of an RGS party following a woman who had lost her cool on a particularly exposed *Via Ferrata* while just behind her James Slater warbled James Blunt's line, 'There must be an angel with a smile on her face…'

But these are sporadic and relatively minor events compared to the memorable beauties of an early rise above Chamonix with the light glowing over the glaciers, while experiencing a tranquillity not found elsewhere, or the satisfaction of traversing great Alpine glaciers from one country to another, or looking down from a Cuillin summit at Scotland's jagged, subtly-coloured coastline and islands. You do not have to go too far, indeed, nor be able to see very much at all to acquire memories which are durable, as *The Leith Hill Adventure* describes so convincingly.

All of the leaders in this modern period are agreed that, perhaps as a reaction to the intensity of term-time life, the emptiness of remote places creates a special kind of intimacy and encourages the kind of reflectiveness which the hurly-burly of term-time does not so readily permit. All of us hope that by giving RGS boys past and present the opportunity to enjoy the great mountains and wildernesses of our own country, and far beyond, we are giving them something of great pleasure and enjoyment for the rest of their lives.

---

4. *Bergschrund:* German, 'mountain crevasse', ie the long and gaping hole where a glacier intersects with the base of a mountain face.

DEATH ZONE

Death Zone: Introduction

The expeditions covered by this section involve high-altitude climbs and very high-level treks. The altitudes are so great, from around 6000m up to above 8000m, that the body cannot readily renew the cells or energy which it loses, with the result that any time spent at that elevation is to dice with death.

The first two contributions are epics of extraordinary physical and mental toughness. They are very modern expeditions: Mike Norris's solo, oxygenless success on Cho Oyu, at 8201m the sixth-highest mountain in the world, is a breathtaking extreme achievement; Rupert Dix's near-success on Gasherbrum, at 8035m, the thirteenth-highest mountain on the planet, accurately and excitingly describes the techniques now used for the 'post-Alpine' style of ascent which has replaced the 'Alpine' style, it in turn having superseded the classic 'siege'-style expeditions which led to the first ascents of such great peaks as Everest, Nanga Parbat and K2. Both contributions offer a rich mix of emotions, such as frustration, anxiety, despair and happiness, as well as physical impressiveness of the most remarkable kind.

The second kind of expedition is seen in Jonathan Stuart's contribution: the high-level trek. This is a real adventure. Put together on a shoestring, enduring immense travel discomfort, rat-infested hotels and bureaucratic hassles, Jonathan (with Rupert Dix) trekked all the way to nearly 6400m on the North Face of Everest and encountered snowstorms, swollen rivers and any number of other hazards on the way. The jaunty nonchalance with which this pair met all the extraordinary, never-ending difficulties and dangers of the trek makes for an exciting narrative.

The final contribution is of a different kind: Alex Way scarcely describes the physical surroundings on his first ascent of a 6300m peak on the Tibetan Plateau. The climb (which he shared with several others), was situated in country not particularly remarkable or particularly beautiful, but it is fabulously remote; this latter quality clearly had a strong effect on Alex's imagination: rather than describe the physical world, he chooses to take us on his mental journey as the grind up the glacier gives way to anxious moments on the face followed by elation on the summit then exhaustion once a safe return to Advance Base has been accomplished.

This section is not for the faint-hearted, but it shows very strongly what extraordinary physical and mental feats the modern OG is capable of.

Cho Oyu: Oxygenless and Unsupported
by Mike Norris

*Life is brought down to basics: if you are warm, regular, healthy,
not thirsty or hungry, then you are not on a mountain. Climbing at
altitude is like hitting your head against a brick wall – it's great
when you stop.*

Chris Darwin

It is 8.30am, September 2005. I am standing at 8201m on the summit of
Cho Oyu, atop the sixth-highest peak in the world, one foot in Nepal
one in Tibet…

Clear blue sky, little wind, no more 'up' to go, the panorama is stag-
gering. The north-east ridge of Everest shines in front of me with its snowy
pyramid sparkling 650m above my head. Looking south, Shishapangma
rises above its neighbouring peaks…for the first time in days my head
feels clear. But more urgently, my euphoria is tempered by the lack of
sensation and a deathly white look to the fingers of my left hand. I need
to get down and I need to get warm.

The plan had been hatched nine months earlier with my best mate and
climbing partner, Seba, during an invigorating bush walk on the Coromandel
Peninsula, New Zealand. An 8000m peak seemed quite a pleasant and
achievable dream in the comfort of a balmy summer's day.

Reality bit quickly, though. Peak fees, transport in Tibet, the logistics of
the gear needed: all were troublesome and expensive. We settled financially
and ethically for the only viable option. We would get to Advance Base
Camp (ABC) through an outfit, *Project Himalaya*. From there, we would
be on our own: no guide, no Sherpas, and no supplementary oxygen.

Reality bit harder. Seba broke his ankle on our last training trip in New
Zealand, just three weeks before our departure for Nepal. Quite incredibly
though, he stuck with me (on crutches!) as far as ABC, and continued to
offer me moral support. It was too late to pull out: the flights, peak fees,
and everything had been paid.

The first 'mountain' encountered by all who enter Nepal is the city of
Kathmandu. Route-finding is merely trial and error, and confusion lies at
every turn. There is no slow approach route, no time for acclimatization.
We have three days to gather all we need. Among the curving red-bricked
walls and endless streams of rickshaws, hawkers, kids and cows, we unearth

'Shona's' where we can hire home-made (but effective) down suits and other essential hardware not readily available or affordable in New Zealand.

Then to the back-alley chemist; the pharmacist knows what is necessary and I scribble down the instructions hurriedly.

'Nifediprine and dexamethazone: treatment for cerebral and pulmonary oedema. If vomit blood, bad head ache, no sight, no can talk; take one each, drink water, go down.'

The blend of broken English and medical jargon is startling.

'Amoxicillin – blood infection. Perimox – throat and chest infection. Diamox – 500mg slow release better – prevent Acute Mountain Sickness (AMS) two per day. Start these now. Okay?'

I take the white paper bag containing all my life-saving ingredients, like a lolly bag. I am now the expedition doctor and hope things are really going to be that simple.

The journey from Kathmandu (1300m) to Tingri (4300m), the turn off to base camp, takes three days, mainly due to the gain in altitude. Upon leaving Nepal at Kodari (1873m), the road rises sharply along the Friendship Highway to the Tong-la Pass at 5120m. This initial stretch is exhilarating as the unsealed and potholed road climbs the immense green valley, passing under waterfalls and skirting huge drop-offs.

At each stop we take the opportunity to acclimatize and walk up the valley walls. There, we come across local Tibetans living traditionally. Otherwise, we are assigned where to sleep, where to eat, and which vehicle to travel in. Not surprising: everything is controlled by the Chinese.

Above Nyalam, as if by magic we turn a corner and the lush green coverage transforms into a vast barren moonscape. Before long, the imposing glittering teeth of lofty peaks soar all around us above the expansive brown plains.

By now the endless throbbing headache has set in for the next two weeks as we struggle to cope with the altitude. Acclimatisation is our sole mission as we prepare to take our first steps on the mountain. Even strolls up moderate hills leave us breathless and nauseous, with our heads pounding. The diamox is possibly helping, but I am soon to give up taking this because of the extreme pins-and-needles it causes. *(See Plate 5)*

From Base Camp, not far from Tingri, we are excited to be leaving the vehicles and finally to start hiking. Khampas, nomads from Tibet, will be herding some yaks for us. They are all armed with foot-long knives and look impressive with their braided hair to which they add yak hair, red wool, turquoise and bones. Temperamental yaks are saddled with sprawling packs. Still, they navigate the jagged loose moraine expertly as we start our two day approach to Advance Base Camp above the Nangpa La. This pass, connecting Tibet and Nepal, has long been used by pilgrims and traders, and still is today. It became infamous in 2006 when Chinese troops shot dead a number of pilgrims crossing the border here.

We are not the first to reach ABC (5600m): the maze of green, red, yellow and blue Buddhist prayer flags trails across the sky. Below them stand bright tents clustered in families like limpets clinging to the rocks. This is our relatively luxurious base for the next ten days. We enjoy fantastic views right up the north-west face of Cho Oyu, allowing us to take in the entire route. Flat, rocky slabs are carefully positioned for maximum comfort. Our mess tent and sleeping tents soon also become festooned with prayer flags. A *puja* (devotional ceremony) is held around a rapidly erected *stupa* (burial monument) with offerings of rice, beer, candies and Pringles. A multi-tasking Sherpa guide who is also a lama leads the ceremony; the crack of the first beer can draws a crowd of porters and guides from all around camp. An 8am drinking session at this altitude leads to me feeling very sick, very quickly. This quiet time before the ascent involves acclimatisation walks, plenty of discussion about tactics, and drinking copious amounts of water to stay hydrated. I say farewell to Seba as he leaves for home.

Day one of my climb to Camp One (6500m) is my hardest of the entire trip. Emotionally, I feel alone, and physically I have to tackle the eight hundred metre soul-breaking 'killer' slope of loose sliding scree with a full pack. This pack is laden with a tent and all the supplies I will need to stock Camp One. I vomit repeatedly on the way up. Nearly collapsing at camp, I dig out a platform, assemble my tent and turn back down for the night. It is dark when I traipse into ABC and sleep heavily.

The next mission is to sleep at Camp One (6500m) and then proceed up to Camp Two (7200m). The 'killer' slope goes better this time and I am looking forward to getting onto the snow above it. The route above Camp One follows a distinctive broad ridge before climbing over a fifty metre sérac (ice tower), with Camp Two not far above. The sérac is pleasurable to climb, with sound ice and a fixed rope in place, an exciting change to plodding. The altitude is really hitting me: leaden feet and gasping lungs. But I just have to keep my rhythm and clip onto the fixed line on the steep sections. My thoughts stretch no further than my endless mantra: 'Ice axe, jumar, left foot, right foot…ice axe, jumar, left foot, right foot.'

I make Camp Two in good time and decide to continue up to Camp Three (7600m) in order to drop off my tent and some provisions. I bury my gear deep (and mark it with a bamboo pole) to ensure that it will not blow away and that it will be safe from scavenging crows. I know the next time I see the tent will be on my summit bid. Pleased with myself, I hurry back to ABC for a well-earned rest!

After two days of complete bed-rest at ABC, I set off for the big push. My adrenaline is pulsing in waves. I feel prepared and confident. I know the only real obstacle remaining is the Rock Band: the crux, a vertical thirty metre rock chimney at 7700m. *(See Plate 6)*

At Camp Two (7200m), I share the tent of a German climber whom I met at ABC. I hungrily devour the tepid water I have melted from the snow. The stove is struggling with the extreme cold and low atmospheric pressure. It takes two hours to boil water and prepare a disgusting freeze-dried meal. It takes almost as long to stomach the revolting fodder I know is essential to fuel my tiring body. Still, I have nothing else to do. The next morning, I am the first to rise and I break trail the whole way to Camp Three. The crust is thin and I break through the snow to my knees. It is exhausting. My chest heaves in a coughing fit.

Camp Three (7600m) is grim. Toilet paper, frozen excrement, cans and plastic packaging swirl around in the wind. Oases of orange urine stains circle the tents. Perched on a 35° slope, I make use of a platform carved out of the snow. I brawl with my tent like a drunkard, wrestling the material down flat. My mind is befuddled. The view for 3000 metres down to Advance Base Camp (ABC) peels away from below my feet. Every five minutes I slump to get my breath back. An hour later, I can crawl inside my tent. Another hour, I melt snow. I am wary of dehydration. At this altitude, there is the constant fear of cerebral oedema (a blood clot in the brain) or pulmonary oedema (flooding of the lungs with blood). It is vital to judge whether the ever-present pounding headache and dry hacking cough may in fact be the symptoms of something more sinister.

I attempt to get some sleep. I am wearing a full down suit and down slippers inside my down sleeping-bag. Still, my toes are freezing. The alarm is set for midnight. One hour to make a brew and then set off for the summit at 1am. I needn't have set the alarm … no chance of sleep.

It is around 2am and about -35° Celsius. I am just below the rock band

and have stopped to be sick. I force myself up. 'Ice axe, jumar, left foot, right foot…ice axe, jumar, left foot, right foot': back to my mantra. Soon, I look up at the rock wall standing between me and the summit. I clip into a fixed line. The metal of my crampons scratches at the rock, screeching like nails on a blackboard. But they hold solid. I brush away snow to uncover handholds. My ears roar with my rushing blood. Between my legs, the hollow circle of my headtorch shows only blackness. I inch upwards, tentative at first. My fingers warm with the exertion. My spirits begin to warm, too. After all the anxiety of facing the crux, here I am doing it. In fact, I am loving it. This is what climbing is all about. It is all over too soon when I step out over the top.

Above the crux, there remains only the painful trudge upwards. My breath is heaving, my muscles are aching, yet I am hardly moving. I have to keep to my target of ascending 100m every hour. It is awkward to grip my ice-axe and clip on and off the rope. I take off my down mitts. At 8am, I step over the lip onto the summit plateau. I pause to take in the view of endless peaks from the roof of the world. The intense sun glares into my eyes. I take off my layers of gloves to rake out my sunglasses. The fingertips of my left hand are ghostly white. I bite them. There is no feeling. I begin to flick and slap my fingers, and then thrust them under my down suit, under my armpit. I am minutes away from the true summit and then I will go down to repair my numbed body.

At the very top, elation wells up and a flush of fulfilment burns within…

Now back home, my fingers have fully recovered and I no longer focus on the pain of the climb. Rather I am thrilled by the personal limits we can all stretch to. I would like to thank Mr Cowx, Scout leader at RGS during my school life, who was the first to widen my horizons in the hills. Our adventurous trips to the wet windswept Welsh hills and beyond opened the doors of adventure for which I am very grateful.

Gasherbrum II: Testing the limits on an 8000m peak
by Rupert Dix

The wind howled around my goggles and bit into my cheeks. I stared down between my legs. All I could see were the front crampon points carefully nestling on the edge of a narrow ledge. My down suit was keeping the worst of the cold out, but my toes were numb and my hands – one wrapped around my ice-axe and the other clutching my ascender – were just solid blocks of bone. I should never have taken my mitts off to free the last karabiner... Perched at 7400m, I still had over 600m to climb; it was now 5am and I had been climbing since midnight. How did I get here?

More than ten months earlier, I had finally convinced myself and my employer that I was due a two month 'sabbatical' to pursue a dream. Having been working for AgustaWestland (Helicopters) for the past fourteen years, they were used to my mountaineering exploits and so were not surprised when I approached them for some company support to enable me to pursue yet another mountaineering challenge: my first 8000m peak.

My passion for the outdoors, and mountaineering, began through the CCF at school, with Dai Jones introducing me to ten-man ration packs, Easter Camps in Wales and awful weather during the Ten Tors on Dartmoor. I had also been fortunate, for twenty years, in having undertaken major expeditions across Nepal, Tibet, Ladakh, the Karakoram and the Patagonian Andes as well as local climbs in the UK, Spanish Pyrenees and Italian Dolomites, but I had yet to attempt one of the fourteen 8000m peaks that, with equipment improvements, have now become more accessible since their first ascents in the 1950s. I had been an avid reader of the great mountaineers' and explorers' exploits, but to actually 'climb' an '8000-er' without any support beyond Base Camp had become my final goal.

Our team, comprising eight climbers, four cooks and three High Altitude Porters (HAPs), was to spend two months together in the most concentrated high-altitude mountain region in the world. This high performance team had been pulled together by Phil (now a US citizen, although of UK origin), with over twenty-five 8000m expeditions to his name. It was his job to plan all the logistics to enable seven other climbers: Wally (Canada), Tachi (Italy), Freddi (Sweden), Sammi (Finland), Arian (France), Max (Argentina) and me – at thirty-nine years by no means the oldest member of the team! – to work together and support each other, to summit Gasherbrum II, at 8035m, the world's thirteenth-highest mountain. Only twenty-five climbing permits had been issued for Pakistan in 2010. In 2009 there were seventy-five; 2008 saw two hundred and fifty, this decline reflecting the global financial crisis as well as the political situation.

Preparations

After a period of intensive training extending from the London Marathon through rock-climbing in Wales to ice-climbing in excellent conditions in Scotland, I landed at Islamabad on the morning of 8 June 2010. There, I met some of the team; we loaded our bags onto a lorry which headed off to Skardu via the Karakoram Highway: we would not see our kit again for two and a half days. Two days later we flew up to Skardu, our last chance to shop for provisions and other supplies. For two days we arranged all our kit: the rope (perhaps two kilometres of it!), tents, kitchen tents, high-altitude tents, food, food, food galore for eight hungry climbers and three high-altitude porters, all our personal climbing kit, clothing, sleeping-bags, down suits and everything else. All were very keen to get on the trail, but, as we waited for some cargo to arrive, it was still uncertain when we would depart. Finally, we left Skardu on the morning of June 13, my birthday, and endured a six hour jeep ride through some amazing scenery to our camp at Askole at the start of the trek to Base Camp. I had completed this trek before, but it remains absolutely unforgettable. On the way, we saw the famous Trango Towers, Masherbrum, K2, Broad Peak and Gasherbrum I as we approached the Base Camp. The views of K2 were the best I have ever seen, with the most amazing photo opportunities!

We arrived at Gasherbrum Base Camp (BC) at about 8am on Sunday, June 20. There was a perfect view of Gasherbrum I (Gasherbrum II is hidden at BC), through the clear blue skies. French-Canadian, Korean and Polish teams were already established. The French, having fully acclimatised in Nepal over the last two months, were going for the summit already. We had to sit things out, however, as being camped at about 5000m, our bodies needed time to acclimatise. I was extremely apprehensive. Six of the eight guys had attempted over forty-three 8000m peaks between them; their experience was vast. Max had still to join us: his visa had been held up, but we decided to push on regardless.

We were all getting on very well, with good banter. Two of the guys had fever or nausea, but we were otherwise generally pretty fit. The cold at night started to bite. Once the sun goes down, everything freezes quickly. At the higher camps, I would sleep in a lightweight sleeping-bag, while wearing my down suit in temperatures as low as -40°C. We were going to bed at about 7pm and waking at 6am. I would spend these days refreshing my crevasse rescue techniques with one of the guys, as it would be highly likely that we would have one or two 'incidents'! Tomorrow we would start the first 'rotation' or leg at 4am by ascending the Icefall.

On with the climbing!
We planned the 'rotations' as follows:
- The first would take us to Camp 1 to sleep at 6000m (a 1000m gain in altitude); sleep there, then return to BC at the end of day 2.
- The second would take us to Camp 1, sleep, then to Camp 2, sleep, then return on day 3 to BC.
- The third (and hopefully final rotation), would take us to Camp 1, sleep, Camp 2, sleep, Camp 3 (7050m), sleep, then set off at midnight on day 4, go for the summit (8035m) and return to Camp 3, sleep, then Camp 1 or BC, depending on strength. The summit day would last about sixteen hours, at extreme altitude and cold, with major ice work.

We had about one month to complete all three rotations. If the weather remained good, we could do the whole climb in two weeks. Acclimatising properly and passing through the Icefall safely (we should only have to do this three times, always early in the morning before the sun came out) would be critical. The avalanche risk would always be there, but we should be fairly safe if we started early, and our campsites were chosen to minimise this risk.

Rotation 1
So the climbing started on the morning of June 24. This is what I had been pondering for ten months, not knowing what to expect, how tough things would be, what the conditions, obstacles and scale of things would really be like. That morning, I was wrestling with my high-altitude boots at 3am, checking my kit over and over again, making sure that I had not forgotten anything, yet realising that my pack weighed too much. I decided to take as much equipment up to Camp 1 with my first carry (the first rotation) as possible (including warm clothing and a down suit, which would not be needed until much higher), so that I could build up my kit for the higher camps. Others carried much lighter loads, but I figured that my strength

would progressively be sapped as I would have to do the route three times minimum from BC to Camp 1.

Head-torches on, crampons, harnesses and axes at the ready, we were off by 4am, before daylight; we worked our way through the vast Icefall, our crampons crunching on the ice. The scale is not really comprehensible, with the ice séracs, crevasses and massive ice blocks hanging off the side of other mountains, waiting to avalanche, day and night. After thirty minutes, I caught my first glimpse of Gasherbrum II – wow! It looked majestic, with its huge triangular summit. (The mountain is hidden until you enter the Icefall.)

We had sent up our three High Altitude Porters at 2.30am. They would place bamboo canes every 100 metres, so that we could navigate our way through the safest route. These guys are, with their lengthy experience, invaluable: they carry a very large amount of the group kit (ropes and tents for the higher camps), since they would be returning to BC on the same day and so would not need any personal kit.

Crossing crevasses was one of the greatest risks on the expedition. Some were 1–2 metres wide (with concealed edges) and 50–100 metres deep. We would set up a rope over the huge gaping hole and carefully jump across while belaying each other. I roped up with Sammi and Tachi. We kept the rope taut between us, ready to ice-axe arrest if any of us were to suddenly break through into a crevasse. My crevasse rescue training was still fresh in my head, so I was acutely aware of what I was doing.

We had to make over 1000m of altitude gain by navigating through about ten kilometres of Icefall, a massive jump in acclimatisation. The effort and energy needed were immense. Our rope team took five hours fifteen minutes (seven to eight hours, normally). So we were doing OK, but my final few hundred metres were really tough: my head was pounding with the altitude as I arrived at Camp 1, just shy of 6000m. I have to say that day was a real endurance test. All that London Marathon training barely took the edge off it! Fortunately, the sun was barely out by the time that we arrived at Camp 1, so at least we were not overheating.

We then spent about three hours melting snow by our tents while preparing our drinking and cooking water. The views were astounding. The Golden Throne, Gasherbrums I, II, III, IV, V and South were each peeking out behind the clouds. The route up Gasherbrum II looked formidable. I could see Camp 2 and Camp 3, and the line right up to the summit. Extreme. The route now became a lot more direct, a 70° snow slope requiring ice-axes, with a pack on your back, the wind beating you down and the thin air from 6000m to 7000m to contend with. I didn't even want to think about the effort needed for the summit push on rotation 3! *(See Plate 7)*

We were then hit by a huge snowstorm. All that could be done was to batten down the tents and try to keep warm. We cooked a freeze-dried meal at 5pm and were all asleep by 6pm. My head was buzzing all through the night with the altitude, but this was to be expected... I now had to repeat the same thing at least twice, for the second and third rotation, plus the higher camp climbing.

On the morning of June 25, we were cramponed-up by 5.30am to return to BC. There was no visibility; it was gently snowing and our eyes were focused on finding each bamboo cane to ensure that we were following the correct route. It was a fairly gentle return, taking about three hours, although we noticed with alarm that some of yesterday's crevasses had widened. At 8.15am came the welcome sight of BC. Our cooks had prepared a good breakfast spread (if you eat eggs). It was great to just chill out in our dome tent and recover.

So that was rotation 1 complete. We were all hoping to go for rotation 2 on June 28. The weather had turned a little harsh, however, and we needed to acclimatise further. The French team had reached Camp 3 on June 14, then started for the summit, but had to turn back as the weather closed in. I guessed that they would have to return to BC and wait for the next weather window.

Rotation 2

We set off on June 28 for the next phase, with the main purpose of gaining further altitude and carrying some of our high-altitude equipment to the higher camps, to be ready for the summit push. This was going to be a testing time for me, physically and mentally, and the climbing was going to be more extreme. The team of five comprised Phil, Arian, Tachi, Wally and myself, with three HAPs helping to move some of the high-altitude kit and tents. The other three, Sammi, Freddi and Max, were working independently, a day ahead of us.

The route to Camp 1, just like the first rotation, took us through the Icefall again. Some of the crevasses had opened up further, dropping perhaps over seventy metres, so we all remained as vigilant as ever. The weather was not great, but we had seen the beauty of the cwm last time we came through. At Camp 1, we returned to unenjoyable freeze-dried meals, then got on with lots of snow-melting throughout the afternoon to prepare our cooking and drinking water.

A 5am start was needed next morning to make the best of the conditions before the sun started to melt the surface snow. This was the real thing. Within thirty minutes, we were starting the 500m–600m ascent up 70° snow slopes. *(See Plate 8)*

The route required some vertical rope work with ascenders; some traverses needed only ice-axe and crampons: you realised the extent of the drop if you did not ensure a secure ice-axe placement! Finally we topped out on the famous Banana Ridge – another wow! Progress was slow, however, as we were now operating at over 6000m, with continuous cutting of snow steps and some fairly hair-raising traverses. After about four and a half gruelling, sweaty hours we arrived at the lower Camp 2. Some tents, covered in snow, were already pitched here, on a very exposed ledge that could only be four metres by fifteen metres.

Phil wanted us to push on for another hundred metres of ascent, to the higher Camp 2, where the winds would be ferocious, but with less snow exposure. This last climb of the day was really tough for all of us. When we arrived, the tent placement was much better, but the winds were already building up. The altitude here was 6550m, my personal record to date.

The normal routine then set in at Camp 2: melting snow and getting ready for the night. Looking up towards Camp 3, I could see the snow build-up was immense, and ready to avalanche at any moment. The French had misled us and had not laid any ropes at all, which meant that we would need to; this would require a further rope carry from Base Camp.

So we decided to spend a rest day at Camp 2 on June 30 to help acclimatise. This was fine, but spending from 6am when you naturally wake, until 7pm when you sleep, on a small snow ledge is not easy. We played cards; I managed to do some reading and spent time keeping the tents secure from the winds. The wind speed rose to 70mph: we had to brace our backs to the tent walls for many hours of the day to stop them from caving in. The snow build-up was huge, and the noise was indescribable!

We went to bed at 7pm, but my body was not used to the freeze-dried meals which meant having to go out into the winds and snow at 1am to use the 'hole in the ground', four metres from a huge, sheer drop, with a crack forming through the middle of it. My rear was very cold. Not an experience that I will rush to repeat!

When we woke at 5am on July 1, the conditions were still 'whiteout', but the winds had subsided and we needed to make some tracks before the snow melted. The descent was epic. Movement was extremely difficult on the fresh snow, when much of the route needed rappelling (abseiling), as the snow would just give way around our feet. I slid often, sometimes on a rope, sometimes just with my axe, but we worked really well as a team. I had a small fall into a sudden crevasse, but was on a rope and managed to brace myself by jabbing my axe into the side wall and catching my crampons on a small ledge – yikes! There was a sudden, terrifying silence... then I heard the team above shouting my name. I had only fallen about three metres, so I could (just about) laugh at the situation!

What should have taken us an hour and a half took four and a half hours, even with every team member completely focused. I felt much stronger than previously and my rope work and technique seemed generally fine. Throughout this descent it was snowing, which meant that my 1998 Chris Bonington Berghaus Goretex Jacket was needed, attracting the usual raised eyebrows from Phil following the grief he had previously given me over my 'retro' 1986 Karrimor rucksack! I also needed to wear ski-goggles which were a blessing in the whiteout conditions when all you wanted to focus on was keeping both hands on the rope.

We all made it to Camp 1 safely, dropped off some gear and then made a three hour walk back through the Icefall (with very soft snow, now, so lots of waist-deep falls) to BC. Every single one of us was shattered. The milk tea at BC was fantastic. A shave, general pamper and quick burst on the i-pod were all that was needed to rejuvenate!

So Rotation 2 was a success. We had acclimatised well. The route and equipment were in place. We still believed that only one more rotation for the summit was needed. The thought of having to do a fourth did not register with me. The critical thing now would be the weather window. We might have to sit it out for a week for this. So we were going to fix some ropes with the other groups from Camp 2 to Camp 3, depending on when the weather improved. We would have to wait and see. The official forecast suggested heavy precipitation or high wind speeds for at least a week; the good weather could be from July 8... It looked like a long wait at BC.

The long wait and mini-rotation

So, back to some reading, a shower (well... hot water in a bucket), some much-needed 'home cooking' and some lower-altitude sleeping. This was a tricky game. Physically, I thought I was going to be OK. Mentally,

I was focused and felt that the team was coming together well. But many other factors needed to be aligned if we were going to be successful. Typically, everything now depended on the weather. The other problem was that our tents were still at Camp 2 with our down suits inside, and the wind speeds could blow them away: did we need to head back up to strike the tents?

Now July 8. After a week at BC, with a lot of banter, cards, reading, washing, eating and resting, the first summit window came. We had been studying the weather forecasts provided by a professor of meteorology in the USA, with our primary concern being the wind speeds. The precipitation levels were low, and the heavy snow of the last few days should have consolidated enough to avoid avalanche or landslide conditions; the temperatures at 8000m seemed reasonable, but the wind speed and direction did not look good. The wind, coupled with the low temperature, could produce a worrying wind-chill factor; the winds, however, were forecast to drop on July 12, the best bet for our first summit attempt.

Our team had acclimatised better than most of the others. We had spent two nights at Camp 2. We would only spend one night at Camp 3 (which is normal) at 7050m and then go for the top. If any of us felt rough at Camp 3, we would descend and go for a fourth rotation later. There were so many unknowns, even the push from Camp 2 (6550m) to Camp 3 which is fairly steep and on quite an exposed section.

From Camp 3 to the summit, we intended to traverse to the side of the summit and then make a very tough push to the top from about 7450m. The descent would be critical: after turning round, we would have been going for ten hours and would be fatigued, with the sun on our back, dehydrated... we would have to be very careful. Our fixed ropes would be in place from Camp 3 to Camp 2, but most of the route down from the summit to Camp 3 would be without ropes.

The other teams had been watching us with interest. The Swiss (whose leader had never climbed an 8000m peak) were desperate for conditions to improve as they had to leave on July 13: they were waiting for us to fix the ropes from Camps 2 to 3 and had been urging us on, regardless of the weather. Some of the French had stayed on at Camp 2. The Slovenian, Italian, Czech and South American teams all had their own agendas. Hopefully our patience and wisdom would pay off. We intended to set off at 7pm on July 12, using head-torches, to avoid the sun during the day and to ensure that the Icefall and ground were solid.

On July 9, we heard that the wind speeds were not dropping sufficiently. The Jet Stream remained at a good distance, but the windspeed forecast was still for about 30–40mph for July 12, 13 and 14, and 20–30mph for July 15, 16… This was intensely disappointing. The wind-chill factor at 7500m–8000m with wind speeds of 30mph is extreme, almost guaranteeing frostbite in hands and feet: once you have lost your core temperature, that is the point of no return. On Everest, the windspeed limit in order to summit is 30mph, but most climbers are using oxygen, which warms up your body, so in reality, the threshold is about 20mph. Here, we are not using oxygen…

So, on July 9, having had a week at BC, most of us agreed that we needed to exercise. We therefore set off for the third time through the Icefall. I was a little reluctant to do this, knowing how much that 1100m altitude gain would exhaust me, but I also knew that my body needed to be conditioned for the summit push. I opted to walk at night through the Icefall, as the thought of sitting in the cwm throughout the day with an early morning start just saps energy: there is nowhere to hide from the sun…

We set off at 6.30pm, an hour before my normal bedtime, and pushed up through the huge Icefall as the snow was starting to harden after a day of softening in the sun. The going was good, with a few soft challenges, but once the night was black we followed our rays of head-torch light, roped together, listening and waiting to dive to the ground to prevent a colleague from plummeting into one of the huge chasms, treacherous enough in the daylight, that were opening up. Some seemed to go down over 100m, with a dark, sinister feeling sweeping over your body as you precariously jumped a one- to two-metre gash, hoping that the cornices would hold…

In the distance, we heard a huge avalanche release itself from Gasherbrum VI, which then presented itself to us about forty-five minutes later, with lorry-size blocks being illuminated by our head-torches. Navigating through the debris was desperate, as the marker wands had been mostly been wiped out. Then our head-torches caught the reflection of a marker wand about eighty metres away and we were back on the route again.

I arrived at Camp 1 at about 11pm, with numb fingers and feeling completely exhausted. All that I could do was remove my harness, rope, crampons, boots and soft shell and crawl into my sleeping-bag. I felt dehydrated, cold and uncomfortable. I had no energy to re-cut the sleeping platform, so trying to sleep on an angle of 10° with my body continually rolling off-balance, while a horrific high-altitude cough sat on my chest, amounted to not the greatest night I've ever spent in the mountains!

I woke at 5am (having had about thirty minutes sleep), wrestled my climbing equipment back on and then headed back down the cwm to BC. The enormous scale of the avalanche debris was now visible. All the six beautiful peaks of Gasherbrum looked majestic in the early morning sun. Huge white trails winding their way through the ice séracs, gaping crevasses – it all looked truly spectacular. We looked like small dots, nimbly working their way through this maze of nature. Back for breakfast at 8.30am!

On reflection, it felt good and was a necessary exercise for the summit push. The depressing thing was realising that we had returned to the waiting game... A shower, some reading, and then a few hours in the cooking tent teaching the cooks some more English: I had covered modal verbs, six major verb tenses, comparatives and superlatives, general conversation and so on. This had gone on for weeks!

Some of the French team had stayed behind, and were at that moment experiencing those 30–40mph winds on the summit ridge. We hoped that they would return with all of their fingers and toes and that they would not radio for rescue. If they did, our summit chances would be quashed, as all energy would be spent on getting them down safely. I could understand what they were thinking: they had been at BC since June 6, and so they had endured a lot of waiting. They were due to leave within days as they had already extended their trip. At least they should have a shot at the summit, within reason: they knew what they were doing.

The Swiss, on the other hand, lacked experience and team spirit. I had seen some of their party returning through the Icefall alone, so therefore able to plummet to their death in a crevasse with an unheard scream... The Swiss had returned from Camp 3 the night before, shattered and demoralised. I think that they were heading home. The Czechs were also desperate, now: they needed to depart soon... The Italians, Polish and South Americans were somewhere in between.

The new plan was to await the forecast on July 12, and hope that the wind speeds would at least briefly lessen; then it would be decision time. Maybe the forecast was making the situation seem worse than it was... a possible summit on July 15 or 16 was our latest chatter. We were becoming restless. I was running out of books, but the guys had managed to rig up one of the high-altitude laptops for us to watch films. So we would leave the dome tent at 7–8pm to go to bed, having just been watching a movie for two hours. The food was getting really quite tedious and I had lost an awful lot of weight despite eating three meals a day.

A further set-back

July 12 turned out to be an all-time low for us. We thought that the new weather forecast would give us the news that we had hoped for, but unfortunately it didn't. I went to bed on the evening of July 11, thinking for the second time that we would push for the summit the next morning. It then snowed through the night and I could hear the chatter round the campsite the next morning which told me that the forecast from our professor in Seattle was not good news. The window would last one day, with wind speeds confirmed at 25–30mph, not 20–33mph, so guaranteed to be 25mph: extremely dangerous. After this window, the windspeed would increase, however, so the real damage would occur after summit day. I was learning the boundaries of this cruel game.

We had also heard that some of the other teams summited on July 11, but one climber fell 300m and a call had to be made to Islamabad. We were not sure, but suspected that the incident involved the French who had been here at BC since June 6. We didn't know if they had any frostbite problems, but in our opinion, the risks they were taking were too great. While none of the stories were confirmed at that point, we would still wait for the weather to improve. On Gasherbrum I, two of the most experienced guys in the climbing fraternity, Don Bowie (Canada) and Alexey Bolotov (Russia), both having been successful on K2, turned round at 7600m because of extreme winds; thus, for them to turn round in the same winds (very wise) makes the G2 story seem all the more remarkable.

Waking up on the morning of July 12, I felt so low. The next forecast was for July 16 and we had no idea what it would be, but we were hoping to be home after seven weeks, not eight! The thought of another week at BC was extremely tough. I had read most of my books; the conversation about the weather went round and round; I just spent a lot of time thinking about being back home. We had confirmation that the French had summited. One of the Poles had injured his leg in the 300m fall, but managed to stay on the Pakistani side of the mountain. He made it off the mountain a few days later. The Swiss had now gone home, having abandoned their attempts. We also received reports that one of our tents had been damaged at Camp 2: this would necessitate a replacement equipment carry.

On July 14, we all made a decision that we would definitely head up on July 16/17 after the final forecast. We would probably go direct from BC to Camp 2 in one day on July 17 (1.5km ascent) to avoid too many nights on the mountain with freeze-dried meals! Then Camp 2 on the evening of July 17, and push for Camp 3 the next day. We could then evaluate on July 19 how close to the summit we could get. If the conditions were good, we would go for it. If not, we would clear everything off the mountain. In any case, back to BC for July 20. That was the plan!

Rotation 3 and the summit push

On the morning of July 16, we received the final forecast from Seattle: zero precipitation from July 16–19, with horrific weather after that. The wind speeds at 7500m and above were 'predicted' at 20–30mph: still a little strong, but our last opportunity for a summit attempt. What we did know was that a summit bid on July 19 would need a 1.5km descent to Camp 1 on the same day if we were to avoid the following bad weather patch, as descending the Banana Ridge in poor conditions could be lethal.

At 3.30am on July 17, we were buzzing around in our tents at BC (5170m), preparing for a mammoth three days, with our only summit push in mind. Breakfast at 4am, then en route at 4.20am. The route through the Icefall to Camp 1 was as treacherous as ever, but we were at least avoiding the sun, so the ice was reasonably hard to walk on. Four hours later we arrived at Camp 1(5950m). There, we collected some high-altitude equipment, then drank and ate, before another four to five hours up to Camp 2. The Banana Ridge climb was hard work, but we arrived at Camp 2 (6550m) at 3.15pm. We had climbed for almost twelve hours, with over 1.5km of ascent, in one day. We repaired our damaged tent then consumed a freeze-dried meal and all of our high-altitude goodies (a tin of sardines, some apricots and chocolate, in my case) and were asleep by 6.30pm (not that you really sleep at that altitude).

At 6am on the morning of July 18, we started to break our first trail to Camp 3. The snow conditions were terrible, with heavy snow slopes. We needed to use ropes and a lot of very focused attention! Some ice climbing, some deep snow (up to our waist) and an ascent of about five hundred metres in four hours made for hard going, with continuous step-cutting and one ice-axe placement after another. I was fuelling on power shots (glucose) and chocolate, with jaded energy levels, but nevertheless enjoying it. Arriving at Camp 3 (7050m) at 10am, I was now to share a three-man tent, which was going to be cosy. The tent is the only place to shelter from the sun, as the intense midday rays strike your tent. The plan was to get our heads down and prepare at 11pm for the summit push. Who knows what the wind would be like?

At 11pm, already in my down suit, having 'slept' in it for four hours, I was frantically stuffing everything into its available pockets as I did not want to carry a rucksack. I carried two litres of water, energy food, different goggles for different times of the day, emergency acute mountain sickness medicine, personal radio, head-torch and batteries, cameras, sun cream for later, various mitts and gloves, balaclavas, plus a harness with climbing equipment, crampons and ice-axe. It was now two minutes past midnight on Monday July 19.

It was crazy, this line of nine climbers (our team of five, three HAPs, and one independent), with head-torches on, climbing up mixed snow and ice slopes in the early hours of the morning. What on earth were we doing? The going was extremely tough. We would all take ten steps, wait for twenty seconds, then continue. My biggest problem was not the altitude, but the cold, which approached -40°C. My feet, after 300m of vertical ascent, were frozen solid, just because the pace was not quick enough (but couldn't have been any quicker). I had to remove my thermal mitts at every rope change (not easy to unclip an ascender with a glove whose size would not seem out of place at a baseball game). After almost five hours of climbing, I could finally see the summit's east ridge, but my fingers and toes felt as I feared they would in these conditions, and I certainly did not want to lose them. (The Old Guildfordians Rifle Club would never have forgiven me.)

The wind howled around my goggles and bit into my cheeks. I stared down between my legs. All I could see was the front crampon points carefully nestling on the edge of a narrow ledge. My down suit was keeping the worst of the cold out, but my toes were numb and my hands – one wrapped around my ice-axe and the other clutching my ascender – were just solid blocks of bone. I should never have taken my mitts off to free the last karabiner. Perched at 7400m, I still had over 600m to climb; it was now 5am and I had been climbing since midnight.

Shortly after, those winds began to pick up (the estimate afterwards was 50–60mph). The summit seemed so close. I stopped beyond the Camp 4 graveyard of battered old tents. I was now at the back of the group and could not feel my hands or toes. This was serious. I was now on my own. What should I do? This is the situation that you read about in the books: pig-headed climbers who sacrifice their digits for an ascent. We knew that it would have to be 'on the day': would we be lucky with the wind? I stopped for twenty minutes to try to warm up my hands so that I could radio Phil and discuss my options. I made the call at 5.45am from an altitude of 7500m. Phil told me to wait for the sun to come out, then evaluate my situation. I pushed on and called again thirty minutes later: the response was: descend, descend, descend!

Everyone was experiencing the same challenge with the wind. Sammi (one of the top climbers in Finland, climbing independently of us) decided to go for it – his choice. Phil had never seen winds like that on an 8000m summit day: our collective decision was to get off the mountain to save our digits. *(See Plate 9)*

I was demoralised. After weeks of waiting for our only window, I was defeated by the winds, not the altitude or my physical ability. The route down was harsh. I focused on good rappelling, some 'back climbing' (where you descend with axe and crampons, facing the rock, one step at a time) and kept my fingers and toes moving until the sensation reappeared. I did not want a slip or fall here – that would be terminal. My digits were going to be OK. I hit the tent at Camp 3 at 8.30am, shattered. I checked my feet: they were not black. My judgement had been just about on the money. Thank God. I got back in the tent, melted some snow for water and tried to get my head down. *(See Plate 10)*

The others returned within the hour and by 2pm Sammi arrived, triumphant (this was his fifth 8000m peak). He reflected that he had taken a big risk, but had been moving much quicker than us. The winds on the summit ridge were horrendous, he said, but he got up and down as quickly as he could. He had been frostbitten on Manaslu last year, so he knew the risks. At 4pm, towards sunset, we started our epic descent, moving on abseil points and snow anchors as best we could. Camp 3 to Camp 2, where we struck the tents. Camp 2 to Camp 1, arriving in the dark, having descended over two kilometres by abseil and back climbing for four to five hours. Shattered, exhausted, just needing to sleep. The time was 9pm.

Return to Base

On the morning of July 20, we returned to the trail from Camp 1 by 6.30am, all completely drained, having not eaten anything substantial since the evening of July 17. We navigated our way through the Icefall for one last time. The precipitation had struck. No visibility whatsoever, as predicted by our weatherman. He had been spot-on throughout, except perhaps the strength of the summit winds. These had not dropped below 30mph in the last month.

In the distance, thirty minutes from BC, I could see Sirbas (one of our cooks). He had ascended the first part of the Icefall with a large kettle of cold orange squash. I imagined that this was how Sir Edmund Hillary felt on seeing the team on his return from Everest's summit in 1953! My rucksack (over eighty-five litres) weighed a ton, as all my climbing equipment, our rubbish, our non-consumed food and so on was packed within. I finally crawled into our 'home', dumped my pack and consumed a very large breakfast. We reached BC by 9am; inside the tents, we knew it was snowing. Food, a proper wash, a shave – it was good to be back!

After three days recovering at BC, with a continuous snowstorm, five of us (three stayed on to attempt Gasherbrum I) undertook a rapid trek back to the roadhead: walking for many hours a day, we completed the trek out in just three days. The glacier, peaks and trail looked very different from what we remembered, yet we barely had time to take it all in as we were focused on our feet, step by step across the terrain. On arriving in Askole, we enjoyed our first coca-cola for weeks, as well as some soup, before distributing our unwanted rations and clothes to the locals. It was good to be back in civilisation, but we were not prepared for what lay ahead.

Leaving Pakistan

Back in Skardu, it turned out that the weather had delayed a number of flights to Islamabad, and it looked as if we would have to go overland. We waited for another day for an improvement but it did not get any better, so on the second morning we readied our driver and ourselves for the two day journey. After more than ten hours' driving we approached Chilas, our overnight rest spot. A large number of trucks, buses and cars seemed to be congregated by a bridge; on arrival, we saw buildings and village debris flooding underneath us within the huge grey torrent of the River Indus. The locals were muttering that a complete village had been washed away. We now realised that Pakistan was experiencing its worst floods for the last fifty years. More than a million people were already homeless and the death toll was rising. The Karakoram Highway was officially closed, with six major suspension bridges down and the only alternative pass, where the trucks were stopped earlier, was now not passable as there had been a series of landslides. We were stranded.

So we headed back to Chilas, this time deciding to take the situation into our own hands. We had heard that some of the landslides on an alternative route had been cleared and that 'ferry systems' with jeeps between 'islands' had been set up to bypass destroyed bridges. We had also been advised that this was an unsafe area of potential Taliban activity, but it was probably our best hope for evacuation. We arranged three jeeps, fully loaded with our equipment, and headed across some of the roughest terrain that such vehicles could drive through.

We drove for twenty hours, sometimes through Taliban country, over the second-highest pass in Pakistan, with makeshift road or track repairs. We drove along some rivers, with a depth of 75cm of water, for twenty minutes at a time, down roads that had a two-metre subsistence fault line, where mud ramps had been made! Whatever it took to return to Islamabad. Two suspension bridges had been washed away. There, we abandoned our jeep on the riverbank, waded across with all of our kit, and picked up another jeep on the far side. The roads were still caving into the river, crumbling at the edges. I gave these back roads another few days before they too would be washed away.

Finally, we picked up a decent bus and drove like madmen, weaving past all the cargo trucks at breakneck speed. We arrived at 11pm at our hotel in Islamabad, and headed straight for 'Domino's Pizza' (first meal without rice and dhal in two months: heaven!). I was given a motorbike lift at 1am to a cash point, followed by a drive to Islamabad airport to buy a ticket. The only flight for days was from Lahore; it was to leave at 8am. That would need another five hour journey to make the 400km trip by car through the night. Further adventures followed, but I made the flight, and the economy seat in the back of the PIA flight felt like the most luxurious treat one could wish for.

All in all, I may not have made the summit, but it was quite an adventure and a truly memorable and testing experience, enriched by the scale of the planning, the invigoration of the climbing, the contrast between mighty nature and fragile man, and by the quality of the friendships made along the way.

The Highest Trek in the World

by Jonathan Stuart (accompanied by Rupert Dix)

I felt oddly happy and carefree as I walked along the Ronghpu[5] glacier in the harsh, clear air at 17,000 feet. I admired the immense mountain scenery that surrounded me, set against the vivid blue high-altitude sky and it was only much later that I realised I had no right to feel like this. I reflected on the ridiculousness of my situation: not many people on Earth were higher than me that June afternoon in 1994, and I reasoned that none of them was strolling along battered and soaked in just sandals, boxer shorts and waterproof jacket. The thought made me laugh aloud, although Rupert ('Roo') Dix, my trekking companion and fellow Old Guildfordian, lay at the extreme other end of the emotional spectrum as he wondered whether he would see me again.

The build-up to this moment had started a year earlier. A mutual close friend died unexpectedly and, even with the benefit of hindsight, without warning. Barely twenty-two and having lost a gifted best friend, the rest of 1993 remained a dark time: it seemed unremittingly negative, but the new year brought renewed optimism. All aspects of life seemed to be heading in the right direction again; this virtuous circle felt great after such a bleak time. Then, in late spring, Roo asked if I wanted to join him on a trek to the Everest region of Tibet. Despite being excited at the suggestion, on any other occasion I might have found a dozen reasons not to go or would have spent too long worrying about 'what ifs'; the timing fitted perfectly, however, and I was ready for such a challenge.

There followed a thrilling few weeks, planning the trip and scraping together equipment on a student budget. For someone who likes to organise and plan and always enjoys a new challenge, this was a great time. Somehow, even the four subcutaneous rabies injections were exciting: they were received in one session rather than the usual two because of a lack of time before the trip, and I'd be happy never to have them again!

I had always loved mountain country. My decision to go to Stirling University was heavily influenced by the proximity of the Ochils, Trossachs and, further afield, the Highlands. I was as happy, however, to walk among mountains as to reach their summits and drew the line at 'proper' rock climbing. At school I had enjoyed the camps that took us to Wales and

---

5. Rongphu: this name of the access area to the northern side of Everest was formerly Rongbuk. Ed.

60

Dartmoor although they sometimes pushed me rather too far. I remember one Easter camp, when we walked up Cader Idris. I was concerned to find that the descent was a long slide down a steep, snow-filled gully. This prospect was slightly alarming but became inevitable when the teacher pointed out it was a long walk back to do alone! Eight years later I was about to embark on the world's highest trek, indeed one of its remotest, but by now anything seemed possible.

The aim of the expedition was to progress as far and high as possible on the Tibetan side of Everest. This was deliberately vague: given the political situation in Tibet we couldn't even be sure we would be allowed into the country. Once there, the pair of us, with limited equipment, would be attempting a trek that the guidebook warned should be 'attempted only by extremely fit and thoroughly acclimatized parties' and was 'best left for a professional trekking company to organise: the food and equipment requirements are more than most people want to carry at these elevations'.

In May 1994 we flew to Hong Kong, then still a British territory and thus a perfect base, especially given that Roo's sister was living there and kindly allowed us to make our base in her apartment. While Everest was our focus we couldn't miss the chance to see China and spent three fascinating weeks slowly exploring this vast country by boat, bus and train. While signs of redevelopment and change were everywhere in Beijing, most of China had yet to see significant change; tourism was still limited. We were often quite a novelty: being fair-haired and left-handed Roo sometimes drew a bemused crowd when writing his diary!

In 1994 there were two routes to Tibet from China. We could fly from Chengdu in the west or take a gruelling high-altitude forty-eight hour bus journey from the north. Given the risk of altitude sickness and the journey time on the bus we opted for the flight as our one luxury on the trip. There was nothing certain about gaining access to Tibet: the Chinese would randomly refuse access or close the border. Buying our plane tickets, however, was uneventful and, having splashed out on the tickets we checked in to Chengdu's cheapest hotel, the infamous Black Coffee. This was a dark, dank and rat-infested converted bomb shelter but it was cheap. We left the Black Coffee before dawn and were glad of the poor lighting because that meant we didn't see the rats squeaking and scratching around our feet as we left! A few hours later, and after a flight over spectacular mountain scenery, we touched down in Lhasa.

It was a relief to be in Tibet, and not just because this felt like a shift from tourism to trekking. China had been beautiful and fascinating but also hard work, noisy, polluted and at times brutal: we saw someone beaten up in the back of a truck and a dead body floated down a river as we passed above it on a train. Tibet was serene in comparison and the people unbelievably warm and friendly, something remarkable given what they see as the Chinese occupation and oppression of their country. We met a Canadian lady at the airport: Cindy was planning to go as far as Everest Base Camp so we joined forces, largely because there were so few Westerners in Tibet at that time.

We spent four days in Lhasa visiting the sights, exploring and making short treks. These were all unmissable in themselves but also enabled us to acclimatise to its 11,450 feet of altitude. Roo had plenty of high-altitude experience but my only trip higher than the Scottish Highlands had been a cablecar trip to the summit of Mont Blanc while in the first year of school! We both coped well and, apart from a few mild headaches, suffered no ill effects. The lack of air sapped our strength and fitness: even going up stairs was hard work; the only strategy was to take things slowly.

While in Lhasa we prepared our kit and bought the last few items, such as paraffin for our stove. We hadn't had time to test the new MSR multi-fuel stove; a lack of experience and dirty fuel caused us a frustrating and worrying afternoon. Without a stove the trek wouldn't go beyond Base Camp but with a lot of cleaning and fiddling the stove roared into life. This was good experience because once mastered the stove proved totally reliable and quickly boiled water regardless of the fuel quality or altitude.

On June 12 we started our two day bus journey to the trek's start. At Shigatse we acquired the necessary Alien Travel Permit from the Public Security Bureau and sent letters home. The following day we took a bus to Shekar[6] on the Friendship Highway, a road which continues to Kathmandu in Nepal. Despite it being Roo's birthday this was a day like any other on a Third World bus: hot, noisy and cramped. And then the radiator pipe burst. A rudimentary repair was effected, the radiator water refilled and the bus struggled on. It crawled up hills and the engine sounded as if it would give up at any moment, but eventually we made it to Shekar. Now we readied ourselves to jump off and looked for our navigation markers: through the

---

6. Shekar: formerly Shekar Dzong, the 'White Glass Fort' mentioned in early Everest accounts. The early expeditions approached it from the east having travelled through Sikkim. In transliterating from Tibetan and Chinese, Tibetan uses 'Sh' where Chinese uses 'X', so Xigatse/Shigatse, Xixapangma/Shishapangma, etc. The sound in either language is close to English 'sh'. I have stuck to the Tibetan forms. Ed.

police checkpoint, continue for another four miles and get off between road markers 494 and 495. Other passengers thought we were mad and tried to dissuade us, but as the bus pulled away it was late afternoon. We were standing on the roadside in the middle of nowhere. *(See Plate 11)*

There are a number of routes from the road to Everest base camp (BC). We chose the four day trek over the Pang La. We could have attempted to get a ride in a lorry or a four-by-four to BC, although we saw virtually none of these, but we wanted to walk from the road to be totally self-reliant, and this walk-in was a fantastic trek in itself. Most importantly, it helped our ongoing acclimatization that would be vital if we were to trek as high as possible beyond BC.

It was a fantastic four day trek to Dza Rongphu (Rongbuk) monastery. We were constantly surrounded by high peaks. The land was uniformly barren and consisted of grey/brown rock moved and ground down by thousands of years of glacial action, leaving behind a gritty landscape with numerous large stones and boulders. An easy walk in the late afternoon after leaving the bus took us to Chay (14,600 ft). This was a friendly village. We stayed the night in a simple single storey local house. Our strategy was to stay and eat in local houses as far as possible to preserve our food supplies.

The next day was a tough reminder that the hard work had started. The walk to Phadhruchi (13,800ft) required us to go over the Pang La (16,800ft). This was hard going in the thin air, especially as our rucksacks were at their heaviest, being full of supplies, and we hadn't yet reached full fitness. To compound our difficulties, I suffered from stomach cramps throughout the morning. The effort, however, was worth it: we saw a Himalayan panorama from the top of the pass with views of Makalu, Cho Oyu and, centre stage, Everest. It was the last view we would have of Everest for a few days but it provided the necessary motivation and encouragement.

We stayed in a small, dirty and very basic lodge in Phadhruchi. On the following day, we continued our trek to Chhosang (14,800ft). My aged and heavy rucksack remained relentlessly uncomfortable and the thin air and daytime heat made our progress slow and hard work but we slowly followed the track up the valley. We had read that Chhosang was a den of thieves and that a stay there was not recommended; we couldn't reach Dza Rongphu, however, in one day and perhaps didn't like to believe such a generalization. On arrival at Chhosang in the late afternoon we witnessed a Tibetan wedding. It was fantastic to see the traditional dress and celebrations. Aware of the village's reputation, we carried all valuables when we left our room and later found our rucksacks had been searched and 'valuable' chocolate stolen.

Following that experience we quickly left Chhosang the next day, excited at the prospect of reaching Dza Rongphu Monastery at 16,350ft. By now we should have been seeing ever more spectacular views of the North Face of Everest. The north side rewards trekkers with the most dramatic views possible without climbing the mountain, although low cloud persistently obscured it. We had followed a fast-flowing river of glacial melt water from the Rongphu Glacier for much of the trek and now had to cross this. It was not deep, coming no higher than our knees, but it was cold, wide and fast-flowing; we were relieved to reach the other side.

That melt water also provided much of our drinking water. Travelling light and cheaply we disinfected our drinking water with iodine and never suffered from illness. The taste became increasingly intolerable, however, almost making me retch, so blackcurrant flavoured rehydration salts were occasionally added to give some flavour. Cindy had a small purification device that we pumped to suck in dirty water and emit clean, fresh drinking water. This was welcome but strenuous work, especially as the filter frequently became blocked with the fine rock flour that is contained in glacial melt water and gives the rivers their characteristic milky appearance. I remembered my A-Level Physical Geography teacher, Chris Pafford, telling us not to drink such water because far from being pure it contained this rock flour. But now, other than after a long and slow pumping session, we had no choice but to drink grit!

We arrived at the remote Dza Rongphu monastery to find a pair of Australians already there; we played football and frisbee with them. A rest-day followed to ensure we didn't overreach our acclimatization. We ate the local *tsampa* and prepared our kit. A few unnecessary items were stashed at the monastery and our rucksacks repacked. Our vision of travelling light meant that we didn't have a tent and had planned to sleep open with a bivvy bag beyond the monastery. This now seemed fanciful and more appropriate for a *Boys' Own* adventure than reality. Fortunately the monks had a store of old equipment left by climbing expeditions and we managed to hire a used but functional Wild Country tent.

The weather had now cleared and we were treated to awe-inspiring views of Everest's North Face and west ridge at the head of the Rongphu Glacier. This really is the classic view of Everest; it was an incredible treat to have this as the backdrop to our world. We left the monastery and now had to be completely self-sufficient until we returned to this small settlement. *(See Plate 12)*

An easy morning's walk led us to the Everest BC at 16,900ft. The BC is a rambling, unremarkable stone strewn area that is no doubt used as BC because it is the last large, flat area before the Rongphu Glacier begins. There we met a Himalayan Kingdoms (now Mountain Kingdoms) expedition attempting a late season ascent of Everest via the North Col. In 1993, Himalayan Kingdoms had been the first British company to 'guide' Everest, putting seven paying clients, six Sherpas and two guides on the summit. The Himalayan Kingdoms team was beginning to establish their camps beyond BC and were shuttling supplies up the mountain. As the only other people now beyond the monastery it was good to know they were there and interesting to see a professional climbing expedition at work.

Our food for the expedition was basic and designed to provide energy while fitting in our rucksacks. The mainstay was a 2kg bag of rice and bags of flavoured noodles we bought at Chengdu. We had also bought PLA (People's Liberation Army) high energy biscuits although these tasted like medium density fibreboard! Our noodles were boiled up for lunches, and on most nights we ate rice. To add flavour we had brought an eclectic selection of small, lightweight snacks and flavourings from the UK. These included stock cubes, casserole sauces, Marmite (decanted into empty film canisters for easy carrying) and a tin of sardines! The Marmite was my idea and I think Roo initially thought it odd, but it proved to add flavour to all sorts of meals and even made the MDF biscuits slightly more interesting!

On June 19 we walked from BC to Camp 1 at 17,900ft. This involved a long, steep climb up scree slopes and outcrops to get to the camp shortly before the snout of the East Rongphu Glacier. Despite the altitude of this trek it involved no climbing and little scrambling, but there were plenty of other challenges. The thin air was the biggest problem. I found a rhythm that worked for me physically and mentally where I breathed slowly and deeply and took one step per breath. This made for slow but steady progress: like this, we could continue all day if necessary. Roo was slightly faster than me and often in front. Depending on my mood it was either useful to use him as a pacemaker or irritating to see the backs of his white legs constantly in front of me!

It started snowing shortly after we pitched the tent at Camp 1: we were grateful we had it. The stove had a tendency to flare up when first lit because it was difficult to preheat it sufficiently, so we never risked using it in the tent. That night we couldn't cook our rice so got into our sleeping-bags and shared the tin of sardines! We both had headaches from the altitude but were otherwise in good spirits.

The following morning the valley looked even more beautiful and tranquil with the monsoon season's first light covering of snow. It was cold, and the sun took some time to rise sufficiently to penetrate the base of the glacial valley. We packed quickly and continued our journey. For the next two days we would proceed along the East Rongphu glacier, initially along its south-western edge and then keep on a line between it and the Changtse glacier. Here we felt exposed and were aware of constant dangers. As the day warmed and ice melted, rocks became loose on the valley walls and came tumbling down like rough bouncing bowling balls. There were constant noises as rocks moved; we had to remain alert to the threat. Fortunately nothing came too near us but it made the progress harder because we couldn't put our heads down and walk in a hypnotic rhythm.

We met the Himalayan Kingdoms yak train taking supplies up the mountain and also the expedition leader Nick Banks, who had summited Everest in 1979, then Nga Tembu Sherpa, who had summited in 1992 and 1993. Nick kindly commented that we were fitter and more expedition-ready than some from his team: nice to hear. That night we slept at Interim Camp at 18,900ft. Although only 1,000ft higher than Camp 1, an important rule to help avoid altitude sickness is to sleep no more than 1,000ft higher than the previous night. In any case, at this altitude and carrying rucksacks weighing at least 25kg we couldn't have travelled any further.

During June 21 we continued our slow progress up the East Rongphu glacier. We were now trekking along the moraine between two glaciers; the first ice séracs were appearing. The guidebook describes these as resembling 'dozens of Sydney Opera Houses sailing on a choppy grey sea', a very good description. The séracs became bigger, sometimes reaching 40ft in height, as we progressed up the glacier: they would be a serious obstacle for anyone needing to cross the glacier, but fortunately our route took us along the lateral and medial moraines.

Camp 2 at 19,600ft proved hard to find. In theory we could have camped anywhere flat enough but the reality is that there aren't any flat areas in this jumble of rocks and ice. The camps are just flattened areas of ground developed over the years by the expeditions that have used this route. We wandered around, looking for the camp, for what seemed like ages when all we wanted to do after a tough walk was rest and have a brew. Eventually we found the camp, which was a rough and only vaguely flat area of rubble with sad remains of old cans marking its use by previous expeditions.

Some rubbish, however, becomes interesting if left long enough. Here and there beneath the rock and ice can be found communications cables left by the British expeditions from the 1920s. These early expeditions included legendary climbers such as George Mallory and Andrew Irvine who pioneered this route. Radio equipment was not used until the 1933 expedition: the pre-war climbers laid cables along the entire length of the glacier. I found fragments of the cloth-covered cables and stowed them in my rucksack to bring home. It was incredible to think of those early pioneers climbing in their tweeds, undaunted by the technical challenges of attempting to climb Everest.

The night at Camp 2 was incredibly cold. We had camped at just under 20,000ft and were surrounded by ice and valleys down which cold air must have flowed. At that time technical clothing was expensive and, on our budget, prohibitively so. I had one layer of genuine fleece; the rest were cotton T-shirts, shirts and jumpers. Perhaps with hindsight our clothing was closer to that worn by Mallory and Irvine! I wore seven layers on my torso that night. We stayed just about warm enough although later photographs showed our faces to be strangely blue. Roo's kit was similarly mixed: while he had what I saw as an exotic Goretex waterproof he was still sleeping on a three-quarters length Karrimat from school days. I always sleep well and, exhausted at the end of each day, had no trouble sleeping on my borrowed inflatable Thermarest. Unfortunately Roo found it harder to sleep at altitude, and was not helped by his thin and short Karrimat.

We had walked for four consecutive days since leaving the monastery and ascended around 3,500ft. Ideally we would now take a rest day and not overstretch our acclimatization. That was never in the plan, however, because our objective was now only a day's walk away and we would be able to return to Camp 2 to sleep that night. We also didn't have the food or time to take a rest-day. We left our tent at Camp 2 and carried only what we needed. We followed the lateral moraine of the East Rongphu glacier as it curved around Changtse, the peak immediately to the north of Everest. Every step took us slightly further round Changtse; the immense North Face of Everest gradually appeared.

The enormous size of this mountain cannot be overstated. We had travelled a long way and were approaching 21,000ft yet the summit was a further 8,000ft above us. As we got closer it dominated us and the landscape until our field of vision was entirely filled with Everest's bulk. We could clearly see the famous pinnacles where Joe Tasker and Peter Boardman (two of Britain's greatest climbers) lost their lives when pioneering the north-east ridge route in the early 1980s. Craning your neck to look up at one and a half miles of near vertical rock and ice is breathtaking and leaves one speechless at the sight of something so absolutely vast. From nowhere and inexplicably, it brought tears to my eyes, not because of any satisfaction in our achievement – we were too tired and breathless for that – but simply a response to the enormous dimensions of the mass in front of us.

We moved slowly; the three of us became spread out. Taking a step per breath was now too much and frequent stops were needed to get more oxygen into the blood. We really were at the limit of our acclimatization: the warning headaches returned. I found a comfortable resting position where I would slightly bend my legs and lean forward, resting the palms of my hands on each knee. This took the weight of the rucksack off my back and gave me relief as the weight was transferred down through my arms and legs. Most importantly, it left the lungs free to take full and much needed breaths.

Soon we reached Advance Base Camp (ABC) at 20,800ft, which is the last camp accessible without ropes or a climbing license. It was good to see the Himalayan Kingdoms mess tent there; we joined their climbers for a brew and some chocolate. We enjoyed talking with them although the leaders obviously had some concerns about the varying abilities in the team and the lateness in the season of their climb. Unfortunately the monsoon snows later repeatedly covered the expedition's fixed ropes and they eventually had to abandon their attempt. We were determined to travel as far as possible so, after enjoying a celebratory tin of tuna, continued beyond ABC. We slowly walked as a group until our way was blocked by vertical ice that marked the start of the ascent to the North Col. Having reached 21,300ft we could go no further and had fully achieved our main objective. *(See Plate 13)*

We returned to Camp 2 exhausted but buoyant and glad to be losing altitude again. Despite our exhaustion Roo was sleeping worse than ever and the tent felt cramped as we all struggled to be comfortable. The next day, June 23, we made great progress but of course we were fit, acclimatized and moving downhill. We passed Intermediate Camp and Camp 1 and stopped at Yak Camp, a little-used spot at 17,400ft between Camp 1 and BC and once more within the main Rongphu valley. Roo and I had a secondary objective: to visit the Advance Base Camp for expeditions tackling Everest's North Face; that was a day's trek from Yak Camp. Cindy had been moving slowly and had gone far further than originally planned so she left us at that point and returned to the monastery.

The tent felt comparatively luxurious that night with just two occupants and a campsite 2,000ft lower than we had endured for the previous two nights. June 24 started well. We left the tent at Yak Camp and trekked with our essentials stuffed in day packs. We soon had to cross the glacial melt water stream flowing from the snout of the East Rongphu glacier; beyond there, the route became a vague path through a jumble of sharp rocks. Light rain fell as we trekked, perhaps another sign of the incoming monsoon, but we made good progress to the North Face ABC at 18,900ft. Walking felt easy because we were fit and acclimatized; psychologically we knew we had achieved everything we had hoped for.

We started back to Yak Camp and soon reached the East Rongphu stream. It was, however, now afternoon and the day's heat had accelerated the glacier's melting: the small stream had transformed itself into a wide and deep raging torrent. It was noisy and boiling and brown with the dirt carried down by the glacier. We weren't so naïve as not to know the river level would be higher in the afternoon but I was concerned by how much it had grown. Our preparedness for the crossing extended to having carried sandals with us! We took off our trousers and walking-boots and donned the sandals ready to wade across! Roo went first and struggled in the near waist-deep water. He faltered once or twice but made it across.

I threw my boots and trousers to Roo but one boot fell short and dropped in the river. The trek out would be interesting wearing just one boot but Roo reached out with his legs and, at full stretch, just managed to rescue the boot before it was carried away. The river boiled down the slope from the East Rongphu valley in front of me. We were crossing just after a bend where the river turned through 90°. Behind me and to my left lay a wall of moraine from the main Rongphu Glacier that was slowly being eroded by the river. Further to the left the river turned another corner back towards the Rongphu valley and disappeared down a steep slope.

In almost all areas of life, from business to sport to Tibetan river crossings, self-belief is as important for success as raw talent. Unfortunately, having watched Roo's crossing and having almost lost my boot I was feeling far from certain about this traverse; that doubt naturally became self-fulfilling. I started my crossing. The water was ice-cold, fast-flowing and was carrying lumps of rock. As I got deeper the water pushed harder against the full length of my legs until I took too tentative a step and was instantly punished by being rapidly carried away downstream. I struggled back to the bank and picked my way along the wall of crumbling moraine back to the starting point. I tried again but with my confidence dented the same thing happened. This time I was carried further downstream and out of view from Roo on the other side of the river. It was clear to me that I wasn't going to get across. Another attempt might just take me to the middle before being swept away by the river, which downstream disappeared underneath the glacier. The consequences of that didn't bear thinking about.

The noise of the river made communication almost impossible. I shouted and signalled to Roo that I would attempt a crossing lower down, but, unbeknown to me, he could neither see nor hear me. I then climbed over the moraine and disappeared. I walked down to the Rongphu valley and felt positive because I was in control of events again. The ridiculousness of my appearance – sandals, bloodied and bruised legs, boxer shorts and waterproof jacket – made me laugh and added to my positive mood. I followed the river while looking for crossing points but there was nowhere suitable. Eventually I reached the Rongphu glacier; the river disappeared underneath it through a tunnel cut into the glacier's side. I could now climb onto the glacier and back down to the far bank of the river. I started up the mixed ice and rock slope above where the river flowed under the glacier. Half way up I had second thoughts, retreated and saw the ice and rock break away and tumble into the river, to be carried away under the glacier. I tried again and this time climbed directly up the side of the glacier so that I could walk further in before turning along the glacier and then cutting back down to reach the other side of the river. This kept me on much stronger ice; I was relieved to climb back down off the glacier to the other side of the river.

I climbed back up moraine and scree slopes to Yak Camp to find Roo sitting there, with an emergency beacon of bright coloured clothes positioned on a high point, wondering if I was alive or dead. I had been gone forty-five minutes and I'm sure that time had been worse for him. Once I abandoned the river-crossing I was in control but Roo had seen me disappear and was left not knowing what was happening. He had had visions of trekking out without me and all that entailed. The relief for both of us was huge. Roo embraced me, patched my legs, made some food and a brew, offered some medicinal whisky. We rested for a while, absorbing the situation as we recovered from the shock. The temptation was to stay at Yak Camp but we knew we would be grateful to be back at the monastery so we started a slow, tired walk. For the first time the trekking dragged. We were weary and impatient to get back to the monastery and were relieved to finally reach our destination as the last light faded.

The journey back to the road was easy. After a day at the monastery we were rested and recovered. The following day we walked back to Phadhruchi, with the help of a local farmer's horse and cart for some of the route. We passed through Chhosang because we had no wish to stay there again and, since we were acclimatised and heading downhill we could easily cover the additional ground. Our incentive was that during our last stay in Phadhruchi we had eaten dinner in the home of a man who had such luxuries as potatoes and eggs! This time we stayed in his house and enjoyed another rest-day the following day. We spent the day eating potatoes and eggs and drinking sweet and moreish 'chang' (homebrewed beer). This was luxury and a fantastic end to the trek. In mid-evening Roo and I stepped outside for a chang-induced pee. The night was pitch black and there were no streetlights for hundreds of miles. I looked up and was struck dumb at the astonishing number and brightness of stars. With a lack of atmosphere and no stray light the night sky was simply incredible; that vision will remain with me as clearly as seeing the vast wall of Everest at our feet.

On the next day we completed our trek. We indulged ourselves by 'hiring' cows to carry our rucksacks over the Pang La on the basis that this was allowed on the way out! Having taken in our last view of the high Himalayas we soon found ourselves back on the road, with about 5km ahead of us to the police checkpoint. We tried to hitch a lift but none of the limited traffic showed any signs of stopping that night. We finally arrived at the police checkpoint where we took a room. We urgently needed to rescue the film from the camera I was carrying when swept away. Having turned off the light we risked taking the film out of the camera and manually wound it back into its canister. When processed back in the UK the pictures showed some water damage but the Tibetan night was so dark that no light had affected the film when we manually rewound it!

Next morning, cramped in the front of his cab, we found a lorry driver willing to take us to the next major town. From there, we boarded a local bus and after two days on the road we arrived back in Lhasa and at last were able to enjoy a hot shower, wash our clothes and eat well.

Looking back on our exploits, it had been a fantastic trek and something we will never forget for so many reasons more than having achieved our goal of trekking as high as possible on Everest.

The Hidden Summit
by Alex Way

My memory of participating in the school's expedition to Tibet in 2003 is divided into snapshots, which is perhaps unsurprising coming from the expedition's photographer. My most vivid recollection is that of reaching 6293m in the Longpo Kangri range, the highest point on the expedition and to this day one of the greatest physical achievements in my life. I still view the summit through the same snow-goggles I was wearing that morning: the omnipresent and hostile orange snow – an appropriately hazardous colour for a surface that all too often gave way on our descent; the rocky outlines of the surrounding peaks, swathed in a mist of condensed exhalation, and the arid valley below awash with the rippling ponds of perspiration.

Another prominent image is of our summit party's return from the assault camp, at the foot of the glacier, and the hero's welcome that greeted us upon arriving back at Advance Base Camp, a couple of kilometres further downhill. Our descent, once off the glacier, was a swift affair which left one elated and exhausted in equal measure. Understanding the physical achievement was, however, the easy part. The wider significance that this whole adventure would have in my development as someone reaching the 'peak' of his school career was, at the time, incalculable and little helped by the ensuing exhaustion and altitude-induced hallucinations.

My own goal achieved, I recall spending much of the remaining time at Base Camp and the subsequent Advance Camp gazing at the peaks. Their serenity, a silence rarely experienced anywhere in the developed world, was disturbed only by the wind and the BBC World Service's unique output of hiss, crackle and the occasional trace of something intelligible, provided courtesy of the small transistor radio I had bought from a newly opened Chinese-run electronics shop not far from the Potala Palace.

I busied myself with the duties of expedition photographer, helping to fulfil the aims of the expedition that stretched well beyond just summiting mountains: the Expedition Leader, for example, wanted photos for her record of Himalayan plants. Another team member wanted some taken of the nomads who were camping just a kilometre downstream from us for his report on Tibetan ethnology, and said nomads wanted photos of themselves (displayed on screen, at least), one presumes, for curiosity's sake alone. I shall never forget their unfailing smiles, their interest in our (temperamental) western gadgets and, for that matter, ours in their ornate and intricately carved trinkets. Being invited into a nomad's tent, lit by a yak butter lamp, to share a cup of yak butter tea while seated on a yak hair cushion around a yak dung fire and studying the face of the yak herder and his mother, prematurely aged by an unforgiving summer sun and some of the harshest winters on the planet, remains one of the most insightful cultural experiences of the trip. Knowing that I was one of very few westerners that these people had encountered was humbling. I felt almost embarrassed, wary of patronising or intruding any more so than we already were by clambering all over 'their' mountains. I found something worryingly paradoxical in the way we would eye up each other's respective cultures with envy – we, theirs for its simplicity; they, ours for its supposed labour-saving advances – knowing that their desire to ape us westerners would ultimately lose them the identity which attracted us westerners to their most beautiful country. Unspoilt, Tibet is not. Rapid development, much of it enforced by government, was already causing widespread pollution of the most hideous sorts. I have no doubt that, were I to return there tomorrow, much of the Tibet I experienced then would have disappeared.

What I could not see back then was that my own greatest achievement had, in fact, not been climbing the equivalent of three-quarters of the way up Mount Everest, but making the difficult decision to do so the previous night.

The day before our first, and successful, summit attempt had been one of glacier training – an opportunity for our fine climbing guide, Rupert Rosedale,[7] to assess the risk of crevasses and plot a route upwards, and for the rest of the party to don our crampons and clasp our ice-axes for real for the first time. The weather was cloudy but not at all inclement, a far cry from the menacing conditions that had greeted us during our winter training exercise in the heart of the Cairngorms. There we had experienced blizzards and gale force winds strong enough to snap the poles and rip the canvas of the 'strongest tents on the market'. Our ice-axe training had been in earnest but turned out to be unnecessary given the apparently fine conditions. Everything augured well for the following morning, or so it seemed. The fine conditions alone could not overcome the fatigue from

---

7. It is still with great sadness that, despite it occurring doing what he loved most, I record that Rupert was killed on the North Face of Ben Nevis on December 30, 2009. Ed.

which I was at that point suffering, brought on partly by altitude and partly by a limited diet of variable quality while on the road of spam, pasta and cheese each night at camp. It is difficult to gauge one's metabolic needs at 5000m. My paces on the glacier were heavy and, at times, faltering. Although roped securely to a fellow climber both in front and behind, I struggled to orientate myself, my vision being obscured by the goggles and the surrounding whiteness. With each plod I felt my legs giving way. This was, after all, the same afternoon that we had brought all our kit up from ABC, having gained several hundred metres in height over a short distance. Our Assault Camp was already only just shy of 6000m and my body was in mutiny. Although our short exploratory probe of the glacier was safe enough, the afternoon sun had softened the surface sufficiently to make each foot drop up to a half a metre when placed. Our kit had been packed away, and while taking a moment's rest before an early supper and bed, I decided I was the weak link in the chain of far more experienced climbers and it would be best for me not to continue with them. Questions ran through my mind by the dozen. Who was I letting down more by not pressing on? My fellow climbers, or me? In the end, I decided the guilt of only making it half way up and forcing the entire party to return unsuccessful would have been too much to bear, so I informed Rupert of my decision.

Had the expedition been solely about making it to the top and gaining records for first ascents, I expect my decision would have been accepted gratefully. But it was not just about that. The expedition members had been selected carefully and the team's strength lay not only in its diversity but in its cohesion too. It was as much about realising potential as it was about mountaineering triumphs. I had come so far, training for months before departure with tenacity and verve I did not know I had. I had always wanted to be part of a summit team, and in any case the fatigue that I had experienced on the glacier that afternoon was not exclusive to me, as I was to find out later. I owe much to the efforts of Rupert and my fellow pupil members in convincing me not to give up.

At five o'clock the next morning, with the sun only just stroking the pinnacles of the valley walls, I was attempting to stomach a breakfast of Muesli in Tang orange cordial. Within half an hour we had set off. *(See Plate 14)*

I learnt more about mountaineering courtesy of this incident than any one moment spent on a glacier. Mountaineering is first and foremost an expression of physical achievement. The emotional and psychological interpretations we so often attach to mountainscapes evolve only with temporal and physical distance. Yet to reach the summit requires not merely physical strength but a fullness of character and a determination of spirit. Resoluteness and a readiness to assist one's fellow mountaineers is a must. The knowledge of how to reach the top must be underpinned by the knowledge that the only successful expedition is the one where all members return home safely. Dealing with failure – regrettably a dirty word in the present social and political climate – ranks alongside the ice-axe as one of the mountaineer's most important tools. For me, this expedition was an opportunity to leave behind the ordinariness of Guildford life for a short time in search of something else, somewhere unknown. Few gap years can rival what we achieved in those seven weeks, and our achievement was a manifestation not only of personal success, but of a collective success for the school too. To become the successful mountain explorers that we did compelled each of us to draw on the entire range of experience that we had been fortunate enough to gain through the school: the precision of the mathematician, the perseverance and team spirit of the rugby player and the discipline and attention to detail of the CCF cadet. Our expedition to Tibet encapsulated the essence of the Royal Grammar School in its entirety. On the one hand: ambition, expectation and high standards. On the other: support, openness to others, good humour, solidarity and commitment, a willingness to nurture talent and produce a roundedness of character. It is little wonder that Royal Grammar School pupils are among some of the finest mountaineers Britain has to offer. *(See Plate 15)*

HIGH AND REMOTE

High and Remote: Introduction

In this section, we wander over several continents, to the unusual and obscure nature of the climbing situations: Gareth Stewart describes the tough ascent of Antarctica's highest peak, Mt Vinson, a privilege denied to most; Ian Ferguson's narratives range from the crumbling shales and a 'hard man' Russian sub-culture in the Caucasus to the Tien Shan, an immensely long range which probably contains more unclimbed peaks above 5000m than any other on Earth.

Ian's achievements are followed by a nervous first ascent of a beautiful peak in the Chinese Pamirs. And the account of the circumambulation of the 'navel of Asia', Mt Kailas, by the RGS Tibet (2003) Expedition might be compared with the kernel of Colin Thubron's most recent book, *To A Mountain in Tibet*.

But one might equally enjoy turning to Mike Smith's prolific ascents and explorations in South America, described with precision and youthful exuberance in a combination of subjective interest and objective description.

An entirely different note is struck by Bruno Marques who describes what is still one of Earth's more obscure corners: the unclimbed ranges where central Bhutan meets China. Bruno's quest was to find Gangkhar Puensum, a complex of peaks likely to remain as the highest unclimbed summits in the world for quite some time to come.

Altogether, then, this section will give much enjoyment to the connoisseur who appreciates that the ascent of certain kinds of mountain is an art form and not just a desperate physical and mental grind; and it will be appreciated by the aspirant climber who wishes to go beyond Alpine mountains to penetrate the more obscure and higher parts of the planet.

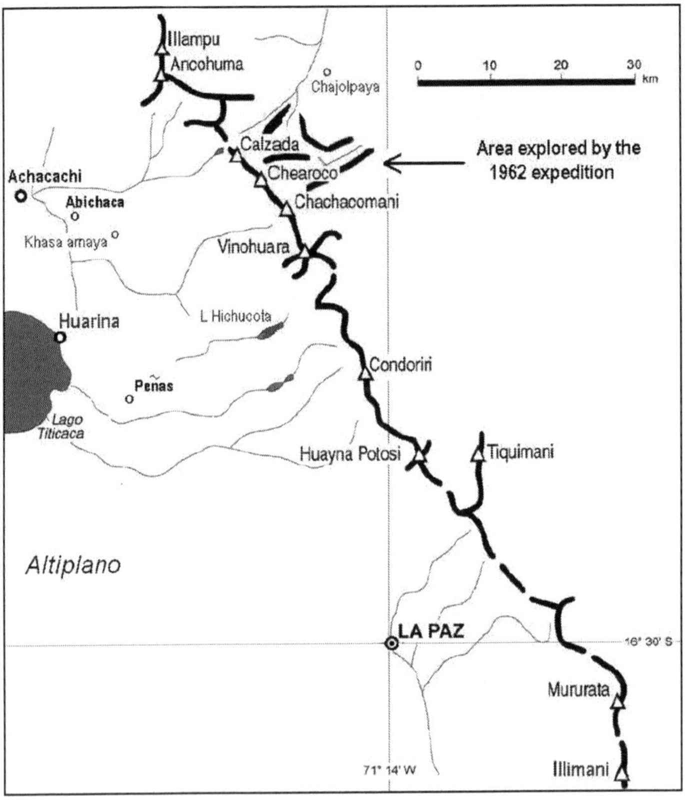
Illampu
Ancohuma
Chajolpaya
0 10 20 30 km
Calzada
Area explored by the 1962 expedition
Chearoco
Achacachi
Abichaca
Chachacomani
Khasa amaya
Vinohuara
Huarina
L Hichucota
Condoriri
Peñas
Lago Titicaca
Huayna Potosi
Tiquimani
Altiplano
LA PAZ
16° 30' S
Mururata
71° 14' W
Illimani

Cordillera Real [based on a map from Neate 1994]

Exploring Real Mountains in the Bolivian Andes
by Mike Smith

Recollections of an Adventure in Bolivia's Cordillera Real
by the Surveyor on Reading University's 1962 Andean Expedition

We landed in a cloud of dust. The final stage of our journey to Bolivia's capital, La Paz, had been accomplished in a Panagra Airways propeller-driven DC7, flying low from Lima over a barren Andean landscape decorated with the occasional gently smoking volcano.

Our objective was to explore a remote area of the Cordillera Real to the north of La Paz, which on all available maps at the time of our 1962 expedition was still an empty space sparsely occupied by a vague cluster of question marks. Our task: to explore, to map and to climb. Our remit: to report our findings to our sponsors, namely Reading University Exploration Society, the Royal Geographical Society and the Everest Foundation. It was the first week of July and we had ten weeks of cool, dry Bolivian winter days and nights before us.

The expedition and its results have been well documented by its leader, Ron Hunter, and others in such places as the *Alpine Journal* and the annals of the Royal Geographical Society (see bibliography below). This *Anthology* provides an opportunity for the writer to pen a few recollections from his own experiences as the expedition's surveyor.

The dust settled to reveal a stunning first sight of the Cordillera Real from the ground. At 4062 metres above sea level the stony airport runway at El Alto was already breathtakingly high, but beyond and above the city of La Paz – its conurbation almost entirely hidden in a ravine to the southeast – towered the majestic Illimani (6438m), dazzling white against the clear blue Bolivian winter sky. I was soon to enjoy the view again, this time framed by an open window at the Rancho Inglés and accompanied by hummingbirds flitting around on a creeper just outside. But, not for us, Illimani. Our uncharted territory lay to the north, beyond the looming Huayna Potosi (6094m) and the evocative Condoriri (5656m).

The Rancho, a large and empty house made available to us by an Anglo-Bolivian friend of the expedition, was to be our base for the next few days. At least, that was the plan. In the event, however, a few days became more than a few days as Eddie (who had accompanied the expedition's equipment and supplies from Liverpool on board the steamship Reina del Mar and then by steam train overland from the Chilean port of Arica) tested his Spanish to the limit to negotiate and barter these necessities through Customs. Meanwhile, the other five expedition members got to know a little of La Paz, its people, culture and food (the pasty-like *salteña* is especially recommended!), with significant support and hospitality from members of the Club Andino Boliviano. The delay also gave us more time to acclimatise to living at 4000 metres above sea-level. For Ray, who had bravely taken on the responsibility of expedition doctor, it brought the responsibility of keeping a watchful eye on our inquisitive interest in such hazards as the local fire-water, *singani*, and the street markets' ubiquitous heaps of dried *coca* leaf.

The delay was not wasted time for the surveyor. I seized an early opportunity to hitch a lift to a village named Peñas on the Altiplano, some sixty-three kilometres north-west of La Paz and within sight of the perimeter of our hidden terrain. To the west of the village lay a rocky ridge from the heights of which I could see, simultaneously, the main chain of the Cordillera to the east and, to the west, the southern shore of the great Lago Titicaca. It was from this vantage point that I was able to formulate a strategy for my task. I could see a reasonably level area on the Altiplano for my initial base line. Then, on Lago Titicaca's shoreline I spotted a clearly identifiable point which, at 3814 metres above sea level, would provide my vertical reference. And the high place at which I was now standing on the Peñas hills would become an important triangulation (trig) point for subsequent geometrical sightings using the theodolite we had borrowed from the Royal Geographical Society. I built a stone cairn with a unique profile on the spot before descending. *(See Plate 16)*

By the morning of Thursday July 12 we were ready to go. All the equipment and food, the latter organized by John into balanced weekly rations, had been packed into tough ex-Royal Navy and Royal Air Force kitbags. Our hired truck stood loaded on the Rancho's drive with the six expedition members perched on top. The driver was charged with the no mean task of getting us and our load to a point as close as possible to the Lago de la Calzada, situated ten kilometres from the foot of the Calzada Pass, a gateway into the uncharted mountain hinterland which was the expedition's goal.

Our route from La Paz north-west across the Altiplano was in no doubt as far as the village of Achacachi, thirty-three kilometres beyond Peñas, a distance of around ninety-six kilometres in total. While the road would be unsurfaced, it normally presented no difficulty for the trucks which regularly carried goods, livestock and people (usually a fairly uncomfortable mix of all three) to and from the communities in those parts. After Achacachi, however, we would need to change direction, turning east into river-furrowed foothills heading up towards the Calzada Pass. From the highly cautious advice we had received from our sources in La Paz, we knew that this section of the proposed route would present us with our first 'known unknown'. The earlier reconnaissance of a possible route 'A' by members of the Club Andino had resulted in both a broken axle on their *camioneta* in the region of Coromata and a 'no go' verdict on the route. We were now on the way to having a first look at a possible route 'B', there being insufficient time remaining for the luxury of further reconnaissance. Would route 'B' go?

The answer was 'no'! As Ron records in his piece for the Alpine Club's journal: 'Our intelligence sources … proved considerably inaccurate and we were dropped some twelve or fifteen miles farther from [the mountains] than we anticipated. Without porters, and with some four dozen loads weighing eighty to a hundred pounds apiece, this inaccuracy cost us several days and considerable perspiration, but was an excellent if brutal way of getting fit.'

Right about the perspiration! And at no time more so than during the immediate aftermath of the truck lurching to a halt near the hamlet of Khasa-amaya. The driver had decided his vehicle had taken more than enough punishment on a trail which had for some time become more of a mule track than a road. But, so far short of our target and hoping to win a few more miles, we tried to persuade the driver that a reduced payment might be on the cards. The driver stood firm on full payment (justifiably, I would say with hindsight) and the argument began to develop heat. It was at this point that we were about to learn for the first time that within the sparsely populated vastness of the Altiplano interesting news can travel with the speed of light. The next thing we knew – there on the skyline was a cluster of figures, coming out of nowhere and heading in our direction.

Led by a rather dangerous-looking character dressed all in black, our unexpected visitors soon outnumbered us by three to one. With their interest quickly turning towards the contents of our kitbags and other important cargo on board the truck, it didn't take us long to realise the game was up. We paid our fare in full and were relieved to be left without loss, free to set up camp for the night, albeit a night without too much sleep. Particular credit for their performances in this episode must be given to Eddie for his knife-edge negotiating and escapology skills, and to Robin who, as our dedicated cameraman, did not allow himself to get side-tracked into the business of resolving the problem. He just filmed it!

For all of the next five days we toiled, lugging pack-framed load after pack-framed load, moving our gear and our campsite incrementally forwards and upwards towards the distant Cordillera. Five days too many for the climbers. But not entirely so for the surveyor. On the fourth day, high above Khasa-amaya, we were passing through the area I had judged from Peñas to be most suitable for my survey base line. So, it was now the surveyor's duty to take time off from the yomping in order to make a closer inspection of the surrounding terrain. Such a pleasant duty! And the terrain was good. I decided on the best position for the base line, built small marker cairns at each end and on the following morning, July 17, employed surveyor's tape and theodolite to obtain its length, which I calculated to be 1723 metres. Further work with the theodolite established the distance between my two main triangulation points on the Altiplano: the cairn on the hill above Peñas and the summit of another prominent landmark, the Cerro de Abichaca, to its north. The intervening distance was calculated to be a healthy 28.8 kilometres.

On the sixth day, our luck turned. It was fortunate indeed that we had invited Alfredo Martinez and Peter Tichauer from the Club Andino to join us for a few days' climbing around the Calzada Pass. They trekked out, as planned, together with Venancio, a multi-talented Aymaran Indian also from the Club. When they reached the pass and found we had not arrived, the high-plain telegraph was soon working again and, thanks to Venancio's savvy, this time it worked to our advantage. What shouts of relief we raised when, on the morning of the sixth day, they appeared over the brow of the unrelenting slope, first just three distant figures, but quickly multiplying to reveal a large herd of llamas and a gang of drovers. We were back in business!

The llamas were fabulous. Loaded with heavy kitbags, two apiece, they just carried on as normal. In other words, they just carried on behaving much like a flock of long-necked sheep. The flock was cajoled and steered up over the hill and down through a maze of boulders into the valley running up to the pass. This feat was achieved with remarkable precision by the drovers, employing a combination of Aymaran vocabulary and small stones propelled from a llama rope sling (the *q'urawi*) to ping off rocks about the llamas' ears.

We set up our first base camp at the foot of the Calzada Pass, just above Lake Carizal at a height of 4740m, on the evening of Wednesday July 18. *(See Plate 17)*

Two prominent mountain groups guarded the pass above our camp: the Nevado Casiri to the north and Nevado Calzada to the south. Above their glacial defences, both groups bristled with summits, most of which were without record of prior ascent. While the main business of exploration lay over and beyond the pass, the immediate opportunity for climbing was irresistible: the opportunity to sample Andean rock and snow, the possibility of some first ascents and the prospect of an early glimpse of our uncharted target area away to the south-east. So, the next couple of weeks saw us scale the three summits of Nevado Calzada, including a first ascent of its principal summit (5820m) achieved jointly with our Bolivian friends, Peter and Alfredo, plus a number of minor peaks on and around the Nevado Casiri.

Among many memories from those early climbs, two remain particularly vivid. One is of the strange stalagmite-like structures called *nieves penitentes* which we encountered on the steep snow slopes of Nevado Calzada. These near-vertical spiky flakes of icy snow, up to a metre in height, are the bizarre product of freeze-dry physics in the Dry Andes sub-region and seem to have been devised by nature to impede a climber's progress in almost any direction. And so they almost did! A second and more romantic recollection is of the silent arrival of a condor, also on Calzada, circling slowly on thermals in the airy space below us and extending to full advantage its massive three metre wingspan. *(See Plate 18)*

Our high-altitude exertions were well supported at supper time each evening in the communal bell-tent at base camp. In some respects our carefully thought out expedition diet was at the cutting edge of early '60s culinary technology. That was certainly true of the freeze-dried meat which had been donated to the expedition on a trial basis by one of the Ministry of Agriculture's research stations in Scotland. Nevertheless, we were already getting a little tired of the all too consistent quality of this excellent product and were wondering what the local condors might be eating. Well, among other things no doubt the occasional *viscacha*, a rabbit-like member of the chinchilla family, abundant in the Andean uplands. How nice to add the occasional *viscacha* to our menu! And so it was. Taking advantage of my membership of the University's small-bore rifle club together with a good deal of youthful naivety, I had borrowed a pensioned-off BSA lever-action .22 rifle, had purchased (as I was at the time licensed to do) a box or two of high-velocity ammunition and had added these items to one of the packing cases destined for La Paz. How Eddie got this weaponry through the Bolivian customs I still don't quite know! But he did, and by our second evening at Calzada base camp we were tucking into wild game, skilfully skinned, jointed, pressure-cooked and pan-fried by Venancio. *Viscacha de la Calzada*! The first of many.

But now it was time to move on. Time to cross to the eastern side of the Cordillera and to seek a passage into that uncharted hinterland, into that empty space on the map. Accordingly, on July 29, a reconnaissance party comprising Ray, Eddie and myself set off over the Calzada Pass at the crack of dawn and returned that evening with exciting news.

On the far side of the pass we had followed the track which descends to the village of Chajolpaya while looking continuously for chinks in the defensive walls of rock on the southern side of the valley. In due course, we found the breach we were looking for, a wild but accessible valley heading back at an acute angle behind the Calzada massif. This valley climbed and bent to the right on reaching a fork. The branch to the left looked the more promising and we took it. It rose steadily towards a snow-covered col. Fired with excitement and anticipation, we climbed the steep final slope to reach the col and blinked in wonder at what we saw.

We were gazing down into a boulder-strewn glacial valley running at right angles to the col. To the left it became quite wide and grassy as it ran away to the south-east. It was completely devoid of trees; devoid of any signs of habitation; empty. To the right, it culminated abruptly in cliffs, ice-falls and snowfields. But what had us spellbound were the chains of glistening peaks which lined both sides of the valley. This was everything we had been hoping for. We could not resist the temptation to clamber up a rocky spire on the west side of the col, from which we could now identify the distant silhouettes of the giant Nevados Chearoco and Chachacomani. Eddie marked the occasion by naming the spire from which we viewed this panorama, Verity. We would in due course learn that the valley below, soon to become home for our second base camp, bore the Aymaran name Negruni.

Back at the Calzada camp we didn't hang about. First thing the following day, Venancio headed off in the direction of the Altiplano to find llamas. Kit was reorganised and packed for transit; tents were readied to follow suit. At this point, once again, the surveyor took leave of the

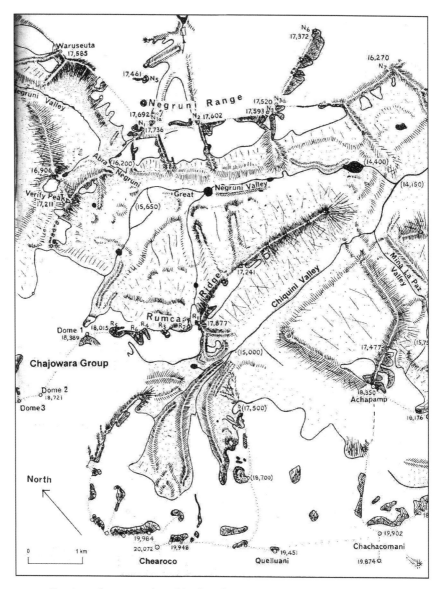

Portion of map produced by Reading University Andean expedition
[published 1963 with minor amendments 2011]

main company. He had unfinished business on the Altiplano, including a first visit to his Cerro de Abichaca trig point for essential angle-gathering with the theodolite. This and the return journey via a deserted Calzada, then over two passes to our new base camp in the Negruni valley gave me the memorable experience of a three-day solo trek. One of the nights was slept in the open under the most amazingly clear three-dimensional high-altitude sky while watching the silent screening of a non-stop display of shooting stars.

The communal bell-tent had only just been reinstated when I arrived at our new base camp. Apparently, the poles had gone missing during the llama march. Venancio, astute as always, had taken appropriate action. He had correctly calculated their whereabouts and advised the community's elders that they would be receiving a visit from the military if the poles were not promptly forthcoming. Sorted!

Everything stops at night in the Negruni valley. First, the evening's banter in the communal bell-tent. The sun has long dropped below the summits of the Chajowara group to the west as the temperature plummets under the ever-clear winter sky. By the time we are in our sleeping-bags the only sound in the desolate valley is the tinkling of the small stream near our cluster of tents. No sound of wind in trees. Very little wind, no trees. Now the stream falls silent, turning to ice in its tracks. No sound at all, except for Eddie's quiet breathing. Then Eddie stops breathing! What's going on? I give Eddie a nudge. Eddie breathes, complains gently to no-one in particular and drops back into his slumber. Eddie stops breathing again and this time I allow him to die for a little longer. Five seconds; ten seconds; eleven, twelve … and his breathing kicks in. As it always did, thankfully. I am learning to recognise the strange normality of altitude-induced Cheynes-Stokes breathing.

Had it not been for Ron and John's failure to return to base camp, I probably wouldn't have climbed Negruni-1. Part of the Warawarani group, Negruni-1 (5406m) is the highest of three summits which connect to form a chain on the north-eastern side of the Negruni valley. Its symmetrical profile was my inspiring first view of the day as I looked out each morning through the tubular doorway of my red, ex-Everest '53, mountain tent. Its precipitous triangular face of fluted snow and ice rose high above a chaotic hanging icefall of a glacier, which reached (in those days, not now) half way to the valley floor. *(See Plate 19)*

Early on the morning of August 7, Ron and John set out from base camp to climb Negruni-1 by way of its west ridge. A short time later I followed in their tracks as far as the Negruni Pass, then turned my back on the beautiful N-1 to clamber up Verity and set up my theodolite on its summit for a day of blue-sky triangulation. Robin, Ray and Eddie were busy bagging peaks in the 5400m to 5700m range along the Rumca Ridge and in the Chajowara massif opposite, while Venancio prepared *viscacha* (*de la Negruni*) for later. All according to plan, yet when Venancio called us in to join him around the cooking pot that evening, Ron and John were missing. Come nightfall, they had still not returned to base.

At first light the following morning we scanned the sharp triangular silhouette across the valley and realised that three more of us would be climbing Negruni-1 that day, but this time as members of a search party. We set off – Robin, Ray and myself – with light packs and were soon atop the Negruni Pass. We paused to home in on Ron and John's tracks, clearly imprinted in the crisp snow which rose up to join Negruni-1's west ridge. We followed them to gain the crest of the ridge, which we climbed at an easy angle until on a level with the bergschrund below the mountain's exquisite south-west face to our right. That was the end of the easy climbing. From that point onwards up to the summit, the ridge was a finely honed cutting edge of snow and ice, frequently steep to the point of vertical. We made full use of the steps chipped out by Ron and John's ice-axes the previous day and were encouraged to find similar evidence of our friends' good progress all the way to the snow-capped summit. Then what did they do?

Their options for descent were three. First, to down-climb the west ridge. Not a good idea and no evidence of that. Second, to descend the south-east ridge to the high col between Negruni-1 and Negruni-2, thence down a steep hanging glacier and terminal moraine into the Negruni valley. They would have weighed up that option. We soon came across tracks, however, suggesting they had chosen option three – to test the visibly less challenging terrain on the eastern side of the mountain and risk a longer hike back to base. This conclusion was confirmed just moments later when, right on cue, we spotted flashes of reflected light way below in the Negruni valley. The source was just discernible as two figures. No mistaking who!

Infused with relief, renewed optimism and floods of energy, we promptly decided upon option two for our own descent. We were soon down to the col where we organised a good anchor, made quick work of breaching a cornice and roped down a modest step onto the glacier below. Then, lucky with our route finding, we sped on down through a maze of small crevasses and ice-cliffs, skipped over the terminal moraine and were soon reunited with our friends, celebrating a good day with large quantities of weak high-altitude tea, back at base camp.

When you're mapping a mountain landscape, you need names: names for all those valleys, rivers, passes and summits. And when that landscape is remote, uninhabited and has never been mapped before, the surveyor finds himself hunting for names day and night. Every opportunity was taken to discover the local name, if there was one. Every rare encounter with an Indian passing through the area was seized upon to obtain name sounds. Venancio did his bit to help. Our map contains the results of this research. Exceptions to the rule include the summit named Verity (inspired by Eddie) and the three Domes (uninspired by me). But, what about Rumca Ridge? Rumca sounds like an Aymaran name, surely? Indeed it does, but some might also get the hint of an acronym for Reading University Mountaineering Club! Either way, it is pleasant to note that *Filo Rumca* appears quite frequently in present-day maps and descriptions of that part of the Cordillera Real.

With most of our tasks completed, we had just a few days left to indulge in something special. Two items headed the list of special things and their names were Nevado Chearoco and Nevado Chachacomani. At 6118m and 6066m respectively, these are two of the most royal summits in the Cordillera Real. They had been almost continuously within our sight, in the distance, on the south-western side of our area of exploration.

On August 17 we descended the Negruni valley, dropped into the Chiquini valley and ascended to the tip of the glacier which falls north-east from the col between Chearoco and Quelluani (5929m), a peak at the north-western corner of the Chachacomani massif. At this point we separated into two teams of three, one team for Chearoco, the other for Chachacomani, and progressed in parallel up the two lateral moraines to set up advance camps at similar altitudes (circa 5000m) on opposite sides of the glacier. We were allowing ourselves two days to forge routes and complete ascents of our respective summits.

The Chachacomani team, Robin, Ray and myself, was unsuccessful. On the first day we were too slow in finding a route up onto the high glacial plateau, the white wilderness which stretches three kilometres to Chachacomani's twin summits away to the south. On the second day our progress was terminally impeded by the web of crevasses, many of them huge, spread wide over that vast plateau. Our sole recordable achievement was a minor summit of some 5700m (aneroid) on the Quelluani side of the massif. *(See Plate 20)*

By contrast, Ron, John and Eddie achieved notable success on Chearoco. The crux of their climb was an overhanging ice-cliff which they encountered at around 110 metres below the summit, towards the end of the first day. Defying both gravity and the cold, they managed to engineer a passage across this obstacle, an achievement which they supplemented with a fixed rope. Then, as Ron records, 'early the next morning we retraced our steps up the mountain, performed a swinging Hinterstoisser traverse … and gained the summit snow-field by midday.' (Mindful of some serious Alpine history, they left the fixed rope securely in position for descent!) Theirs was the first recorded ascent of Chearoco's south-east ridge, a route subsequently graded III/AD+ (Brain, 1999).

Time was now running short. Back we trudge to Negruni base camp to rejoin the trusty Venancio. Pack kit; down tents; the llamas arrive. Down the Negruni valley; down the Chiquini; over a high pass; camp for the night; another pass and on down past Lago Hichucota to the Altiplano. A second night, sleeping rough this time. Daybreak, and we flag down an empty truck on the Peñas road. The next thing, we're back in La Paz. Here, there's time to unwind; time to enjoy hospitality, to recount our adventures and to reflect. And there's just time for the surveyor to make one final visit to his trig point on the Cerro de Peñas!

Then, it's up to the airport, homeward bound. *Adiós a la Cordillera Real! Adiós amigos bolivianos!* We take off in a cloud of dust.

The expedition team:
Ron Hunter (leader), Robin Bradford (cameraman), Ray Fearon (doctor), John Flood-Page (quartermaster), Eddie Quicke (interpreter/ negotiator), Mike Smith (surveyor)

Bibliography:
Brain, Y. (1999) *Bolivia: a Climbing Guide*. Leicester: Cordee, pp.17–21,104–113

Hunter, R.H.F. (1963) The Reading University Andean Expedition 1962. *The Alpine Journal*, 68, pp.219–224

Neate, J. (1994) *Mountaineering in the Andes: a source book for climbers*. 2nd Ed, London: Royal Geographical Society. Available online from: <*http:/www.rgs.org/OurWork/Publications/ EAC+publications/Mountaineering+in+the+Andes.htm*>, chapter/pdf on Bolivia

Getting Hooked: Mount Elbrus (5644m)
Western Summit via Normal Route from Priut 11
4 September 1996

by Ian Ferguson

It might all begin in a rustic but cosy hut, with a good humid fug and flames of gas cooker or open fire. Stiff limbs, grazes and exhaustion would be mellowing under the anaesthetic effects of fat, carbohydrate and alcohol. Humour would flicker: black-edged wit, self-deprecation or solid ribbing, reflecting common experiences and a welcome: a laid-back looking scene in unpretentious surroundings, belying the qualities and narratives of the characters therein. Partners who've judged you and been judged, with whom you've shared dependence on an accurate assessment of each other's condition, capacity, motivation and limits. Who have shared responsibility for your life and dignity, and become companions. Through common pursuit of the utterly futile, a tribute to friends or friendships passed, and a celebration of survival, life and opportunity. Then would come the crazed sparkle of a new idea, a forming plan:

'Shall we try 'X'?'

'D'you think it would go?'

'What's the worst that can happen?' (To which the belayer's standard response is, 'You'll be fed the rest of your meals through a tube; now get on up or let me at it.')

Climbing's sometimes fun, but always nice when it stops, and it gives an excuse to eat a lot and drink beer – but also to brag about how brave we all were (within limits: 'to spray' is a derogatory term for trying too hard, or bragging outside the circle). As the Clash sang, '…and some of it was true….' We climb to earn our stories: for a reserved Englishman, it's a route to flamboyance. Compelling, once discovered – but why ever would one start?

Curiosity, while hard on cats, was rewarding me just fine in early adult life: engineering and flying, extending my school Russian in the never-a-dull-moment early post-Soviet world… During a summer placement at British Aerospace's Research Centre in Bristol, two young scientists joined colleagues at our table in the canteen. They had patchy sunburn, thousand-yard stares, and were regarded with a certain awe. Shyly, they revealed that they had just climbed Mont Blanc… and gradually, I became aware of a new, unscratched itch. Engineer by training, I consulted my well-thumbed International Standard Atmosphere table: air pressure a few per cent lower, temperature: distinctly parky. But what about the sky? Is it really darker? As Eric Idle said to Terry Jones, 'What's it like?'

School days gave few clues of the pleasure I was later to gain from days in the hills. It is true to say that Dai Cowx's showing of *Stone Monkey*[8] – it was supposed to be a geography lesson, or perhaps the Urnfield was a quagmire again – was inspirational: but the reality of a long cold wait for a hasty top-roped fumble at a small damp boulder proved a deterrent. My local Scout Group taught me to navigate to a fair standard, but by and large Ten Tors and Three Peaks school expeditions were conducted by a hairier-arsed group than I frequented. Instead, I thrived on sailing, which I'd long aspired to in preference to hearty, Truly Great Team Sports. Richard Mant's expeditions set a high standard on which to base visits to more mountainous environments than Norfolk, and under his and Andy Kittow's encouraging guidance I learned of the analogous trust and shared commitment needed whether in a climbing partnership or a sailing crew.

Pride and determination lay behind one memorable schooldays ascent. Participating in an REJ Seymour Scout Camp to the Isle of Arran, the option was offered of a walk up Goat Fell. As a very occasional sufferer from summer hay fever, I choked and sneezed my way from the beach campsite to the van. A jibe from another scout was surely not ill-meant, but it stung. I didn't struggle particularly to get to the top, but Chris Pafford and I were around fifteen minutes ahead of the rest of the party by the time we returned to the van, and to overtake him seemed thoroughly unwise.

So what, as a fledgling adult, should I go and climb? I realised that the childhood staple of long family walks was behind me, and that while assuming that outdoorsy hill-climbing activity would be something I'd continue, I'd taken my surefootedness and navigation skills for granted and actually done little or nothing beyond a handful of Snowdonia trips. I knew no-one who was likely to be interested to ask along, so I found myself a commercial trip. Any mountain would do, but one in Southern Russia would be an obvious complement to my interest in the region. Highest in Europe? Eighteen and a half thousand feet? Sounds ample! Ambition combined with near total ignorance proved advantageous: easier on the

8. This award-winning film (1983) traces ace rock-climber Johnny Dawes's boyhood influences and films him on his gritstone masterpieces and on the spectacular Quarryman Groove in North Wales. Winner of five international film festival awards.

nerves, and sparing disappointment if the summit proved beyond reach. Never a voluntary athlete, I even did some training...

While the north-western end of the Caucasus was still comparatively peaceful in 1996, Russia's domestic aviation was probably heading to the nadir of its safety record. Nonetheless, late August found four nervous foreigners arrived safely in Mineralniye Vodiy. Our programme would take in an attempt at a peak on the main Caucasus ridge followed by an idyllic circuit over two high passes. Finally, a four-day sojourn on Elbrus would be our climactic summit effort.

The night in the hotel in the valley is best forgotten, but soon enough we got our boots on and started into the wilds. 'Zelionaia Gostinitsa,' announced Sergei, in his third and fourth words since meeting us several hours previously, as he dumped a vast Bergen at the edge of an attractive grassy meadow. 'Green Hotel,' translated Gia, his charming and more voluble Georgian sidekick, and we set to work to set up tents and other domestic arrangements. Olya, an attractive if lath-thin Ukrainian of limited approachability and, at around twice her own volume, an even vaster rucksack than Sergei, was helped from under her burden and turned her hand to stoves and vegetables. Wary inquiries revealed that she was 'training' for some unspecified personal mountaineering goal next year; she would cook for us on this trip. We flabby, decadent Westerners kept a nervous distance.

We were roused at an early hour with black tea and *kasha* (savoury oat/buckwheat porridge) with salted butter but, with dry glaciers and little snow, not too early. The team set out. Even glaciers can take a diminutive in Russian: '*Lidnichka*,' muttered Sergei in a rare outburst of loquacity as we stopped to rope up. A few hours of steep ascent had passed, and gradually a view north was developing to the point that Elbrus herself could be seen emerging.

Clouds built, and we reached the watershed. One foot in Asia, one in Europe; then an easy, if exposed scramble up a loose arête soon took us to the summit. A big step up from the tourist path on Ben Nevis: 3805m, the summit of Gumachi. Crossed flags of Russia and Georgia, but sadly no view.

Long, long days were the theme of our tour to the north of the Baksan valley. Never breaking 4000m, it contributed more to our fitness and endurance than to our acclimatisation, but drew a distinction between those who were trotting along, enjoying the scenery and the singing of unaccustomed muscles, and those who found it a tiring trudge. Eventually, all seemed to gravitate to the first category, more or less, and Sergei would nod approvingly at the comparatively meagre showing of blisters at the end of each day. It was not the occasion to be breaking in footwear.

Syltran Lake was Arcadian, with the pass at 3400m and a flock of wild goats who did not linger to greet us. This was late season: alpine meadows were not thick with flowers, but nonetheless some mature grasslands and sheltered areas could be found. The Iryk pass was higher, necessitating that we cross another dry glacier to reach a bleakly situated memorial to the Great Patriotic War (Second World War), and what we were told was a bear's footprint in the snow. It looked to us very much as we would expect a bear's footprint to look, and our steps acquired something of a nervous spring.

'Hard Rock Café,' announced Sergei some hours later. He placed his rucksack in another exquisite, if boulder-strewn alpine meadow, at the head of a tiny enclosing valley with a small tinkling stream. Olya set about her catering.

The long, fairly solitary days of walking had given me a chance to cultivate some apprehension. Would my fitness be sufficient? Would I hold us up, or be the cause of the group's failure? Would my boots and equipment, bought with a background of little experience, be adequate? Given my honest curiosity about conditions high up, what might I face in terms of frostbite, blizzard, hardship or injury? What task had I taken on, and why did it suddenly matter to me? On later climbs, early independent fumbles in the Alps, the fact of having passed through this performance anxiety would stand me in good stead, as I would be able to chuckle to myself and put everything in perspective with the reminder that, dammit, I'd already climbed higher than every summit within sight. At that time, the nervousness was real: a caption to a photograph of Elbrus, written at the time, dryly states, 'Still there…'

We had some afternoon left, sufficient to get some rural laundry done against stones in the stream. A shepherd appeared as if from nowhere. No Georgian can miss a chat – or a deal! – and Gia soon called us over. If we all pitched in a few dollars, a sheep could be ours, and Olya's skills could be turned to fresh kebabs. A select party soon departed behind a substantial boulder, and almost an hour later, returned sans ewe but carrying several very heavy-looking plastic carrier bags and a churn.

I drowsed against a stone, and was roused by lowing. Cows were passing through the valley, and one in particular was making off with my drying laundry in its teeth. I gave pursuit, with mixed success, recovering the clothes, but only after the cow had trodden heavily on them. Back to the stream for a second wash...

The valley was proving tiresome in the true style of Freshfield's[9] Caucasian adventures, as a fierce twenty-minute thunderstorm soaked us through. But kebabs on an open fire raised our spirits, and the skies cleared.

The next morning we anticipated sheep's milk (part of our total service arrangement regarding the ewe). But Olya's efficiency was ruthless, with an early, roaring fire ready to rouse us with a brew. 'What milk?' she asked, as it boiled furiously in the churn.

Our rural idyll ended sharply when we descended into the dusty valley. Noisy transport took us to the foot of Elbrus's glowering bulk and a grimy, alarming cablecar. From 3800m, a bleak walk led through a grubby quasi-industrial wasteland; a four-hundred metre climb followed, past the base and beams of an old, ruined shelter to the Priut Odinnadsati, the 'Refuge of Eleven', a capacity of a hundred, three-storey climbers' hut, somehow reminiscent of the Birmingham Bullring, made of plywood skinned in thin aluminium sheets. A horizontal ladder from the slope at the back gave access to the first – or second, in the logical Russian system – storey.

We were allocated rooms in this incongruous spaceship, a beached whale, built in 1939 with a dance floor across which (presumably well-acclimatised) dancers were rumoured to have waltzed while Stalin murdered. It was not warm: we ensconced ourselves in down and fleece and any other cosy fabrics we could find, to wait, cross our fingers for health and weather, and stay hydrated. *(See Plate 21)*

This last act had consequences, and before dark fell, I headed out to investigate the possibilities. 'Long drop' describes the mechanism, but insufficiently encompasses the horror of the actual *skithus*,[10] festooned in grimly-coloured (happily, frozen) stalactites; at least the stalagmites sufficed to provide some grip where it was desperately needed. A narrow wooden beam as support above the void. Scrawny guy-ropes lashed the tiny weatherbeaten affair precariously to the side of the hill, and, if the door could be held shut, gusts of trans-sonic spindrift were the main threat to any exposed flesh. Constipation could have been justified purely on the grounds of personal safety.

---

9. Douglas Freshfield (1845–1934), one of the great early Caucasus explorers, and a President of the Alpine Club and the Royal Geographical Society. He was the first western European to reach the mysterious and still dangerous region of Swaneti, in the Georgian Caucasus. Ed.

10. A Swedish term for a particularly repugnant form of outdoor lavatory. Ed.

Next day held an acclimatisation excursion for us: to the Pastukhov Rocks, just short of 4800m. Out we trudged, grimly slow. 'Rest step to success' was a slogan I had read in something related to Nepal, and Sergei's skill in setting a metronomic, tortoise pace was commendable. To this form of progress was added the grim monotony of the constant angle, a significant disadvantage while climbing volcanoes. The accomplishment was to mentally escape from the circumstances, to create a lively inner life to allow the mind to fly free from the repetitive plod, and let respiration find its own, consistent rhythm.

Any significant blisters, sunburn, chafing or pain from other injuries acquired over the last two weeks would be trouble here, as the insistent goading would distract the distanced mind to make every minute a misery. And the summit walk would require dull, patient hours. I counted to a hundred in French, German, Russian – repeatedly. And wished I had some Spanish...

Views of the main Caucasus ridge were spectacular as we descended: Ushba, Shkelda, the Bezingi wall. Georgians being cooler than the rest of the world, Gia skied back down.

We were back by noon, to pass more hours of nervous anticipation cocooned in down.

Early evening, nervous of Elbrus's reputation as a cold mountain, I made experiments with my footwear. My hiking heritage had specified two pairs of socks be worn inside any sturdy leather boot, although I'd noticed radicals among my companions were using only single pairs. Perhaps, for tomorrow's circumstances, I should forestall frostbitten toes by wearing three pairs? In my naivety, I tried it. I know now that restricted circulation would have added really seriously to my problems, but luckily for me, three pairs really weren't going to fit. I settled to checking my other kit. Balaclava, sunglasses, second woolly hat, inner gloves, big fleece-lined outers, gaiters: earnest-looking equipment, carrying a promise of exploration, extremity, the unknown, at least for me.

Alarms were set for horribly early hours, and sleep came surprisingly easily despite the gasping dry air.

A grim-faced Sergei told us to douse our alarms, and get another hour or two of sleep, as the wind was too strong to start on time. Our stomachs did sorry flips, at the thought that even the attempt might be snatched from us at the last minute. Disappointment took some quashing.

Some time later, he roused us and told us to get kitted up, noting only that we'd 'give it a go'. Nerves by this point were jangling, but preparation and mental checklists kept things on the way, and we soon emerged into the freezing darkness.

As always, the first twenty minutes were bitter, but by now, we knew what to expect of Sergei's trudge, and personal admin – taking off and stowing hats and gloves, opening of zips – could be neatly timed with respiration to keep gasping and coughing to a minimum.

Hours passed. Light came, but visibility was never significant. We moved slowly up inside our ping-pong ball, a gentle breeze toying with us, concentrating on the person ahead and maintaining the pace. Step, step, clink of the ice-axe shaft against the crampon if any snow appeared to be sticking between our crampon spikes, to hamper their penetration of the surface.

The Pastukhov Rocks passed. Sergei had never been given to frequent breaks, but this morning was something of a personal best for continuous motion. A brief consultation with Gia, and on we go. *(See Plate 22)*

Wind strength was not decreasing, and some loose snow was beginning to fly by us. More time passed, each of us in their personal world, 'Are we nearly there yet?' being the thought we dared not consider.

But we were nearly there, and the conditions were pressing. Sergei's body language was the clue, and perhaps he fractionally increased his pace, as a catch in my throat had me retching, spitting breakfast. Concern from Gia and Sergei, but not a thought to turn back for, within a hundred metres the angle had reduced, we were walking not climbing, and Sergei was looking about, to find a little stone pillar.

We were the highest people in Europe.

Hard on the liver: Kazbek (5035m)
by the Normal Route (PD+)
10 September 2001

by Ian Ferguson

' It's a church, Jim: but not as we know it.' There was no Jim: a conse-
quence of solo travel relying on one's own limited skills in the local
languages is the foundation of an ongoing inner dialogue. Several tens of
cash dollars had changed hands at Tbilisi airport as agreed in advance; four
ready-looking locals and I had then travelled a few hours by UAZ (an old
form of Russian military jeep; a spartan form of SUV) up the old Georgian
Military Highway, and we were now trudging towards the snowline. The
Tsaminda Samebo church bisected the long spur behind us. It was almost
an English country church, but for the exotic barrel-shaped tower, conical
roof and commanding view of the wide, grassy valley leading to the main
pass of the Central Caucasus, whose uncompromisingly snowy peaks
glared down towards East and West.

An English non-specialist education in the Ancient World peters out
in these parts. To the north, there are unruly Russian borderlands. A few
dozen miles to the south-west, Noah's Ark came to rest near Agri Dag
(Mount Ararat) in Turkey. 'Here be dragons' – until a local's slaying of
one had qualified him to be patron saint of part of a damp island in the
North Sea. Even the Greek gods considered it a fair Alcatraz, or perhaps
Guantanamo: as punishment for having shared the secret of fire with the
human race, Prometheus had been chained to a summit in order to undergo
a daily regime of eagles pecking out his liver. This summit was Kazbek,
towards which we were headed.

At 5035m, Kazbek demands a respectful period of acclimatisation. I
knew this would be done on the mountain itself, and anticipated some dull
and repetitive plodding. I was pleasantly surprised: while Agri Dag's lower
slopes are sufficiently capacious and convoluted to conceal a whole Ark,
even Kazbek had diversions worthy of a couple of days' outings. First,
a hermit's cave: ample accommodation for several, hung with woollen
tapestries in Orthodox iconic designs, illuminated by candlelight and
approached by several metres of steep and crumbly Severe or Hard Severe
climbing. A small modern church: its aluminium construction revealing
an aircraft, rather than a Portakabin, ancestry. But its guy-ropes hummed

and our jackets began to crackle…as subscribers to a meteorological rather than spiritual explanation, we flung ourselves down the scree slopes and ran for the safety of our Base Camp, a substantial concrete building.

In the clean, thunderstorm-washed air of the early evening, the old Soviet bosses of the former Meteorological Station arrived, every pocket bulging with cork-stopped bottles of clear liquid. Having checked and fettled our gear, we turned in early in anticipation of Summit Day, and the small-hours 'alpine start'. To this day, Kazbek is hard on livers: when we arose a few hours later, the bosses had reached the high plateaux of their inebriation. It was difficult to refuse 'a hundred grammes (of vodka) for the route'.

'Oi, Englishman, are you a Christian?'

Mumbled circumlocution along the lines of 'brought up in that faith, yes'.

'Well, at least you're not a (expletive deleted) (offensive epithet for Mohammedan?).'

No; fair to say I'd not leant in that direction.

'Well then you know what the Trinity is. Get another two hundreds down you.'

And so the first couple of hours' ascent passed painlessly. *(See Plate 23)*

It was a well-chosen hill for exotic tourism and to increase my high mountain experience. Climbing with a single client this late in the season, my guides had chosen to bring along a pair of junior colleagues to build up their experience. We were well-acclimatised and didn't linger. The final slopes of hard ice provided a welcome mildly technical diversion for a young, confident and happy team. Better yet, perched between Europe and Asia, we were blessed with a view. North-east, their borders defined by the Military Highway and the watershed, we peered into Chechnya and further Dagestan. South-west lay the less-publicised troublespots of Swaneti and Ossetia. As I basked a few hours later in the glow of accomplishment and looked forward to a few days' exploration of Georgia's lowlands, I reflected on what an endlessly fascinating but turbulent region the Caucasus was. But it was September 10, 2001.

The First Ascent of Moby Dick
by Catherine Moorehead

As we headed for the Chinese Pamirs, we knew that we were trailblazers, or at least something similar. Inspired by Chris Bonington's *Kongur*, which described the First Ascent of one of the highest peaks wholly within China, and wanting to break out of Munrobashing, I thought that a group of nameless, unclimbed peaks in the depths of Central Asia would be an ideal way forward.

There were two other bits of excitement in the mix. The Karakoram Highway from Rawalpindi to Kashgar, a particularly dangerous branch of the Old Silk Road, had been opened in 1988 thanks to a joint Sino-Pakistani undertaking, at a cost, it is said, of one human life for every one of its 800 kilometres. We were, therefore, among its earliest travellers. The rough track had been blasted out of the cliff-faces of the Indus and Hunza Gorges – where the walls are sometimes 3000m high – through what is perhaps, geologically, the most unstable country in the World. (I was once told by an Oxford geologist-climber that the vast nearby range of Nanga Parbat (8126m) was moving at a frightening 8cm a year!) From time to time, we could see, on the opposite bank, traces of the old track where travellers were blindfolded to divert their terror away from the drop. Above the Khunjerab Pass, on the Pak-Chinese border, at nearly 5000m, one of the highest regularly used roads in the World, the countryside changes to a plateau. Mustagh Ata (7546m) and Kongur (7649m) can then be seen soaring above a couple of dozen or so glaciers. The base camp at the Karakol Lakes was a stupendous place, with one of the best views in Central Asia, marred only by the local Kirghiz who wanted to pry everywhere.

Six months before, a friend and I had flown to Beijing to negotiate a deal with the Chinese Mountaineering Association. (No emails in those days. It seems almost unimaginable now, but, apart from that visit to Beijing, the whole expedition was set up by letter!) That successfully completed, and the usual visits to the Great Wall, Summer Palace and Temple of Heaven having been concluded, we celebrated at a magnificent banquet laid on for us by the CMA. Chinese banquets are rightly interspersed with frequent toasts. Knowing of the appalling Chinese human rights record, I had to think rather carefully beforehand about what my toasts should be. In the end, I chose 'To the youth of our two nations!', which seemed to be acceptable. At the banquet, egalitarian China was also in evidence. Professor Guo Xin, the dignified Vice-President of the Beijing University of Geosciences, sat next to our student translator and, on his other side, sat pretty little Wu Wei, our city guide, who could not have been more than sixteen. Youth and egalitarianism, however, made a different mark only eight months later when the bloody horror of Tienanmen Square erupted. (One of the Beijing geology students who joined our expedition reported that on the night, he had heard 'six hours' of unbroken gunfire.) With only one month to go before our expedition, it appeared that China was on the verge of civil war.

On the somewhat idiotic grounds that the Pamirs were 'a long way' from Beijing, and because Health and Safety had not at that time been invented, and because there was no direct link between the Foreign Office website and the viability of travel insurance, I decided that the expedition should go ahead. (We had no trouble; there was, apparently, some arson and militant protest in Kashgar while we were there, but we saw no sign of it.)

To reach the Chinese Pamirs without going via Beijing, your best bet is to start in Pakistan. This approach of course needs extreme patience when tackling Pakistan's bureaucracy, especially in 40° heat and unspeakable humidity. But we were armed with 'many, many rupees' a good deal of bluster, and helped by my room at the historic Flashman's Hotel having one of the only two Foreigners' Alcohol Permit offices in town.

A week after arriving saw us trundling over the rolling hills beyond Islamabad towards the Indus Valley. From this road, you can see Rakaposhi, Nanga Parbat, Haramosh, Kongur, Mustagh Ata and Chakraghil. There may be only two comparable places in the world. The crawl along the precipices was, however, an odyssey of terror which will live with me for ever. Not so some of my team-mates: they chose to sit on top of the roof-rack, and at least had a breeze in their faces – though they had to remember to avoid decapitation by the frequent overhangs.

After a stopover at Gulmit to get some cricketing practice in ('you are out if the ball goes into the Indus') and to make an acclimatisation walk up the Pasu Glacier, we said goodbye to our Pakistani minders and changed to Chinese vehicles at the Wild West outpost of Pirali. The Pamir Hotel in Tashkurghan ('Stone Fort') lived up to its character of being at the ends of the (Chinese) empire: pillows filled with sand, dirty sheets and crockery, headaches all round, hot water for only two hours in the evening – the Chinese got there first – and excellent food.

An easy few hours on a fast open, alpine desert road then brought us to the Karakol Lakes where we set up Roadhead Camp on a sandy beach, with a backdrop of caramel and purple hills leading to the unattainable higher tops.

I never thought that I would say this, but after a few days of acclimatisation walks, I found myself leading a train of twenty-three adult and two baby camels, and a number of ponies, up the Konsiver River valley. We made our Base Camp, after two straightforward days' walk, at Aktash ('White Stone'), next to a massive earthquake fault.

The next thing was to find the mountain. Three reconnaissance parties set out. I took mine towards what I thought was the Karatash Pass; we got the valley wrong, however, and ended on a glaciated col at about 5100m, having struggled up 1000m of rocky stream-bed, with the most enormous precipice I have ever seen dropping away from it. I'm sure no one has been there before or since.

The recce parties reported that an approach to our mountains was possible. (The recces were necessary as we had no map better than 1/250,000 – Stanford's finest – to go on. The Chinese had a 1/50,000 map, but we were not allowed to see it. An irony, as you can now buy it in Stanford's.) We would, however, have to set up an Advance Base in a higher, though still grassy valley. To reach it, we had a difficult river-crossing, then had to follow a meandering shepherds' track rising for about 400m. A shuttle arrangement for hauling all the food – the country is an Alpine desert; we had brought a ton and a quarter of food, in forty-nine barrels, with us – and equipment was carried out. ABC, in a pleasant valley at about 4500m, was established. We were watched by a pair of Himalayan griffin vultures, a pair of lammergeyers, and two Kirghiz shepherds ('Frank' and 'Film Star') with almost equal wonder. *(See Plate 24)*

We had two peaks in mind, both about 5400m. They were not named on the maps. Following a word we often heard the Kirghiz use, we decided to call them Orina I and II, though looking back on it, having found out that 'orina' is Spanish for 'urine', I would rather we had come up with something a little more dignified.

One party reached the top of Orina I, in perfect conditions. As Heroic Leader, I had given up my place to someone else not so much on the grounds of altruism but because I had been acclimatising fairly slowly. By the time the successful party returned, however, I was rarin' to go, to attempt Orina II, or, because it resembled a gigantic snowy whaleback, Moby Dick. *(See Plate 25)*

From the alpine valley – the only other European at that time to have been through it was, of course, Bill Tilman on his way from Kashgar to meet Eric Shipton for their attempt on Mustagh Ata – we struck up a lateral valley over steepish scree and rubble. After about 400m, the valley levelled off as a hanging glacier approached. We camped on its tongue.

During the night, I failed to sleep very much. The storm outside the tent, the pork stew for supper and the edgy feelings about the next day's climb combined in an uneasy drifting in and out of consciousness....

The storm had abated by morning. We saw that about 10–15cm of new snow had been deposited. The world was silvery grey, but the sky was clear. And it was something to remind myself that every one of the dozens of pink-tinged peaks that I could see was unclimbed. As we strapped on crampons, peaks across the valley then turned molten gold with the first rays of the sun.

We trudged up the easy, almost crevasse-free glacier. My thoughts drifted again...From the glacier, we had to zig-zag up a face of sometimes quite deep, fresh snow. It was not just avalanches on everyone's mind... The snow appeared to be making strange echoing noises...

'We're maybe above a cathedral hole,' opined Nick.

'A what?'

'A 'cathedral hole'. You know, where instead of the usual crevasse, there's a hole the size of St Paul's Cathedral below you.'

'Oh.'

At that point it somehow became easier to concentrate on the imminent danger of avalanches.

Leaving these dangers behind us, for the time being, we reached the summit ridge. If he had had one, this would have been Moby Dick's backbone. The ridge ahead was narrow, though not too tricky. The problem was steering a line high enough to stop the bulging leeward slopes from peeling off and precipitating us 600m down to the glacier yet not too high, so that we could avoid breaking through the wavy cornices. *(See Plate 26)* I recalled the early climbers' description of the Inaccessible Pinnacle: 'there is an infinite drop on one side, and an even greater one on the other'! I was also reminded of an outing to snowclimb the cliffs of Coire an Lochain, in the Cairngorms, with Forfar and District Hill-walking Club (motto: 'far i'wi'noo?') when one of the club's stalwarts had peeled off near the top. And as the Club President reported, 'He fell 900 feet and d'ye ken, he swoor a' the way doon!' (Said member, having bounced down on snow, picked himself up at the bottom and recommenced the climb.)

We edged our way along the summit ridge. Cloud was bubbling up from the ABC valley. Testing every step, we reached the summit, albeit in swirling mist, at 11.30am. It was intensely quiet, until Matthew started going on at length about how quiet it was.

Retracing our steps over the protruding leeward slopes, where our upward steps had no doubt already marked out a potential avalanche split, was even more nerve-racking than the upward climb. We were mightily relieved, though elated, to reach the Assault Camp again. Then the hard part of the day started: we had to pack and lug back to ABC all the Assault Camp material which had been carried up by three times as many people as were now available. I must have been carrying about 30kg, a tricky and unpleasant business when descending steep rubble and scree. Still, the joy of having done our peak, my first First Ascent, got the better of the physical pain.

A couple of goats slaughtered and eaten in the Szechwan style; a mind-boggling trip down the Gez Gorge to Kashgar for the Sunday Market; a bit of earthquake avoidance as we approached the border again; the wonderful emerald hillsides in post-monsoon Pakistan; violent illness after eating dodgy chicken at the (allegedly) 'best' hotel in Pakistan; all these little surprises have now faded as the mountaineer's Bad Memory Elimination Syndrome kicks in. There is no emotion comparable to that of completing your first First Ascent.

Travelling Hopefully: Central Asia First Ascents
by Ian Ferguson

Karakoram:
Central Kharut Peak (6540m) Pakistan/China border between Sella Saddle and Windy Gap, above the Godwin-Austen glacier; 6 August 2005

A t seventy kilos wet through, my fate in glacier travel is usually pretty clear: first on the rope, human crevasse-probe. It's enough to make a man climb with girls. As the old joke goes 'Why do mountaineers rope up? To prevent the sensible ones from running away.'

In fact, the mental effort of judging the likely layout of crevasses and picking the best line is usually a pleasant diversion during long trudges up glaciers. On this route, body and mind were getting the full workout. Since the helicopter left us, two metres of snow had fallen. In my tent that morning, I had woken to a strange silence, choked and gasping, with a fine headache. The tent structure was standing firm but my tent-mate and I were hypoxic: we punched and shouldered our way to the surface. Our team then enjoyed a pleasant morning's joinery and construction work digging out and reconstituting the Mess Tent. A little cosier than the designers intended, but with some Modernist/Brutalist drying racks from unrecoverable bent poles…

We had delayed departure from Base Camp for twenty-four hours to let the fall consolidate. The wait was not dull: every ninety seconds, avalanches could be heard tumbling off the surrounding bowl of crags. When the snow stopped and visibility improved we began to get used to the idea that tiny sloughs raised a disproportionate racket, but every half hour or so a real monster would let loose, so no-one became blasé. Even as we trudged up the glacier, a square half mile of the south face uncurled itself from the cliffs, some remnants of spindrift and icy blast chilling us some two minutes after the most massive wreckage had plunged into the bergschrund.

Breaking trail in fresh armpit-deep snow, one leans forward and then probes gingerly with the leading foot, trying to make an early judgement about whether it will take weight. If not, quickly squat back onto the other foot and decide whether to shuffle the back foot a half-step forward in the hope of bridging the crevasse, or try a ninety-degree turn to tack along to a better spot. In any case, neither foot is ever stable and twenty steps will leave the leader sprawling repeatedly, swimming and covered head to foot in snow. In fact, the occasional breakthrough into a crevasse at least recovers the attention of the rest of the rope, and shares the dampness and frustration a little.

We shared the leads between two ropes of three, but a ten hour day carrying overnight and technical climbing loads was enough for everybody. That was before setting to with shovels to establish snow bases consolidated enough to erect tents for High Camp, only a few hundred metres below our target summit.

The next morning would prove a culmination. Ten years of alpine mountaineering had contained some satisfying climbs and attractive summits alongside some spectacular shared experiences and rewarding friendships. At some point, however, any moderately ambitious mountaineer's thoughts turn towards the Greater Ranges, and the logistics that expeditions to those destinations entail. To me there seemed to be two fundamental problems: the intractability of synchronising motivations, abilities and substantial allowances of annual leave with suitable partners, and the binary nature of expeditions to Big Peaks.

Also needed was at the minimum a month of gasping squalor, potentially dismissed by the simple question, 'Did you get up it?'

Characteristically, I'd thought hard before finding my own solution.

Personal curiosity had led me to professional adventures in Russia and Central Asia, where a working knowledge of the Great Game and the travels of the geographers, mountaineers, agents and warriors between British India and the Tsar's realm had been a pleasant backdrop, and a potent fuel for the imagination.

Islamabad: permits, porter arrangements and July heat. 'Try and do one thing a day,' said my tent-mate, who had been in Pakistan summer temperatures before. 'No fewer than one, but no more.' Sound advice with an interesting visit to a squalid zoo as we awaited climbing permits, before tempting the fates with a two-day journey along the Karakoram Highway. The rushing Indus: Nanga Parbat and the Fairy Meadows, inspiring scene of the Messner brothers' struggles. Some bonus ranges to glimpse: not only the Karakoram, but the Pamirs and even the chance of a short walk in the Hindu Kush. Tantalisingly close to Hunza and Gilgit, but even without setting eyes on the historic forts themselves, ample atmosphere: glacial erratics covered with drying apricots, precarious terraces of irrigated wheat, sparse, goat-toughening country under Galen Rowell's luminous skies as we headed towards his Mountain Gods' throne room.

Ancient pitons, battle-scarred axes and even single high-altitude boots under the 'Long Life Mountaineering Equipment' sign in Skardu, a frontier town, before another day's travel, pausing to tie ropes to the jeep's roof-rack to keep it upright while traversing streambeds, bridges long gone, as we headed for the last grass at Askole and Urdukas. *(See Plate 27)*

Names to conjure with: Cathedral; Trango; Masherbrum; Angel; Laila; Gasherbrum. And then, with the corner turned north and out of civilisation's sight, a realm where imagination had failed: prosaic Broad Peak; atomic, essential K2.

Our goal was China. Just beyond Broad Peak and east of K2, a 6400m summit defines the China/Pakistan border. Once upon a time, a Japanese expedition had reached almost 6000m: the summit of Central Kharut Peak, an attractive snow cone, remained untouched.

To my knowledge, it remains untouched. Islamabad bureaucracy and intransigent porters had chipped days out of our month, leaving a scant four days of mountaineering from our base camp at K2's foot. Acclimatisation can't be hurried. When day two dawned to a metre of fresh snow, we knew the game was up, never even getting to the foot of 'our' route.

Pakistan was a rude if probably realistic introduction to the Expeditions game, though in every other aspect but the climbing it had met all my (high) expectations.

Kyrgyzstan:

First Ascent of snow dome at 42° 07' 25"N, 79° 38' 22"E, just S of Putevodniy Pass, (4970m); F/PD-, 29th July 2007.

Attempted Ascent of Pt 5005 at 42° 08' 58"N, 79° 36' 11"E on the ridge west of Nansen Peak; reached the ridgeline approximately 500 metres ENE from Pt 5005 and traversed approx 200 metres of the ridge before retreat by abseil, 1 August 2007.

Routes from Base Camp on the Kanjailau Glacier, 5km SW of Nansen Peak (5697m).

Two seasons later, I was ready for another go. Professionally, I'd taken a break from the Russian-speaking world for sufficiently long for a mountaineering visit not to feel like a busman's holiday. On the other hand, I'd once spent a couple of years as a salesman of modifications for big, ugly

Russian helicopters, and yet never flown in a helicopter of any sort. The Aeronautical Engineer's curiosity was piqued...

Via Moscow to Bishkek, the only capital city I'm aware of that's named after a sex toy. (Bishkek's etymological roots may be in the word Pishpek, a stubby pestle that Kyrgyz herdswomen use primarily to stir fermenting mare's milk. Scurrilous but credible rumour reports a second, intimate use.)

From Bishkek, a long drive: past Issyk Kul[11], from which (anecdotally) years before a Soviet torpedo had run amok and leaped, having failed its secret tests, onto a beach where Moscow tourists had had themselves photographed adoringly alongside it. Past roadside sales of apricots and mackerel, dried or fresh, and occasional freshly-sprouted aluminium mosque domes. More common, though, were picturesque encampments of gers (the Mongolian term for a yurt), the characteristic mushroom tent of the region, with the odd Lada or Land Cruiser tethered alongside the horses. Past Turkic graffiti written in Cyrillic; but also, slopped in khaki paint on crumbling pre-fab concrete fence slabs, the inviting slogan 'БИЗНЕС ИНКУБАТОР' ('BIZNES INKUBATOR'). (In fact, such micro-credit agencies made a significant contribution to improving Kyrgyzstan's rural economy at this time.)

A morning in the market spent negotiating for industrial quantities of salami, sprats, bread and vegetables, but avoiding the blandishments of the goat's-head wholesaler. Then, load the truck: reload the truck according to the driver's whim, and eventually make an alpine start for several hours' drive through exquisite, rolling grassy foothills to a long low valley containing the helicopter pad.

Conditions aboard were informal, and as impromptu interpreter 'Left a bit – right a bit – over there looks safe: save us a walk,' I had a plum view of proceedings. The flight was smooth, efficient, loud and intimidating. The pilot was not eager to linger on the glacier at 4000m, and snatched photos of the team unloading the aircraft to show every member cowering and stooped, while the rotors thundered and slashed the air a good twenty-five feet above our heads.

'OK, see you next Thursday!'

'Right! Thursday!' (Shouted.)

An imposing pile of kit suddenly looked very small and quiet as the helicopter departed.

---

11. The purity of Issyk Kul's waters were not helped a few years later when a lorry carrying several tens of thousands of litres of cyanide crashed into it. Ed.

Three days later, success was in sight. Trail-breaking had comprehensively soaked any leather boots in the team, and mine were frozen solid on summit morning. On the other hand, the climbing proved trivial and the weather was smiling. By 9am we'd bagged our peak: first ascentionists of a modest summit a couple of rope-lengths higher than Mont Blanc, in the Kyrgyzstan Tien Shan. Handshakes: a panoramic view including the great marble pyramid of the 6995m Sky God himself, Khan Tengri, highest of the range, and Nansen Peak, our local giant at 5600m. Exotica: Turkic language; a Russian-named Nordic hero in a Chinese range, the 'Heavenly Mountains'. The boots were thawed, and still four days mountaineering to go! *(See Plate 28)*

Other parties coming back to that area have probably traversed the skyline of our bowl of mountains, ticking top after top of accessible, virgin, 5000m summits. Time and supplies limited our efforts to an attractive nearby 5005m snow cone with a view of the South Inylchek glacier, approached by an interesting ridge of more technical climbing. But the ridge turned out to be made of loose pottery shards and to conceal a number of awkward abseils. Our time ran out: when our watches showed that we'd be tackling the snow cone in the midday sun, it was time to concede to the mountain.

Such a 'failure' put 'success' in perspective. Considerable commitments of time and money had won me my 'First Ascent' prize. The heavy snowfall had spared me confirmation of my personal nagging doubt that would never have occurred to anyone unfamiliar with the region: that our summit might have been marked with a cairn of fish bones and empty vodka bottles, as an attractive viewpoint reasonably accessible from a nearby pass on a standard Soviet mountain tourism itinerary. My judgement is uncertain: Soviet mountain tourism was highly regimented, with infractions of the near-border area very unlikely. But no matter: my view from our 'loose pottery' watershed was certainly new to human eyes, its rocks to human feet, and I'd taken my part in some honest, engrossing exploratory climbing.

And, of course, sometimes, the joy really is in the hopeful travelling!

A Shortish Walk Round Mount Kailas
by Catherine Moorehead

It is said that Superhero Messner completed the fifty-two kilometre *parikrama,* or *kora*, or circumambulation, or just plain walk round Mount Kailas, the holiest mountain in Asia, in one go, in something no doubt well under twenty-four hours. We lesser mortals took two and a bit days. But then the track does rise to 5660m, a pretty respectable height if you are just a fortnight away from leafy Surrey.

Kailas, nestling in western Tibet, was intended as our main acclimatisation walk before venturing above 6000m on the Tibetan Plateau; in that, it succeeded admirably. My best moment lay in discovering that (for once) I was not actually the last to reach the highest point. We completed the walk in the conventional clockwise direction. To go widdershins, you stamp yourself as a Bön Animist, ie a follower of the ancient pre-Buddhist pantheistic religion which sees spirits throughout nature, often of a pretty nasty sort, this practice being testified to by intermittent cairns of bleached animal skulls.

Kailas is doubly sacred: for Hindus, it resembles a giant phallus and is therefore a fertility symbol; in Buddhist iconography, however, each of the four faces is named after animals, colours and jewels. The *parikrama* path is buttressed by unimaginably steep dark cliffs, down which waterfalls fall with a clean, awe-inspiring verticality. Beyond these, pristine snow-slopes sweep in graceful curves to the untrodden summit at 6714m.

You start from the collection of hovels known as Darchen. Rice wine, tasting of essence of urban drain after a long, hot summer, can be acquired for 40p the bottle in the shack next to the police station next to the bawdy-house. It (Darchen, not the bawdy-house) is a miserable place, its tawdriness highlighted by the magnificence of its surroundings.

Having spent five days on the rough road from Lhasa, with a fascinating stopover at Shigatse to see the fake Panchen Lama's palace (the real Lama being still under house-arrest in Beijing), and having already ground over several 5000m passes, and having puffed our way up a bit of Kailas to near one of its inner-ring lamaseries the day before, we felt fit enough to go rocketing off on the first day of the walk. In a thought-provoking contrast to our hell-for-leather speed, we soon came across one of the real pilgrims, a Tibetan doing the circuit by successive prostrations (with his elbows and kneecaps suitably reinforced). This sight provoked much discussion about how long he would take. No rest for the active, however: we soon left the vast, sandy steppe of the Plains of Barga on the mountain's south side – always puzzling to see prairies of beach sand with glaciated 7000m peaks behind them – and swung north, though still following a nearly-negligible gradient, into the amphitheatrical canyon which constitutes Kailas's left (western) flank. By mid-morning, we had passed the mighty Darpoche prayer-flag, with its nearby sky-burial ground: here, the locals leave their ground-up corpses out to be picked over and disposed of by vultures and other raptors. At one time, such sites were sacred, and exclusive; now they are approaching the sad status of tourist destinations. We avoided the place.

The verticality of the valley walls imposes itself ever more strongly the further north you go, as do the boiler-plate smooth slabs and contortedly weird rock-pillars in a cigar-coloured 3000m high pair of parallel curtains. After a lunch of marmot-outstaring competitions, we soon arrived, rather less energetically as the heat of the day took its toll, at the Second Prostration Point, something perhaps roughly equivalent to the Stations of the Cross in Christian culture. Another touristy intrusion: a tea-tent where you could buy coca-cola at the same price as the shop next to School back in Guildford! You could devote a whole essay to the incongruities of this situation.

At least, on leaving this point, I began to feel a stronger, more welcome sense of isolation. On the far side of the river, two *gompas* (lamaseries) clung in true Tibetan style to a cliff-face: we were now in a place sufficiently remote for the meditative life to be achievable. As the path swung right and east up a still very easy grass and moraine incline, we approached one of the great sights in the mountain world, the more than Eiger-like North Face of Kailas, an imposing 2500m triangle of striated precipices. Remarkably, it was almost bare, in worrying contrast to Charles Allen's photograph, taken in July (same month as we were there) 1938, when the face was plastered with snow. *(See Plate 29)*

Where on earth were the yaks? They had all our food and equipment, and we were approaching our first camp. No sooner thought than said, a tinkling and a rumbling signalled their approach, urged on by a very purposeful herdsman. Yaks always look as if they ought only to be able to lumber around; instead, they are remarkably nervy and erratic creatures. We met yak-herdsmen at both extremes of competence. The incompetent one caused us horrible problems on a different day in a different valley.

An obstacle had to be overcome before reaching camp: one of the main tributary streams draining off Kailas's North Face. Five years before, in Kazakhstan, when trying to cross a glacier stream on my idiotic own, I had been swept away and thought that the end had come. River-crossings, even in the Cairngorms or Rannoch, had become traumatic ever since. So I chose my spot carefully: wide and shallow, though with fast, bubbly chocolate-brown streamlets everywhere. Gingerly I picked my way over the slippery boulders, and exhaled gratefully – we were now at about 5000m – then turned to see many of the others trotting over a bridge about 100 metres upstream!

Most of us managed a hearty meal at our camp, always a good sign. But as night fell, the storm started. Lightning seemed to earth itself horribly close to the tent. I wondered – when not trying to do something about my sinuses – once the rockfall started, if the whole rotten, bouldery cliff above the camp might come crashing down on us and thereby prevent us ever having to leave the tents at all.

Early next morning, having examined the route ahead and wondered whether I would ever manage it, and consequently believing that I would take more time than all the fit young men in the party, I told my Deputy, ace mountain-doctor Barney Rosedale, that I would leave ahead of the rest if I were to ascend the 700m to the Drölma La and reach the top of the pass at the same time as the rest – as it turned out, a needless anxiety. *(See Plate 30)*

With ashy mouth and bruised nasal tubes, and with not much breakfast inside me, I picked my way over the rickety wooden bridge (with added holes for that extra-close view of the spuming torrent) spanning the main North Face river outlet. After that, the path wound up through extensive boulderfields to a flatter, open area. At this point, true to my Scottish-derived and accurate estimate of the weather prospects, the morning mists cleared and a glorious day opened out. To my surprise, as Kailas's summit and attendant peaks became visible, I found I was actually enjoying myself!

Some of the others caught up, then overtook me, though our heftiest expeditioner could be seen some way behind, toiling upwards in evident pain. At about 5500m, the path steepened considerably, though nowhere did it become difficult. My elevation of spirits did the trick: at no point did I need to take fewer than thirty-two steps without pausing for breath. With a cry of '*Lho gyaltso!*' ('The gods are victorious!'), I reached with surprising ease the Drölma La summit moonscape, alleviated by thousands of poster-paint coloured windhorses, the prayer-flags whose contents the winds carry everywhere. What a place! Wild, savage boulderfields, rugged, soaring cliffs, glaring snowfields, panoramas of distant, scarcely-explored mountains – and a sandwich and thermos of something agreeably hot with which to supplement it!

We all then bumbled with considerable speed down the bouldery slope to the north-eastern corner of the circumambulation, perhaps motivated by the prospect of the tea-tent at the bottom. I named this outpost the Tashi Delekatessen – *'Tashi delek'* being the traditional Tibetan greeting – a brilliant piece of wordplay which unaccountably no-one thought funny. To be back in a greenish and wet valley, having descended from the sterile heights, was much like the feeling I have sometimes experienced of being back in the dense pine forests of Rothiemurchus after having struggled through a storm on the Cairngorm Plateau, rather as though coming round from a disturbing dream into solid reality.

Mud and flowers, and jagged purple cliffs, and our first stone-built house occupied our thoughts over the next few hours as we ambled down the east flank, a generally much more open and benign valley than the western side. At our second camp we were entertained by our yakherders' dogs barking for three hours non-stop, having spotted a couple of very vicious-looking, mangy grey wolves pottering around in their hunt for marmot on the other side of the river.

The final day dawned uncontroversially, and continued so. The path again became easy and pretty nearly level. The rest struck off it to visit Milarepa's Cave, a supposed meditation base for the great Buddhist saint, but whose 'caves' are about as common as Bonnie Prince Charlie's, and just about as likely to have been slept in.

The path added a bit of interest as it clung to the sides of a small gorge, across which lines of prayer-flags fluttered improbably. Having negotiated the gorge, we swung westwards in the direction of Darchen. We could relax and enjoy the splendid sight of Lake Manasarowar (the lake of benign spirits) and Rakshas Tal (the lake of evil spirits) framed by the Mustagh Ata lookalike, in its very long, sustained diagonal summit ridge, Gurla Mandhata (7777m), lying athwart the Tibetan-Nepalese border.

A few hours later, we had set up camp on the sandy shores of the benign one, to begin a pleasant break before heading for a new chapter of adventures on the Chang Tang (the Tibetan northern plateau) and, eventually, Everest North Base Camp, where we still claim the world high-altitude record for fireworks parties on glaciers.

Highest Unclimbed:
Gangkhar Puensum South-East face Trek

by Bruno Marques

The river followed us all the way up.

Having started in lowland farms – bearing in mind that 2620m counts for 'low' lands in Bhutan – we meandered through forests of bamboo, sauntered past Himalayan mountain beaches glinting with quartz-rich sands, scrambled up over rocky paths, pressed on through ancient-smelling pine forests and slogged up the steep, needle-strewn paths they had to offer. The spirit of this particularly quiet, rarely trodden corner of the Earth seemed to change round almost every bend, and through each of these stages of our journey the atmosphere and even the mood shifted accordingly. The same river was somehow able to transmogrify into different guises throughout, reflecting and accentuating this ongoing variation in setting and ambience.

At times the going was pretty easy, and provided ample opportunity to talk with other members of the expedition along the way. This was one of the things that struck me most about the expedition as a whole: how easily everyone got on with one another. We were a rum mix of Old Guildfordians, friends of OGs and even the mother of an OG! A diverse mix in terms of background and particularly of mountaineering experience, we kept together well as a group on the climb and, more importantly, got on very amicably with minimum effort and only a splash of daily gin and tonic. At other times, however, the Bhutanese peaks and their thin air took over all attempts at conversation, removing that pack mentality and leaving me to try and bring my heart-rate down to a calming 100 beats per minute or so from the alarming speeds to which the exertion sent it soaring, even during a slow climb. Having heard the rumours that it is often the younger, fitter members of high-altitude expeditions who give themselves altitude sickness by pushing past their limits, I was keen to restrain myself, and my heart rate, as much as possible, a tactic which later paid dividends.

The third day, our longest day's climb, became something of a defining point in the trek: the atmosphere palpably lifted from the increasingly oppressive dark pinewoods to a vast clearing which stretched out from, then beyond all that had gone before along the lower legs of the ascent. Rarefied caps of the surrounding Bhutanese mountain tops presented themselves to us in the gloriously open landscape which, particularly for a novice 'mountaineer' such as myself, stirred very strong feelings that we really were in the Himalayas: folds of snow-encrusted rock pushed up into the thinning atmosphere as a result of ancient and ongoing tectonic movements. Here we were, very bloomin' high up. While the strength with which this sensation first struck me faded away, the feeling itself did not but rather lay ubiquitously in the background as we pushed on further, past the desolate, and frankly somewhat desperate looking shacks and shelters used by the herders whose lives were spent in transit across these mountain passes. There was no-one to be seen in these structures of river-washed rocks and boulders, a far cry from anything that could remotely be known as 'civilisation', and yet the frequency with which we passed these refuges, all well-stocked with wood fuel, indicated that they *must* still be in use. Indeed, our guide, Karma, and the pony-herders in charge of keeping camp assured us that these passes were still a fundamental part of people's livelihoods.

In times gone by the mountains used to be the only routes in and out of Bhutan and of neighbouring trading regions in this stretch of the Himalayan mountain range, and weather-toughened men would herd their load-carrying charges through the passes, taking refuge where they could find it, in the seasons that dictated their annual commute. This was how wools, spices, rices and other essential commodities, as well as developing cultures, made it in and out of these regions, by the painstaking time-worn efforts of the men and their animals. This is also one of the quintessentially inspiring qualities of the Kingdom of Bhutan: a very large part of it still truly exists in 'times gone by', a fact reflected in many of the good-natured Bhutanese people we saw before and after the trek, and no less in the very team of ponymen supporting us on the mountainside. Granted, they were currently being paid essentially to nanny a group of well-spoken Guildfordians up a mountain that they themselves could happily trot up and down without respite, but then they were also very much living on means by which their forebears lived, those afforded by the mountains. Time-worn tradition is definitely a running theme in Bhutan, with carefully emerging ties to the present (mobile phones, internet, road-based trade and, most recently, democracy[12]) dropping a tincture of modern life into this hidden mountain kingdom whose essence still lies very much in a tranquil past.

---

12. We were in Thimphu, the Bhutanese capital, on the day of their first General Election, and indeed had a chance meeting with Bhutan's first democratically-elected Prime Minister, Jigme Thinley, at a hotel near Trongsa, Central Bhutan, a few days later. Ed.

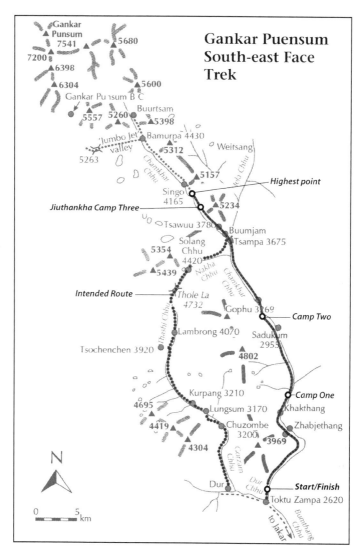

The proposed trek route (conditions permitting!)
Reproduced with permission from Cicerone's Trekking in Bhutan
© Cicerone Press and Bart Jordans

The goal of our trek in this ancient land had from the outset been to reach Bamurpa, a spot around the 5000m altitude mark which has previously served both as base camp and perfect vantage point to view the highest unclimbed mountain peak in the world; no mean claim.

Gangkhar Puensum (with various spellings due to transliteration) literally means, 'Three mountain siblings'; attempts have been made to

117

climb the main peak in the past. After several failures, however, and out of respect for Bhutanese religious beliefs concerning the spirits which dwell and rest on these mountain peaks, further attempts have been ruled out by the Bhutanese king. Thus Gangkhar Puensum promises to hold its unique status for some time, and had certainly kindled excitement among the novice hikers and hardened mountaineers on our expedition alike. *(See Plate 31)*

We continued the long slog up to Jiuthangka in the rarefied air just above 4000m, that same single river still hugging our side, now becoming something of a trusted companion. Arriving with a short amount of light left, we had the perfect opportunity to soak up the view of our expansive camp in its open plain, feeling somewhat grandiose compared to our last camp, couched in a cramped mountainside enclave next to the river. The 'slow-but-steady' approach got me exhausted by the time we reached that viewpoint, but not quite knocked for six. Spanning an area large enough to fit two or three football pitches, this ranked as one of the largest flats we had seen in Bhutan aside from the airport runway in Paro, the only airport in Bhutan, owing more to geographical reasons than economic ones, I suspect. Given the rigours of the day behind us, and the challenge of the days ahead to reach Bamurpa, a good few of us decided to bed down early to sleep off the exhausting efforts of our day's climb and the effects of the considerable increase in altitude.

I for one slept somewhat fitfully, amid bizarre sounds of tent patting, the repeated sweeps of brush on canvas and the squeak-squeak-crunch of powder under foot followed by further baffling 'pat-pat' noises. In the tentative brightness of morning, as sleep drew further away and consciousness seeped in, I pieced the sounds together, bit by bit. Karma woke the group, tent by tent, for our now ritual morning black tea in bed, during which I popped my head out of the tent to see pure, fresh white powder everywhere. Fields, riverside, tree-tops, pony backs, tents, deserted shacks. Covered. Snow had come to visit us in the night, and it had visited us in droves. The ponymen who had chaperoned us up the hill had been working tirelessly throughout the night to keep the snow brushed off the side of our tents so that they didn't collapse under its weight. *(See Plate 32)*

Coming out of the tent into the snow for the morning routine of an open-air topless wash from the hot water bowls brought to us, we were met with blood pheasants scooting about in the distance, breathtaking views of whole vast banks of pine trees, tops dappled with white, and our friendly ponies roaming the now covered plain we were camped in, looking for the few enterprising patches of grass and greenery that had poked through the snow.

And therein lay the problem. Food had been carried up for the ponies to have a daily feed out of their muzzle bags, but they were also reliant upon opportunities throughout the day to graze. After all, they did work hard: each morning we would leave the camp behind for the ponymen to pack it up onto the ponies' backs; they would at some point in the day overtake us further uphill to set up camp ready and awaiting our arrival in the mess tent for hot food and drink; a pretty fantastic level of service and hospitality in this harsh wilderness. Thus the ponies needed plenty of grazing throughout the day, and the snow proved to be a major factor which, coupled with information gleaned from our earlier visit to the small army outpost at the bottom of the mountain, built compelling evidence against the possibility of succeeding in our goal. The mountain pass further up, colloquially known as Jumbo Jet Valley, through which we had been planning our return, was utterly impassable due to snow drift. The ponies could not advance to any camp further up while the snow held. Almost immediately it was declared that this day would be taken for rest, acclimatisation and, ultimately, decision-making.

A meeting of the expedition was held mid-morning, after some serious snowman building had been conducted, and options were laid out. Basically, it was evident that we would not be able to progress further up as we would not be able to set up camp without grazing being available for the ponies. Furthermore, we could not push on to Jumbo Jet Valley and move down to a campsite below the snowline on the other side, as the pass itself was impassable. While hopeful but ultimately unrealistic avenues were briefly explored, more out of good manners than any real decision-making process, the disappointing reality of the situation had silently settled in and imposed itself upon all our minds, and eventually had to be spoken. Our fearless leader, Catherine Moorehead, had to bite the bullet and inform us that we would not be able to make it to Bamurpa, and that we would have to finish our trek by returning the way we had come, by following the same river down that had followed us up. Nothing further could be done, but we all knew that no stone had been left unturned in searching for alternatives, and that the conclusion was, indeed, conclusive[13].

We were all disappointed, and I'm sure the crushing effect of this did

---

13. I'm not sure about the 'fearless' part, but I was certainly extremely disappointed that we were not going to be able to go on and see the great peak and/or the Chinese border. Very few western expeditions have reached the point we did but of course one of the great expedition skills, which certainly needs to be applied here, is knowing when to turn back. CJSM

not escape anyone, least of all Catherine and the Deputy Leader, Barney Rosedale, who had both put so much effort into engineering this unique venture. Acceptance of this disappointment, however, at least allowed the opportunity to explore for one last time, not by finishing the proposed trek route, but at least at snatching a glimpse of our original goal – a direct view of that highest unclimbed, the enigmatic and as yet elusive peak of Gangkhar Puensum.

The possibility of climbing higher for a portion of the day only, unaccompanied by the usual entourage of ponymen, ponies and camp paraphernalia, with a strict time by which to return was opted for by a half-dozen of the more determined (or just more stubborn) members of the group. One of the ponymen had informed us that there was a point on the path about half way towards our intended final camp from which we could get a good view of the mountain trio, if the skies were to clear up. That being such a big, and unlikely, 'if', some of the others were naturally put off and opted for a day of rest and relaxation at Jiuthangka in our veritable luxury camp suite.

Barney, guided by the Head Ponyman and Karma, led the crack-team of Ash, Colin, Justin, Judy and myself on our final mission before settling in for our return to Jiuthangka and, ultimately, back off the mountain and well away from any other opportunity to glimpse this promised peak with the naked eye. While this was a rather sad thought with which to contend, it was with an air of spirited and somewhat playful optimism that we set off. The snow clouds were thick and still coming in, and the real chance of actually seeing Gangkhar Puensum slim, but further sights of snow-clad mountain scenery were guaranteed. Combine this with the ability of the scenery to surprise with a continual renewal of vastly varied landscape views, and the mood was set in a very positive light, despite those rolling grey cloud banks overhead.

Still deep in pine forest, we set off. Boughs weighed down with snow buckled before us to provide a picturesque scene – and endless opportunities to hatch cunning plans… Several of one's comrades who carelessly stood too close to such a laden branch soon found themselves beneath a deluge, with snow in hood and on head. This enclosed forest soon opened, leaving us precariously stepping out into broad, surreally cobbled plains that were clearly designed with the notion in mind that no human feet would ever tread them. Yet more dark stone shacks proved to us that these passes were crossed by men and pony alike, though we were probably the first soft

Guildfordians walking cautiously in the footsteps of altitude-hardened indigenous Bhutanese, especially at this time of year when the ponies could not even feed. As we crossed these lands, I felt like something of a fly-on-the-wall, almost as though we should not really be here and that by some strange and special invitation we alone were permitted a view of this broad expanse of coarsely cracked rock.

Eventually we passed through some narrow turns and dense foliage to a small, innocuous little spot on the slope, with one side clear of obstruction. And we stopped. The same river which we had heard at the start of the trek burbled by underneath, younger, more energetic. The culmination of trickles of melting cap ice. We stood about not really knowing what for, surrounded by nearby bushes and a slightly more distant grey haze. This was our spot. This was our chance to see our peak. At least it had come to feel like it was 'Our Peak'. So much had we pushed and slogged up the mountainside, so much had we seen the scenery change as determinedly as the river followed, and yet this was the highest point and the only point from which we could see Gangkhar Puensum. And yet the group disposition contained no despondency or disappointment, but rather tones of amused irony – we had, after all, set out from Jiuthangka on the cloudiest, most inclement day we had experienced in Bhutan for a cheeky spot of sightseeing. (Though at this point I must confess to still being a little bloody-minded and suggesting we press on or wait around for the cloud to clear: it wasn't going to clear.) Barney led a well-exercised team back down through snow that was turning sludgy, after our mandatory Team Photos at the Highest Point of The Trek and comments that we could always just cut and paste a picture of Gangkhar Puensum into the background. *(See Plate 33)*

On our return to a warm mess tent and hot bowls of noodles, it was evident that not all the rest of the crew had been resting. David, Keith and Jim had been 'holding the fort' while Catherine and Tom had been making arrangements for a special Commemoration Service to be held for Michael Hetherington. Michael had been a dear friend of several of the expedition members and had been set to number among our party on this mountain before he inexplicably disappeared on a hiking trip in South Africa. His disappearance was a mystery and remains a tragedy, and it had long been agreed that a Commemoration Service would be held in his memory. The main Bhutanese guide Catherine had liaised with, Chambula Dorji, was kind enough to arrange for a butter-light ceremony to be held in Michael's memory in a quiet and strikingly beautiful monastery in the Punakha area.

In addition to this, Catherine had suggested that a Christian ceremony be held for Michael, in keeping with his faith, at the highest camp site on our trek, in which a deeply moving eulogy was read which spoke volumes of the varied and rich life of a friendly and kind-hearted gentleman[14]. A prominent rock, with a suitable view of this strikingly beautiful setting, remains with a message carved to Michael and any other travellers who may happen across this site.

The following day came after a good night's rest, and a slightly later start than the strict reveille times of the earlier days of the trek, with a hale and hearty pace taking us down the mountain at speed to reach the first day's half-way point, even leaving Karma's energetic disposition tired enough to be caught 'resting his eyes' with his forehead perched on his umbrella. The following day this opened the exciting possibility of beds, log fires and most important a resupply of our dwindling alcohol stores. I jumped at the opportunity presented, opting to follow Karma down on a rapid return to the hut from which we had set off six days earlier so that he could get in contact with his boss, Chambula, and I could get a well-earned beer. The lower altitude and, crucially, the downward gradient had me feeling like a (reasonably) fit man in my early twenties once again, and for the most part I managed to keep up a pretty decent pace with Karma (though I was back to square one when it came to any uphill legs). Taking only one ten minute break on the descent I was somewhat taken aback to arrive at a strange wooden hut with a nearby school – apparently the cultural equivalent of the Post Office in London Road where we used to buy sweets and cigarettes, and yet so very different – to have Karma thrust a bowl of hot noodles and a bottle of Druk 11000 in my hand. ('Druk' means 'Thunder Dragon', Bhutan being 'The Land of The Thunder Dragon'; Druk 11000 is a powerful Bhutanese lager that boasts the uncertain strength of 'Alcohol content not exceeding 11%': that's quality control for you.) He was then kind enough to buy me another before promptly announcing that he was going to run further down the hill to where he could call Chambula and leave me here with not a soul who could speak English, to await the arrival of others, expected to turn up in a few hours' time. In fact, the inhabitants of this hut did not even speak Dzongka, the national language, but rather a local dialect.

---

14. Although Michael never married nor had any children, he leaves family members whom we have got to know and who have been of great help, in a kindly way reminiscent of Michael himself, in piecing together the material by which he is remembered. (See David Dunmur's Hannibal article.) Ed.

I wasn't left with much to do but drink more Druk 11000 and be befriended by the odd wandering fisherman and strangely inquisitive rogue children who happened to stop by for a beverage (non-alcoholic). Unsurprisingly, by the time the first few friendly Guildfordian faces wandered into the distance to greet my eyes, it was through a reasonably thick haze that I saw them. Unfortunately my over-exhausted wits had left me by around my fourth bottle, though I had enough presence of mind left to keep the others similarly plied until Karma eventually arrived with the proverbial cavalry. Our much-loved and dearly-missed fleet of 4x4s and drivers were greeted with very happy and only slightly tipsy faces, knowing full well our Bhutanese drivers-turned-friends were walking tickets to the height of civilised comfort: bedrooms with personal log furnaces...

To the Top of the Bottom of the World: Mount Vinson
by Gareth Stewart

Something was digging into my ribs and had woken me suddenly. I had probably enjoyed the best night's sleep of the last seven, but a double-down skin sleeping-bag is claustrophobic enough without the ten or so items I had stashed inside to stop them freezing overnight. I pondered for a moment which item it could be... my camera? No, that was under my knee; my water bottles? No, they were between my legs. I concluded that it must be either my sun cream or my toothpaste, both of which I had tried in vain to use the day before, but they had frozen solid; this had been my last ditch attempt to make them usable again. This puzzle was all I had thought about in those first few waking moments; only now did I begin to realise that the whistling outside I had grown so accustomed to had stopped, the tent was no longer flapping and I was surrounded by an eerie quiet.

Our small team, consisting of Tom and me and our well-known guide David Hamilton, had been tent-bound on an Antarctic glacier half way up Mount Vinson for a full five days. We had been waiting for a ferocious storm to abate and had started to realise how very cut off we were: only the previous night we had been calculating how many more days we could hold out before having to take drastic action. We held reserves at Base Camp and had also stashed food at our High Camp before descending to the glacier to sleep (following the climbers' mantra of, 'climb high, sleep low'), but the storm had arrived quickly and the continent had given us a taste of what it could serve up. This was meant to be summer, yet the temperature had dropped to -40°C and the wind had gusted from every direction at 80 to 100mph, with visibility down to a couple of metres as the air filled with spindrift. We had taken as many precautions as we could by building an ice wall around the tent, but even so we had to spend five hours of the first night holding the tent up from the inside while we took a battering. The force had been strong enough to blow us over inside the tent as the wind tried to rip our flimsy canvas home from the ground.

The quiet outside, I hoped, meant that the wind had stopped and that on unzipping the hatch I would be greeted by favourable skies. The performance to get ready to go outside was not a quick one, though I went about the task as quickly and diligently as I could, because I was desperate to see if the storm had released us from its grip. The final exit manoeuvre entailed dislodging the icicles from the tent zip onto my sleeping companions before stepping into the cold Antarctic morning air. I noticed that despite the twenty-four hour sunlight, our tent was still in the lee of the surrounding mountains and as such we were 10°C worse off for being in the shade. Consequently, the mercury in the thermometer on the tent, which registered temperatures as low as -35°C, was still off the scale. I could virtually feel the heat being sucked out of me. Outside, beyond the broken and collapsed protective wall of snow and ice we'd cut and dug around the tent, the crystal landscape stretched away. The utter silence was humbling and the view immense. *(See Plate 34)* After such a long time confined in the odd orange glow of the tent, the world was suddenly so much greater again and my senses were definitely struggling to take it all in. Moving slowly, I stopped and stared in every direction, teeth gritted against the cold, and once again I could feel the excitement of an attempt on the highest peak on this most remote continent rushing back. I thought about going for my camera, but then remembered that if I brought it outside too quickly from the relative warmth of the tent, the lens would have frosted over and the film, in freezing instantly, would more than likely have snapped. The moment stayed just that: a moment.

Antarctica is an extraordinary region, the best description of which is extreme. It is the highest continent, as well as the driest, the coldest and the windiest. Nobody owns it, although seven countries have laid claim to small slices of it, and it has never had a native human population. Antarctica is geographically predisposed towards adventure: the summits on the continent have an allure of their own, enhanced by the remoteness and extreme cold. Although the Ellsworth Mountains that rise imperiously from the Ronne Ice Shelf were first spotted by the American aviator Lincoln Ellsworth while making a trans-Antarctic flight in 1935, he missed the highest peak, Mount Vinson. Remarkably, the 4897m high Mount Vinson wasn't spotted until US navy pilots made reconnaissance flights over Antarctica in 1957. Almost a decade later, in 1966, the American Alpine Club sent a team to Antarctica with the intention of conquering Vinson. Led by Nick Clinch, the four man team was flown into the mountains in a ski-equipped Hercules. On December 18 they battled their way to the summit. Over the next few days the team also claimed first ascents on the second, third and fourth highest peaks on Antarctica, the neighbouring Tyree (4845m), Gardner (4686m) and Shinn (4661m) respectively. Although Vinson is the coveted highest point, Tyree is in fact the continent's most challenging climb.

If it didn't contain the thirteen mile long, eight mile wide Vinson Massif, the Ellsworth Mountain range, which is a mere 750 miles from the South Pole, would only have been visited by a handful of daring explorers. Mount Vinson is one of the world's coveted Seven Summits and as such attracts a strong degree of attention. We were not driven to climb all seven summits: I've never been sure that I could endure the two month acclimatisation period interspersed with eight or so days climbing (if the weather is good) that is required to summit Everest. Similarly, we had not arrived at this point to be the first people on top, although we were still within the first thousand. Rather, we had been drawn by the remoteness and the sense of adventure coupled with the desire to challenge ourselves in such an awesome place. Although having just spent five days in the close proximity of two other men in a space no bigger than a large dining table, which you were not allowed to leave for any reason, I felt I could take anything on!

Our expedition had started under a cloud of ill-luck. We had all begun our trips to Antarctica from different points in the UK, and had all been offloaded from flights and lost vital expedition kit. I had been offloaded in Santiago, Chile: on my eventual arrival in Punta Arenas, Southern Chile, I discovered I had no bags (I still maintain as a result of Barcelona beating Real Madrid 3–0 as I was attempting to transit Madrid International!). Slowly we re-grouped and recovered our possessions; unfortunately we had missed the transit to Antarctica and had to endure a fortnight's wait, seated by the phone, waiting for a weather window to allow us to fly again. Finally, we boarded a commercially operated Kazakh Ilyushin-76 cargo plane and took off for the south. The huge plane is far from comfortable and we had to share the fuselage with a 4x4 vehicle, two skidoos and fifty barrels of aviation fuel. During take-off, the noise was ear-splittingly loud and the ear-plugs we had been issued with merely muffled the racket to a dull roar. The plane is windowless but there are superb views from the glass nose-cone below the flight deck: perched next to the navigator, underneath the cockpit, you feel like a gunner in a Lancaster bomber. Just under five hours later, the landing at Patriot Hills, on the only blue-ice runway in the world, is bumpy and a little bizarre. The plane takes 3km to come to a standstill as the tyres struggle to grip onto the rock-solid turquoise ice band formed by the harsh winds that have stripped the snow from the surface. Stepping out of the plane, we caught our first glimpse of the end of the world.

Patriot Hills is a collection of tents and temporary structures perched on the ice some 600 miles from the nearest neighbour; it is often the starting point for Antarctic adventures. The 4x4 was on a record-breaking attempt to the South Pole; the camp cook was attempting to snowboard a vast distance with a kite, and we were just there to climb a mountain. Lady Luck then decided we had been put through enough tests for the moment: within twelve hours, we were loading our kit into a small ski-equipped Twin Otter before embarking on the stunning one hour flight to Vinson Base Camp on the Branscomb Glacier, to the south of the Ellsworth Mountains. We pitched our tents and caught up with a group of climbers returning from the summit, all of whom looked rather the worse for wear. Complaining of appalling weather and unexpectedly low temperatures, they reported that most of the group had still made the summit. Buoyed by this news, the following day we set off up the glacier with two weeks' supply of food and fuel to Camp One.

There are no porters or pack animals in Antarctica and all the gear has to be carried or towed across the ice on sledges. The surface of the ice appears flat, but is in fact studded with concrete-hard, wind-blown ridges – *sastrugi* – which can be anything from a few inches to six feet high. You travel, roped in a line, one person to the next person's sled, so as to have the best chance of surviving a crevasse collapse. Progress in crampons is slow, although the distances between camps are relatively short; the extreme conditions continually sap your strength. Each night was spent continuously refuelling on as much as you could eat, the only shame being that the cold temperatures made everything feel rather bland, depriving you of your normal sense of smell and taste. The climb, in good weather, was meant to last no more than a week, but to get a settled patch for that period of time was rare, the odds being that at some point things would get interesting.

From Camp One we continued to trek up the glacier and round a corner to the headwall. There then followed an exhausting toil up the steep wall, because the sleds became unusable and all our gear had to be transferred onto our backs. At the top of the wall we had to navigate a sérac barrier and crevasse field. The scenery gets progressively more and more spectacular as you gain elevation and the remoteness starts to eat away at even the most positive frame of mind. The High Camp is situated on the broad col between Vinson and Mount Shinn, a sizeable, shapely peak to the north. Here we stashed additional food and supplies before retreating to Camp One for the night, so as to aid our acclimatisation. *(See Plate 35)* Thankfully we had made it back to the camp before the storm broke and had made as secure a refuge as we could. The same could not be said for an ascending Russian team we had passed as we were coming down. They got caught at the sérac barrier, and had to take refuge under an ice block, only to stagger into Camp One forty-eight hours later, snow blind and frostbitten. That storm lasted five days and made us continually consider our predicament. Despite getting so close we were almost forced to abort the summit attempt.

Five days later, in the cold of the 'morning', I knew it was back on. We had to suffer the climb of the headwall again, but it would be worth it. The drifting at the High Camp as a result of the storm had buried our stash under a metre of snow and the digging to retrieve it and to secure the tent, fearful as we were of a fierce storm 1000m higher up, took a lung-busting three hours. Typically, given the amount of time and effort expended, the 'night' was calm and quiet. At just after nine in the morning we broke camp and set off south up a long glaciated valley that leads to the peak. Having weathered the storm, it was exhilarating to be, at last, on the way. As we were making steady progress along the gently angled slope that leads to the summit pyramid, we abandoned our down clothing. Choosing the slightly shorter, steeper 'right hand route' to the summit we stepped onto a 35° snow slope and climbed for 300m to the West Ridge, a snow ridge studded with rock pinnacles. The descent would be along the 'left hand route,' meaning that we would complete a traverse of the mountain. *(See Plate 36)*

As we neared the top of the bottom of the world, we got to gaze across thousands of square miles of ice cap and glacier, which slowly faded into a distinctly curved horizon. Neighbouring mountains Shinn and Gardner, as well as a whole host of unexplored peaks, broke up the uniform, desolate view, a view that is nonetheless starkly and harshly beautiful. The ridge in turn led to the summit, a broad sloping ledge topped with a cornice, which we finally claimed around seven hours after setting out. In near perfect 'warm' and clear conditions we sat and stared at our surroundings, the memories of the storm long since faded. Sumptuous views of the Ellsworth Mountains contrasted strongly with the seemingly flat, apparently endless plateau that stretches south to the Pole. Quietly we marvelled at the extraordinary landscape before us, humbled by the vast raw beauty of Antarctica.

Plate 1 (see p.13): Pen and sepia drawing of the Punmah Glacier by Godwin-Austen

Plate 2 (see p.18): Colonel Algernon Durand CB, CIE

Plate 3 (see p.19): The British Agent's house, Gilgit

Plate 4 (see p.20): Crossing a rope bridge

Plate 5 (see p.40): Mike Norris acclimatising above Nyalam

Plate 6 (see p.42): Looking up from Camp One. Camp Two lies on the knob above the sérac. The rock band is the horizontal break above that cuts the face. The route then traverses right to the ridge line up to the summit plateau. A forty-minute flat trudge then leads to the true summit.

*Plate 7 (see p.48): Rupert Dix at Camp 1 with a
distant view of the summit of Gasherbrum II*

Plate 8 (see p.49): Climbing the famous Banana Ridge, Gasherbrum II

Plate 9 (see p.57): Summit pyramid of Gasherbrum II from Camp IV

Plate 10 (see p.57): Rupert Dix's view from the high point on Gasherbrum II, K2 centre right

*Plate 11 (see p.63): Rupert Dix and Jonathan Stuart at the
start of the trek to the Tibetan Everest Base Camp*

Plate 12 (see p.65): The spectacular North Face of Everest from Rongphu Monastery

Plate 13 (see p.68): NE ridge of Everest from Advance Base Camp: the end of the trek

Plate 14 (see p.75): The Tarlung Glacier on the ascent of Tarlung Kangri (6293m)

Plate 15 (see p.76): View towards Longpo Kangri (7095m) from the summit of Tarlung Kangri

Plate 16 (see p.82): Altiplano, Chearoco and Chachacomani from Lago Titicaca [photo Maierhofer]

Plate 17 (see p.85): Expedition group at Calzada base camp [photo Tichauer]
Back row: John Flood-Page, Ron Hunter, Venancio, Alfredo Martinez.
Front row: Robin Bradford, Ray Fearon, Mike Smith, Eddie Quicke

Plate 18 (see p.85): Ray Fearon cuts through nieves penitentes
above the ice-cliff on Chachacomani. [photo Bradford]

Plate 19 (see p.88): Negruni-1 from the west [photo Fearon]

Plate 20 (see p.90): Quelluani from the north [photo Bradford]

Plate 21 (see p.96): Priut Odinnadsati, the 'Refuge of Eleven', Russian Caucasus

Plate 22 (see p.98): Mount Elbrus from the 'Green Hotel'

Plate 23 (see p.100): Kazbek (5035m) and the approach

Plate 24 (see p.103): Advance Base Camp on Moby Dick

Plate 25 (see p.103): Peak of Orina I from Moby Dick (Orina II)

Plate 26 (see p.104): Summit Ridge of Moby Dick (Orina II 5439m)

Plate 27 (see p.108): Cathedral Peak and Trango Towers viewed en route to the Chinese border

Plate 28 (see p.110): Ian Ferguson on the 4900m snow dome summit, with Khan Tengri far left

Plate 29 (see p.112): North face of Mount Kailas

Plate 30 (see p.113): Drölma La, at 5660m the highest point of the Kailas circuit

Plate 31 (see p.118): Spectacular views surrounded us as we ascended the deep gorge of the Bumthang Chu (Central Bhutan)

Plate 32 (see p.118): A rude awakening

Plate 33 (see p.121): A photo-shop view of Gangkhar Puensum from our highest point

Plate 34 (see p.125): Midnight sun over the Antarctic plateau

Plate 35 (see p.128): Mt Shinn, fourth-highest peak in Antarctica

Plate 36 (see p.128): Mt Vinson summit ridge

Plate 37 (see p.175): Malcolm Eldridge on Mont Blanc du Tacul

Plate 38 (see p.177): Marion Elmes and Mike Parsons reach the north ridge of the Weisshorn.

Plate 39 (see p.177): Malcolm Eldridge on the summit of Ankogel

Plate 40 (see p.183): The Grandes Jorasses:
the Walker Spur is the central feature leading to the summit.

148

Plate 41 (see p.183): Andy Cole on one of the ice pitches: Walker Spur

Plate 42 (see p.185): Andy Cole and the broken Czech on the summit, Pointe Walker

Plate 43 (see p.188): The Guildford section of the Austrian Alpine Club (Österreichischer Alpenverein or ÖAV) in the Zillertal, 1958. From left to right: Keith Newman, Dave Dunmur, Mike Smith, Dicky Collard, Tim Hall and Andy Wade

Plate 44 (see p.191): The summit ridge of the Zuckerhütl

Plate 45 (see p.191): On the approach to the summit of the Wildspitze

Plate 46 (see p.192): South west ridge of the Wilder Freiger with the Müller Hütte
in the right middle-ground and the descent gully in the foreground

Plate 47 (see p.196): Adrar n'Dern, Mountain of Mountains (4005m)

*Plate 48 (see p.199): Alex Jackson, Edward Knowles (the third member of the team),
and our guide Sylvester*

Plate 49 (see p.200): A view of the rift valley from Mt Nsunzu

Plate 50 (see p.203): The 'Hodaka' traverse with Kitahodaka in the
foreground, the point of Yarigatake distinct in the background

Plate 51 (see p.203): Rotenburo: the perfect cure for weary legs!

Plate 52 (see p.204): The summit of Mt Fuji

Plate 53 (see p.216): The North face of Ben Nevis from the west;
Tower Ridge is the central feature. ©Alex Gillespie; reproduced with permission

Plate 54 (see p.216): Tower Ridge from the summit looking west;
the Tower and Tower Gap are clearly visible.

*Plate 55 (see p.217): The
face below Ben Nevis
summit plateau*

*Plate 56 (see p.217): The
crash site on Ben Nevis*

Plate 57 (see p.224): From the summit of Beinn Bhan looking south-east

Plate 58 (see p.226): Blaven – in the clear

Plate 59 (see p.229): The tarn below Cader Idris

Plate 60 (see p.232): Crib Goch, with Snowdon in the distance
Courtesy of Lou Johnson: www.walkingbritain.co.uk

Plate 61 (see p.236): The maiden voyage of the unnamed coracle transport

Plate 62 (see p.236): The supply-line

Plate 63 (see p.238): The Old Man of Stoer in daylight, and the author's route

Plate 64 (see p.243): A midnight belay looking up pitch 3, Point Five Gully, Ben Nevis

Plate 65 (see p.245): So much beauty and ice

Plate 66 (see p.253): The dreaded Dunes – one of the most challenging sectors of the race

Plate 67 (see p.254): Charles Vivian basks in the glory of a sub-five hour marathon,
after 142 miles and seven days in the desert.

Plate 68 (see p.261): On the 'hard' Via Ferrata Tomaselli

Plate 69 (see p.262): Dolomites Via Ferrata: the Cristallo Ridge

163

*Plate 70 (see p.264): Musk Ox Col on the border of Kazakhstan and China
with the Col centre and Torrance's Top, right*

Plate 71 (see p.269): Greenland: Lyngmarksfjeld with Apostelfjeld on the left

Plate 72 (see p.270): View of Godhavn from the summit of Lyngmarksfjeld

Plate 73 (see p.271): Svalbard: load carrying with pulks on our backs

Plate 74 (see p.271): Crevasse rescue training

Plate 75 (see p.272): A fully-loaded pulk on the ice-cap

Plate 76 (see p.272): Bivvy out at Newtontoppen

ALPS NEAR AND FAR

Alps Near and Far: Introduction

The emergence of mountaineering from the slaying of myths and dragons through scientific enquiry to recreational sport has been documented in many places. Mountaineering may not be the 'sport of kings', but in the nineteenth century it became a pastime for the British aristocracy and the leisured classes, and it started in the Alps. In 1857 the first mountaineering association in the world, the Alpine Club, was founded in London by British gentlemen climbers. This continues to be one of the most prestigious clubs for mountaineers, but today the Alpine Club encourages mountaineering exploits everywhere, not just in the Alps, and supports mountaineers from all backgrounds.

This section includes contributions on alpinism from around the world. The heights of alpine peaks (2000m–5000m) are such that climbing them does not need expeditions with porters, sherpas and pack animals. The routes are shorter, requiring just a day or two, and apart from the occasional bivouac, planned or unplanned, a system of mountain huts provides shelter and food for all who venture forth. Our stories come from the mountain regions of Europe, Japan, New Zealand and Africa; they represent a cross-section of mountain activities undertaken in the tradition of the earliest alpinists as sport rather than exploration.

It is wholly appropriate that the tales begin with a re-run of a famous historical event: the traversing of the Alps from end to end by Sir Martin Conway in 1894. But this account comes from OG Malcolm Eldridge and was completed in 1997. Malcolm also gives a gripping account of a classic route on an alpine north face (the Walker Spur of the Grandes Jorasses). Another classic traverse, on skis this time, from Chamonix to Zermatt (the *Haute Route*) is described by David Benest, while David Dunmur and Mike Smith record peak-bagging in the mountains of Austria by an aspiring group of young RGS mountaineers.

A continent away, the High Atlas rise to just over 4000m, and Djebel Toubkal provides challenge enough for Ian Ferguson who lyrically records the tastes, smells and views of Morocco. Still on the African continent Mt Nsunzu (Zambia) attracted the attention of Alex Jackson and Oliver Garnett, but they left their ice-axes at home and took machetes to tackle the steep but lush mountain slopes.

Still further afield the Alps of Japan gave sport to Himalayan veteran Mike Norris, who tells of a spectacular ascent of the Japanese Matterhorn, Yarigatake (3180m). He also joined the 300,000 people who climb Mount Fuji every year, except that he ascended the revered peak in January in near Himalayan conditions. Finally, Mike Floate introduces us to the famous Alps of New Zealand, no less spectacular than the European Alps, with challenges to suit all.

The Alps from End to End – Again
by Malcolm Eldridge

The idea was simple. Browsing through my bookshelf a few years ago I realised that the hundredth anniversary of Sir Martin Conway's historic trip across the Alps was coming up. Beautifully described in his book, *The Alps from End to End*, I decided to repeat the traverse. Work slipped out of my life; a willing wife and ownership of a motorhome made the trip a possibility. After months of planning routes, collecting maps, arranging partners and sorting all the problems associated with going away for three months, we set off on June 19, 1997.

Conway was a fascinating character. A typical Victorian gentleman, public school and Cambridge were followed by much travel and adventure financed by a wide variety of schemes, although his greater fame was as an art historian, MP and first Director of the War Museum. He climbed in several continents and wrote many of the early alpine guides which gave to peaks poetic names that have been retained by the Swiss authorities. An eminent member of the Alpine Club, he eventually became President. He used the *Alpine Journal* to argue that the prevailing 'Centrist' view of climbing, staying in one place and doing a series of ascents, was inferior to the 'Ex-centrist' approach of travelling through the mountains. For him, the idea of the Alpine traverse came while in the Karakoram on a famous traverse with his long term guide, Mattias Zurbriggen. They mused on the possibility of repeating the experience of travelling through a mountain region a bit nearer home. 'Let us travel the Alps from end to end.'

At the start of June 1894, the party assembled in Turin. Conway and Zurbriggen met Mr E A Fitzgerald with two guides, Louis Carrel and J B Aymonod. Two Gurkhas completed the party, to help carry the loads and learn the craft of guiding. The party chose a line which took them from the Col de Tende in the Maritime Alps to Ankogel at the eastern end of the Hohe Tauern range in Austria. Throughout the trip they used public transport to avoid the tedious bits. My aim was to follow the route as nearly as possible, given that weather and other variables affect journeys. My wife, Judy, would drive us to the head of each valley and then drive round to the other side of the mountain to meet us a day or two later.

We took Conway's advice and started three weeks later than he did, on June 21. The cold windy weather and patchy snow suggested he was right.

The first day or two also showed the wisdom of having guides, porters and an average age of thirty – my aging team of three averaged fifty-seven, and John Kendrick had not climbed in the Alps for over thirty years. Chris Fitzhugh was also past his best. But the mountains were in friendly mood, and the Roche de l'Abisse, Mont Clapier, Argentera and Tenibres gave us superb days in a delightful, deserted area. Conway failed completely in this area. The military kept a close eye on all his activities and stopped him going near the border with Italy, which is where the hills are, and which were in any case too deeply covered in snow.

Our route northwards jumped over the interfluves between a series of beautiful dead-end valleys full of charming historical villages, amazing displays of flowers and sightings of wild animals. We first followed Conway's footsteps exactly on the Pelvo d'Elva, during a day mainly memorable for losing Judy who only needed to drive over a pass and turn left to find us. She spent several hours cursing our lateness, while we toured the local roads in a police Landrover looking over all the unprotected hillsides to find where she had crashed. She had carefully read the directions for the meeting place – for the next day!

Conway's first real triumph was on Monte Viso but vile conditions prevented us getting far above the bivvy hut. He gave few details of the next few days: they were dismissed as unworthy of note. We, however, thoroughly enjoyed our trip via unspoiled valleys to Briançon, crossing some of the passes that Hannibal is reputed to have used. No doubt the RGS expedition in the late '50s[15] which attempted to clarify his route also passed through this area. John and Chris went home. Left on our own for a few days, we relaxed by looking at the flowers in the Nevache valley before a swift traverse took me over a very snowy Mont Thabor to Modane. Here we met Graham Ellis on July 11 for the section to Courmayeur.

Our trip across the Vanoise glaciers was trying, a hot day with deep soft avalanchy snow. Thoughts of climbing the Grande Motte the next day were dismissed, just as Conway had done before us. His experience of Tignes, however, was very different. Where he found a lake with cows and goats and a few chalets, we came down through the clouds to a huge modern ski complex, busy with morning skiing and afternoons of swimming, tennis and skating followed by evenings of partying for the many young people in residence. We appreciated that they were having a wonderful time, but their presence was somewhat alien to the nature

---

15. See p.255

of our trip. Two more days took us up the east ridge of the Aiguille de la Grande Sassière and the south face of Rutor to reach La Thuile and Courmayeur. Heavy rain in the valleys was complemented by fresh snow in the higher hills.

I had set aside a week to do the best possible traverse of Mont Blanc. The plan was to meet Andy Cole, my long-term climbing partner, and to spend several days going over Mont Blanc by the Peuterey Intégral, an ambitious route that we had wanted to try for years. Kurt Diemberger describes it as 'the grandest and most desirable of all alpine routes'. Andy had trained hard for this week. Sadly, the huge amount of new snow and the promise of only three days' good weather scuppered Plan A.

We checked out conditions on a delightful trip up the ordinary route on Mont Blanc du Tacul before traversing Mont Blanc by the same route as Conway via the Gonella hut and the Dôme glacier, a superb climb up easy slopes to the summit which dwarfs everything around it. The poor snow conditions meant that the mountain was less crowded than usual but brilliant weather compensated for the long wade down the Grand Plateau to the Grands Mulets hut and Chamonix. It was at this time in July that the conditions were causing too many accidents, and it was a relief to have the completion of the journey as my aim rather than the ascent of specific out-of-condition routes. *(See Plate 37)*

After a few wet days, good weather returned on Sunday July 27, in time for my next trip over the Aiguilles Rouges to Mont Buet, a brilliant viewpoint full of people in every imaginable interpretation of appropriate mountainwear. I left the crowds and went via the north ridge to the Emosson Lakes. Then a long fast day over the Tour Sallière, the loosest rock I met, and on to Mex, above the Rhône valley.

The next section across the Bernese Oberland was notable for the almost total lack of other climbers. Perhaps this was likely on the less well-known Diablarets, Wildhorn and Wildstrubel, but to traverse from Lötschental to the Grimsel Pass and meet only one other team on the hill was a lonely way to spend the first few days of August. My plans would have led me over the ridge of the Sattelhorn and Aletschhorn but the deep new snow and unstable slopes above kept me on the glacier in the valley bottom. As on the whole of the trip, spending a little time getting to know the area and following the Conway trail added interest – we were shown round the Hotel Nest-und-Bietschhorn in Lötschental and found a bedpan he might have used.

We were now joined by newly-retired Jim Wilson, who had been to the Alps before – once. It seemed unlikely he would cope on the proposed first day. Jeremy Talbot in his ancient Central Switzerland guidebook described Conway's day here as, 'An incredible display of stamina'. When I reached the summit of Galenstock I could see the pass that I had wanted to cross, but my first duty was to Jim, who did not reach the top. We returned to the Belvedere and the Furka Pass, the only time on the trip when I failed to get to a meeting place by the planned route.

Maderanerthal, Hüfihütte, Tödi, Sandtal, Tierfed, Muttseehütte, Ruchi, Hausstock, Elm, Piz Segnes, Vättis: the names will mean little to most British people. But this area was really beautiful, a region little changed in the last hundred years. We were fascinated to find Conway's entry in three successive hotel registers and, as always, an explanation of our venture led to friendly hospitality. This reached its peak in the Hotel Stern und Post in Amsteg. After an excellent meal of locally-picked and -caught food, we celebrated Jim's recent move to Scotland by helping Elizabeth Tresch reduce her stock of malt whisky. We paid the price on the long trek to the Hüfi hut.

My next week would be alone. I intended to improve on Conway's journey. The first three days took me through the Rätikon, an area almost unvisited by Brits, but supplied with many huts linked by excellent paths through Dolomite-like scenery with many superb rock routes. The Schesaplana and the Sulzfluh were my summits in this range, neither reaching 3000m, but making up for their lack of height with wonderful views of limestone cliffs and beautiful green valleys. Then after a day off with Judy in Klosters (we went for a walk), I headed into the Silvretta. The weather now was excellent and my day traversing the Silvrettahorn and Piz Buin confirmed that nine weeks walking and climbing get you fit – it was a quick and confident trip.

The Austrian part of the trip was as much Süd Tirol (Italy) as Tirol. The east-west valleys that Conway used to link areas happen to be south of the main chain so we often started and ended days in Italy. First, though, the classic areas of Ötztal and the Stubai. Mike Parsons and Marion Elmes met us in Nauders on August 23 and a wet walk led us to the Weisskögel Hut and its mountain, which was high and handsome, and gave a pleasant route up the north ridge. The next day we climbed Martinsgrat on to the Wildspitze, not on Conway's list but an essential pilgrimage for me, thirty-seven years after my previous ascent – my first Alpine mountain. I had climbed it on an RGS Scout trip led by two teachers, Jackie Lauder and Derek Deeprose, but instigated by David Dunmur[16], my predecessor as School Cross Country Captain. *(See Plate 38)*

The Zuckerhütl marked a return to poor weather – few views, soggy snow, lots of rain and some welcoming huts on the long walk down towards Sterzing, below the Brenner Pass. The new snow looked brilliant on the drive up towards Hochfeiler, but made the climb precarious. From that summit another long afternoon walk led round the south of the Zillertal range to Ahrntal where Mike and Marion left us. I had been with partners for about half the trip but now we had no more dates and deadlines.

I yo-yoed over a few passes to the foot of the Gross Venediger and settled for the ordinary ascent up gentle glacier slopes to a lovely summit on a perfect day. Once again in hut conversations my venture had been admired and my judgement and sanity had been queried, but the abundant snow of the summer had kept crevasses well covered and the route down to Matrei seemed perfectly safe. With autumn closing in and the knowledge that September had brought huge new snowfalls for the last few years, I hurried on towards the foot of the Gross Glockner.

From the 'tourist' side, this peak makes little impact but approached from the south-west by the Studlgrat it provided a brilliant scramble up a steep ridge with lots of Grade 3 pitches. The rocks were verglassed after a severe storm the previous evening, so I climbed cautiously up icy and snowy rocks to the summit. What Conway called the 'theatrical' part of the mountain followed, the traverse across to the Kleinglockner. Conway claims to have reached the Erzherzog-Johann Hut in seventeen minutes – I didn't try to beat him, and certainly was much slower on the long walk down to Heiligenblut and my mobile base camp.

I was getting really anxious now to complete the trip and for the first time was frustrated by a wet day. But the day off left me sufficiently fired up to rush over Sonnblick with its goldmines and summit observatory, and then on September 9, I set off from Bockstein for one last day. Judy travelled south through a tunnel and up a cablecar to meet me near the Hannover Hut. I scrambled along a loose ridge before joining the normal route to Ankogel, designated by Conway as the last snowy summit of the Alps. *(See Plate 39)*

On this, the last descent, I took off the brakes and beat Conway's time back down. Fizzy wine in the hut added to the feeling of total contentment,

---

16. See p.191

to be sitting once again with delightful people in superb surroundings. Eighty days after starting, with eight hundred miles of walking, thirty-eight peaks, 66500m of ascent all supported by 5000 miles of driving, our trip was now complete. Planning and execution had each taken three months. Integrating seven hundred slides, five notebooks, hundreds of information leaflets, references from books and thousands of memories into a book would take many more. Sadly, in today's publishing climate, you need to be famous or to nearly die to interest publishers. But really, the only thing that counts is having a dream and accomplishing it, successfully.

The *Haute Route*
by David Benest

During my university vacation in 1979, I began my exploration of the Alps, first with a Joint Services meet in Bregaglia, in the south-east corner of Switzerland, where on the first day an RAF squadron leader was killed by a rock-fall while his wife and children remained, unknowing, on a campsite in the valley. I then teamed up with a fellow army officer. After some climbs with him, I decided he was insane: we parted company in unpleasant circumstances at Argentière. My excursion finished at the Vignette Hut in Switzerland and an ascent of the Pigne d'Arolla. I noticed ski tracks disappearing into the alpine distance and asked to where they led. 'To Zermatt, on the Haute Route,' came the reply. 'Where from?' 'Chamonix.' Wow!

After the Falklands war, and realising my own mortality, I abandoned alpine mountaineering for many years but continued to hanker after what might be 'off-piste' over the next horizon. I watched with envy as various groups of skiers took these 'off-piste' routes. Eventually I became rather bored with bombing downhill. On my fortieth birthday, I decided on a change in direction. As it happened, I had just been selected to command the Second Battalion of The Parachute Regiment, an awesome responsibility in itself. Was I really up to it? Well, the only answer was to find out. I thus opted for a week of off-piste training at Argentière and then ski-toured, for the first time, to Zermatt on the *Haute Route*.

I already knew a very experienced international guide, Peter Cliff, from Yorkshire, who had previously run courses in skiing and mountaineering in the Cairngorms. We were a mixed bunch, including a Royal Navy educator, now retired and running Carlisle emergency planning as well as being a member of the Lakeland mountain rescue team. Then there was a Cambridge don, together with his daughter, a fiercely independent lawyer, whose skiing ability was in need of improvement. And in addition came a city businessman and Cathy, an aspirant international guide, who was, I believe, the first female to be so qualified on our trip.

The ski-tour training at Argentière was without mercy. Peter repeatedly made clear that we needed to improve in every possible way if we were to complete the *Haute Route*.[17] Skiing the Vallée Blanche was a wonder and, as we did so, I attempted to identify the peaks I had previously climbed back in 1979.

---

17. That same year, Peter Cliff and I had an interesting discussion about a compass-bearing in thick mist while on the Cairngorm Plateau during a Mountain Leader training week out of Glenmore Lodge. Ed.

Came the day, we set off via the Grand Montet, which at c3000m quickly makes you realise what altitude was all about. We would be skiing and climbing off-piste now for the rest of the tour, skirting through the awesome and avalanche-prone séracs below the Grand Montet and then ascending the Chardonnet Glacier on our skins. For those unaccustomed to ski abseils, it was something of a surprise to find ourselves doing it over the col at the top (parachuting images of '*Green On – Go!*' came to mind) then doing our best to avoid the bergschrund. Another ascent followed, made all the more fearful as a party of lawyers ahead of us found the going distinctly difficult, one luckless victim hurtling past me, chased downhill by his Swiss guide who caught up with him and arrested his fall. The *Schuss* on the Trient Glacier should have been a doddle, but with over 20lb in my rucksack, I piled in – a full-scale head over heels, realising only afterwards that I had injured my knee in the process.

The Trient Hut was lovely, with pasta and wine aplenty. But I could not sleep and woke with a raging headache (too much wine?) then suffered the ignominy of the aspirant guide's scorn when she checked and found that I had not folded my blankets according to mountain hut etiquette. Then we were off again, downhill all the way in a wonderful run to the valley and a bus ride to Bourg St Pierre for our last hotel night before Zermatt. I recall wandering around the village, testing my knee and agonising as to whether I should confess my injury, which I knew would mean instant return to base. I decided against. In addition, I had hastily hired ski-touring boots in Argentière and by now realised that this was not a good idea as blisters were forming all over my ankles and feet.

We set off in darkness the following morning, skinning up towards the Valsorie Hut in filthy weather, almost a white-out. I was much impressed by the two guides' navigation skills, utilising aspect of slope and altimeters to determine our location. I had not a clue; I just prayed that my knee would hold out and began to experience feelings of guilt that I was behaving so irresponsibly in not declaring my injury. Fortunately, we found the hut in the mist and were allowed a day off as well, as the next day saw storms and no visibility.

After this pause, when we next set off we were now skinning very high, with myself attached to Cathy and a cause of much complaint as she, rightly, insisted that the rope between us needed to be tight at all times. My physical fitness was quite good, so I kept finding myself almost alongside her in conversation as we ascended, much to her annoyance. In short, I was a lousy 'client'. The ascent was hugely impressive, my first experience of crampons and ice-axes as ski-poles, with the skis attached to my sac. Then followed a delightful but complicated descent to the Chanrion Hut, where to the consternation of our lawyer, a vegetarian, the menu was of either 'spam' or 'horse', served by a monkish guardian with a distinct lack of humour.

On our next leg we headed towards the Vignette Hut, which I recalled from 1979. This was perhaps one of the longest and hardest days of all, gradually ascending an interminable glacier in hot sunshine, an Alpine version of pre-Parachute selection, or 'P Company', before skiing down to the hut in near white-out conditions. I was again impressed by Peter's navigational abilities, skiing with his altimeter in hand to check our descent. My feet were by now in a pretty rough condition and, again, I was much relieved that weather prevented our start towards Zermatt for another day.

But set off we eventually did, in lovely clear conditions, now on the route I had spotted all those years ago. The cols to Zermatt were all demanding and not easy without *Harscheisen* or ski-crampons. Eventually the top triangle of the Matterhorn loomed into view, becoming bigger and bigger as we gained height on the cols. The final descent was in mushy snow; the only answer was to put my ski-poles together as a rudder to steer by. My final walk down to the cablecar was agony. Quite how the taxi driver endured the stench of our party as we returned to Argentière was beyond me.

I returned to the UK, elated at our success but knowing that I had done some serious injury to my knee. On return to work in the MOD I was seen by a doctor who proceeded to bandage my leg and offer me a walking stick. I was told that the likelihood of an early operation was almost nil. I remonstrated that I was about to command a parachute battalion; this was greeted with a shrug of utter lack of interest as to my fate. The real possibility was that I could not take command.

I phoned the Regimental Medical Officer of 2 PARA, then based in Palace Barracks in Holywood, Northern Ireland. He said something with a strong Scottish accent that I could not quite understand. Within days I was admitted to the Cambridge Military Hospital in Aldershot. There I found myself in a ward, itself stifling in the hot July weather, with mainly civilian patients. I opened the doors, to everyone's relief, and before long we were all sitting outside in the sun, discussing our various operations, much to the consternation of the nurses.

My turn came and I recall an anaesthetic injection for my arthroscopy. I was lying on a hospital trolley, getting rather fed up with what I perceived as a delay, and asked a passing nurse when we were going into surgery. Her reply was that I had already had the operation and all was well. 'Go and command your Battalion!' I did, winning the district cross country veterans race several months later and having undertaken ski-tours all over the Alps ever since!

The Walker Spur
by Malcolm Eldridge

Though the North Face of the Eiger has the biggest reputation, few alpinists would deny that the Walker Spur on the Grandes Jorasses is a finer and harder line. Not as long, not as dangerous, but far more remote. Both were climbed for the first time in 1938, the culmination of many efforts to make first ascents of all the big Alpine north faces. Many lives were lost in that period when nationalistic fervour perhaps drove young Germans and Italians too hard. *(See Plate 40)*

I first tried the route in 1977 after a successful ascent of the North Face of the Piz Badile, another of the famous 1930s climbs. We were fit and experienced, but turned back at the bottom for no particular reason – it just didn't feel right. Exactly the opposite emotions applied in 1981. Andy Cole and I had spent ten days climbing a wide range of routes in the Valais and then Chamonix. One sunny afternoon, as we walked up the glacier towards the Jorasses, I will never forget leaving the main trails on the Mer de Glace and entering the Leschaux Basin, then sitting on a rock and looking up at the Walker knowing that nothing would stop us. A brilliant weather forecast meant that we would have time to overcome the wintry conditions on the climb.

It's about six hours from Montenvers to the foot of the face. We had decided to bivouac after the first few pitches and hoped to get to the top the next day. As we approached our intended ledge we heard Americans shouting to each other, 'Tom!' and 'Tom!'; we knew one of the Toms from a few years back. The other was on his first Alpine climb, but he was experienced, a mountain guide. They grabbed the widest bit of the ledge which meant we were nearer the line of the climb. That was fine, though the sight of the famous Rébuffat cracks, filled with ice, immediately above us, suggested that we would need to be on good form in the morning. This section is perhaps the hardest of the route, with pitches of V and VI or perhaps in the circumstances a quick pull on a bit of gear to make it A1. *(See Plate 41)*

We were at the time on a food regime that seemed very neat. With one pan, and a Pot Noodle each, we coped by having first the Pot Noodle, then soup in the container followed by coffee. In the morning we would have coffee first, followed by porridge, and then chuck the plastic container away. Any possible water source being frozen, we started melting snow, but the cartridge was on its last legs so I decided to change it, then threw the hissing remnants down the Face. We were not very environmentally conscious in those days. On with the new cylinder and ….aah, the rubber seal had stuck to the discarded cylinder and all our lovely new gas escaped. No more water till we finished the climb. No drinks, no soup, no Pot Noodles, no porridge, but we did have a couple of Mars Bars each.

The other remarkable thing that evening was the clear and obvious sounds of a woman and a dog on the deeply-crevassed glacier at the foot of the climb. This, two and a half hours beyond the hut at dusk. When I met one of the Toms years later, I checked: his memory was the same.

A cold clear night heralded a perfect day and we got away quickly in front of the Toms. No breakfast to worry about. Pitch followed pitch. Some hard, some easier, all interesting. Cracks were filled with ice, ledges were covered with snow, scree slopes were ice climbs. At least the ice and snow gave up a little moisture when sucked. The icy 75m Dièdre was followed by a snowy leftward trend before a return right via a diagonal rappel, and an overhang brought us to a ledge at the foot of the next main feature, the Tour Grise. Here we caught up with a team of Japanese and were slowed for a few pitches up steep rock before they grabbed a good bivvy spot while we continued to a poor one. Being experienced and having no cooking to interrupt our labour, we constructed a sort of ledge and tied ourselves to a belay. We always used to put our feet in our rucksacks and just have a duvet jacket on our top halves. At least with weight supported by your sack you could relax and enjoy the brilliant sunset, the stars and the dawn. At which point I discovered I had forgotten to tie in to the belay.

Somehow we let the Japanese get ahead; we admired their technique. Only one wore crampons so he led any icy pitch and followed his leader up the rocky pitches with enormous brio, crampons screeching and sparking as he ran up steep rock. We were more traditional in our approach, both using the appropriate footwear for each pitch, but I do recall one nasty-looking groove where I elected to use a crampon on only one foot. It worked.

The route opened up as we climbed a few delightful pitches in the morning sun, but we were soon back into cold gullies and dank chimneys. In good conditions, climbers scamper up much of the climb in rock boots, but we were having a real north face experience, having to take time with each new challenge. Eventually, approaching an easy couloir near the top, we caught up with some East Europeans who seemed to be in trouble. The last guy was climbing on a rope with knots and using one arm. The previous year a friend of mine had been smashed by rockfall on these last few shattered gully pitches, so I suggested we wait well behind the damaged Czech. Once the way ahead was safe we completed the route, tired but really happy to have achieved such a fine climb. It is a fantastic summit with a superb view of the whole Mont Blanc Range and beyond, south into Italy and east into Switzerland. The weather remained perfect. *(See Plate 42)*

It turned out the Czech guy had a broken arm following stonefall. We helped them down, and let them abseil down our rope. What we didn't expect was that all the other parties, including the Toms, would take advantage of our generosity and abseil down our ropes also. After a wearisome descent we eventually found some melt-water on this, the south face, so consumed the previous day's breakfast porridge, uncooked, as well as pints and pints of water. That gave us the energy to speed on, past the hut, where we said goodbye to our American friends, then carried on down to the Italian Val Ferret; a few lifts got us back to Chamonix. Andy had to leave the next morning for the long drive home for work, leaving me to tell the tales and bask in the memories of three brilliant days on the hill.

Austrian Odyssey
by David Dunmur and Mike Smith

How or why this journey began is lost in time's mists, but its consequences were profound for those involved: for some, it shaped their
lives.

There is no longer any record of the Dalmatian Express, a train that used
to run from northern Europe to Belgrade and possibly beyond. We never
knew exactly where it started or where it finished, but it was enough for
us that it transported us in about thirty-six hours from Calais to Innsbruck.
Over a few years we became familiar with it: a commuter route to the
Alps. Our first experience occurred in 1957: a significant year for Austrian
alpinists, when Broad Peak (8047m) in the Himalayas was conquered
alpine-style without oxygen or porters by a team of four Austrians. All,
including the two mountain legends Kurt Diemberger and Hermann Buhl
reached the summit, but Buhl was killed shortly after on nearby Chogolisa
(7654m).

At the time of our 1957 expedition to the Hohe Tauern – a lofty section
of the eastern Tirol – we were unaware of the dramas being enacted a
continent away in the Karakoram. But, for us, the challenge seemed every
bit as great as any 8000m peak. We were a party of nine RGS Senior
Scouts and two leaders, of whom Jack Lauder, scoutmaster and teacher
of Latin, had inspired and organised the mid-August expedition. Two
days of travelling brought us close to our 'base camp' in the Felbertal, a
narrow, steep-sided valley to the south of Mittersill, at which village we
had tumbled out of a steam-hauled narrow-gauge railway train into a very
much more vertical landscape than we had ever experienced before. The
final ten kilometres of dusty road up to the intended camp were assisted
by hiring the local bus, a stubby little Steyr with an enormous bonnet and
a genial driver. With all our kit, we completely filled this machine, as it
powered us up the Felbertal in fading light to the isolated Tauernhaus
Schösswend. Here, we gratefully spent our first night in the luxury of a hay
barn, before setting up camp the following day in an adjacent field beside
a stream. It was a wonderful location. All the more so for the proximity
of the hospitable Tauernhaus *Gastzimmer*, where we would pass several
convivial and sometimes noisy evenings.

Above our base camp towered our first challenge: the eight-thousander, Zwölfer – 8,000 feet, that is! It was on this training climb that the summit party for the major peaks was selected by our local leaders, Herr Starkavitch and Sepp Hofer. The former was the head of the local *Werkschule* – a cross between Outward Bound and Gordonstoun – while Sepp was a metalwork teacher at the local school and, more important for us, a mountain guide. How this Anglo-Austrian liaison had been established remains a mystery; we were more than happy to leave such arrangements to Jack Lauder.

In the following week, summits fell thick and fast to the rapidly acclimatising assault team: the Tauernkogel, with a summit cross just short of 3000m, and then the Gross Venediger (3674m), the fourth-highest peak in Austria. We had learnt a lot: the rudiments of mountaincraft and how to survive for three or four days on a packet of raisins and a pocketful of porridge oats. Actually the latter lesson taught from firm example by Herr Starkavitch had not been terribly successful: our diet had been supplemented by the *Bergsteigeressen* provided by the mountain huts. On the mountain, the regime had been harsh. Absolutely no drinking of water or any other fluids, but in near terminal cases of exhaustion the suck of a lemon slice was permitted.

From such a tough initiation emerged, remarkably, a 'band of brothers' who would carry the *Edelweiss*, symbol of the Austrian Alpine Club (*Österreichischer Alpenverein* or *ÖAV*), to many mountain peaks in the following years. The hard core of Dicky (R Collard), Dave (D Dunmur), Mike (M Smith) and Andy (A Wade) quickly established back home the RGS branch of the *ÖAV*.

We had already signalled to our Austrian hosts our intention of returning in 1958. And so we did. This time the Zillertaler Alpen were to be the objective, but first we stopped at Mittersill to link with Sepp Hofer, our mountain guide from the *Werkschule*. But this year's expedition differed greatly from before: first, we were a smaller group: just six of us. The band of brothers now comprised Dicky, Dave, Mike and Andy from the 1957 expedition, plus two new aspirant alpinists from Guildford, Tim Hall and Keith Newman. Second, no battle-hardened scoutmasters appeared this time to seamlessly organise what had to be organised, or to sort out any unforeseen snags. The logistics were now our own responsibility.

Starting with the logistics of getting there. For some reason, which we cannot recall, the Dalmatian Express followed a different route that year. Not, as in 1957, steaming and clanking across Belgium and down the Rhine valley when, late into a sleepless night, we had passed time in conversation with a German train conductor and somehow discovered that the English language contains a vastly greater number of words meaning 'drunk' than exists in German. Instead, in 1958, our faithful express took a quieter route through France to Basel, then headed east to Innsbruck through Liechtenstein. After Innsbruck, we resorted to making up the travel plan as we went along, somehow requiring no fewer than two more trains and three buses to eventually reach our base camp of the previous year, high in the Felbertal, on August 13. *(See Plate 43)*

Next, the logistics of finding our mountain guide. The previous year, Sepp Hofer had simply appeared, on cue, from where we were not quite sure. This year we were living in the real world and Sepp was nowhere in sight. At the *Werkschule* we were informed that he had sprained an ankle and were advised to seek him at his house, high up on the other side of Mittersill. We found his house, and his family, but no Sepp. Sepp was in Salzburg. But, to our relief, he had kindly arranged for a friend and colleague, the motorcycling Pepano (aka Pepe), to take his place as our guide. Though Sepp was not joining us in person this time, his friendly Alsatian dog, Rolf, had other ideas and playfully accompanied us for a long, long, way down the hill, until we were at last able to divert his attention towards a group of unsuspecting French hikers.

Pepe was to catch up with us on his motorbike somewhere on the track above Ginzling, south of Mayrhofen in the Zillertaler Alpen, in four days' time. Meanwhile, our journal was collecting surprisingly frequent references to the Café Pletzer, an address in Mittersill which appears to have served as an extension to our base camp. Our journeys always seemed to pass its door and we soon discovered it was the ideal place to review progress and make plans over a coffee, plus some local delicacy such as a slice of caraway-seeded rye bread or maybe even a slice of *Apfelstrudel*. It was a cheerful place and sported a shiny juke-box equipped with a good collection of the rock'n'roll classics of the day. Sociable too, especially when a group of girls from Sunderland happened to be in there. So we tended to forget the time, invariably missing the Felbertal bus, and benefiting from a 10km uphill trek (of which Herr Starkavitch would have approved!) back to the Tauernhaus.

All the planning and fitness training started to bear fruit on August 18, when Pepe roared past us on the track above Ginzling, with instructions to catch him up at the Alpenrose Hütte (1878m) and to take no notice of the dark clouds and lightning playing on the summits ahead. From here on, the learning curve was all about alpinism. We climbed the Schwarzenstein (3369m) and learned, hanging on an exposed ridge in thick cloud and losing no more than one hat in the process, about alpine wind. We climbed the Schönbichlerhorn (3135m) and learned about alpine cold. Our journal records that Mike discovered in this regard that tattered cycling gauntlets and second-hand Foreign Legion desert trousers were 'no good'. We further discovered that Pepe's assurance that lightning in the evening sky was a sure sign of a fine day to follow was not entirely reliable. One very poor day following such lightning we could only resort to building a *Steinmann* beside the path below the Furtshagl Haus (perhaps standing to this day?). When it eventually stopped snowing on the summits above, we attempted to climb the Gross Mösele (3478m) and learned about hidden crevasses. Our rope management skills were tested for real, and one member of the party remains eternally grateful for being saved from completing an unplanned descent into the pale blue icy depths.

The following day we found ourselves back in Mayrhofen, bidding farewell to Pepe, soaking up alpine sunshine, a peach or two and a beer, before heading off in search of the Dalmatian Express.

Between taking A-levels, applying for university or getting jobs, the members of the RGS branch of the *ÖAV* were busy planning their 1959 summer meet. Our mountaincraft skills had been honed under the tutelage of three of Austria's mountain maestros. Apprenticeships had been served, and now was the time to venture forth unescorted onto the high peaks. We felt confident: we had weathered mountain storms, suffered white-outs and even undergone a crevasse rescue.

The great Brenner Pass connects Austria with Italy, by carving its way through the chain of mountains to separate the eastern and western Tirol. Our mountaineering experience had been gained in the less-frequented Zillertaler and Hohe Tauern ranges, but we now felt ready for the heartland of the Austrian Alps, the Ötztal and Stubai. This central mountain area lies to the south-west of Innsbruck, and although two of the highest Austrian peaks, the Gross Glockner and the Gross Venediger, are to the east, the greatest concentration of glaciers and peaks over 3500m lies in the Ötztal and Stubai. These two areas are dominated respectively by the Wildspitze and the Zuckerhütl, and of course both of these were targets for this year's expedition.

These days, Austria's network of mountain huts is well known to climbers and mountain walkers, nowhere more so than in the Ötztal and

Stubai. The hospitality received in the huts is legendary, as is the food, *Glühwein* and communal sleeping arrangements, but in the high season they can become crowded. This was not the case in the 1950s: occasionally, we had the huts to ourselves.

It was a time of revolution in the world of mountaineering: equipment was rapidly changing. Sitting in huts waiting for a break in the weather we became used to local guides approaching us to show interest in buying our Viking hawser-laid nylon ropes hanging in the porch. They were a new phenomenon in the Austrian mountains. Not surprisingly our response was always: *'Aber wir brauchen sie!' ('But we need them!')*

We were, however, always able to come to some arrangement and save the effort of transporting the ropes back to England at the end of the trip. Relieved of the burden of ropes, we would then return encumbered with ice-axes, which were in short supply and expensive in the UK. It was regrettable that our early trading talents were never put to later good use.

Not only was our equipment different from the local climbers, but traditions of ropework also differed. What was the correct method of tying on, for example? Remember, this was before the days of custom-made harnesses. The simple bowline around the waist was favoured by the British, having been taught to boys for generations from the pages of *Scouting for Boys*. The Austrians favoured the chest-harness and we became expert at tying these, though not all in the team were convinced. The benefits of the chest harness, however, were demonstrated when Mike fell though a snow bridge on the Gross Mösele: he ended up with his head above his feet, whereas with a waist-harness it would usually be head down and feet uppermost!

The 1959 team of Dicky, Dave, Tim and a new member, Mac (G McAlister), started from Obergurgl in the Ötztal, at that time a small village. Our first objective was the Hohe Wilde (3419m), sometimes known as the Hochwilder. This mountain has two summits, north and south, connected by a rocky ridge. The north summit is approached from the Hochwilder Haus over the Obergurgl glacier, but the weather defeated us, and we retreated in a white-out and snowstorm. A day waiting for the weather to improve was spent at the Ramolhaus, and then over to the Breslauer Hütte for an attempt on the impressive Wildspitze (3772m), the highest peak in the Ötztaler Alpen. At the hut, such was our youthful confidence and apparent competence that a lone German lady asked if we would guide her to the summit, which we did. Our mountain triumphs were mounting.

Buoyed by our success in the Ötztal, we went back down to Sölden and then up to the Hildesheimer Hütte for an attempt on the Zuckerhütl (3505m). Our luck was holding with the weather and all was set to bag another summit. The Zuckerhütl is the highest peak in the Stubai group and is an imposing mountain from all sides. It presents no particular difficulties, however. The route leads from the hut over the Pfaffen glacier to the *Joch* between the Zuckerhütl and the Wilder Pfaff, and from there the rocky east ridge leads easily to the summit cross. For us, that was to be the final ascent of our season. *(See Plate 44)*

In three short seasons, we had progressed from total novices to confident mountaineers, and our confidence knew no bounds, though our technical skills were severely limited. In retrospect it was perhaps stretching the limits of risk management to propose another guided mountain tour for boys from the RGS. This time, we would be the guides. But risk management had not been invented in 1960, so there was of course no risk.

The guides, Dicky, Dave and Mike from the original band of brothers, would introduce the delights of alpinism to a selected group of twelve Senior Scouts, led again by Jack Lauder and a new scoutmaster and physics teacher, Derek Deeprose. We alighted from the Dalmatian Express at Bahnhof Ötztal on the morning of July 29, hired a bus up to Obergurgl and then continued on foot to the Neue Karlsruhe Hütte. The next few days were spent training the group in mountain techniques, crossing glaciers safely, crevasse rescue, abseiling, and most important, exposing the boys for the first time to the exhilaration of the high mountains. These activities took us to the Hochwilder Haus and the Ramolhaus, and then on to the Breslauer Hütte for an assault on the Wildspitze. All of this was familiar territory for the 'guides'; the main achievement was to lead all the group safely in a traverse of the twin summits in wind-blown snow. With the guided tour successfully completed, the party of scouts left for the cultural attractions of the Oberammergau Passion Play. We had other things to attend to. *(See Plate 45)*

The Stubaier Alpen had excited our interest the previous year, and beckoned tantalisingly. A day's trek took us from the Breslauer Hütte in the Ötztal to the Hildesheimer Hütte in the Stubai, ready for a traverse of the Zuckerhütl and Wilder Pfaff (3458m). This we achieved on August 6, with obstinate cloud partially clearing to give brief, stunning, views of and from the Zuckerhütl's iconic summit cone. Despite carrying all our gear, we progressed further over the Wilder Pfaff, and arrived at the Rifugio Cima Libera, just across the border in Italy. This hut is more usually known by its Germanic names, the Müller Hütte or Karl Franz Josef Haus, for it is firmly situated in Süd-Tirol, the disputed region that was formerly German and is now part of Italy. By whatever name, the Müller Hütte was very definitely Italian. We were its only inhabitants that evening, apart from the *guardiana*, and the *Bergsteigeressen* now came with overwhelming quantities of minestrone soup, the like of which none of us had ever before confronted.

It was a very convivial evening and rather put paid to the 'alpine' start planned for the following day. We did, however, finally stagger out of the hut shortly after 8am, blinking in the glacial glare. The recently reticent sun had today been up for hours, drying and warming the rocks of the south-west ridge (grade II) of the Wilder Freiger (3418m), our intended target. Soon we, in turn, were warmed and stimulated by its rays and bounded up the ridge to complete a traverse, descending to the south and returning across a rather mushy glacier to the Müller Hütte. *(See Plate 46)*

A second more abstemious night at the Müller Hütte followed, and then we were off to the Sulzenauhütte, a final stopping point before descending the Stubai and taking the bus to Innsbruck. Our final descent has been described elsewhere (*Oxford Mountaineering*, 1961):

An Alpine Gully

Our alpine holiday was drawing to a close. We had just completed a peak to peak tour of the Oetztal and Hoch-Stubai, and were staying at a small Italian hut while preparing for our return to civilisation. It was to be a short day's journey: over a col and down a short gully, a tramp down the glacier, and we would be able to catch a bus to Innsbruck. Not more than three hours' walking, the hut warden assured us, and so we were in no hurry to leave.

At last our party of three was ready to depart, and we were soon making our way to the col. Inevitably, after a long stay high in the mountains one feels loath to leave them, and we were too preoc-cupied with these ethereal feelings to notice very much about the gully we selected to descend to the glacier.

We started down the gully of our choice, a short rock couloir of about 400ft. We moved independently and easily, until after 100ft it was apparent that this was no ordinary gully: it was a very active one, for the bed was very loose and obviously in an avalanching mood. We reassured ourselves, however, by roping up, and continued slowly down: after all, we thought, this gully has probably been in this condition for months. Suddenly our confidence was shattered as a flurry of stones came crashing down from above. Our immediate thought was to 'get the hell out', but how? We were now half way down the gully. To ascend meant climbing up avalanching rock, not a pleasant occupation, so our only way out was to continue descending. The gully wall looked climbable, so we crossed out of the line of the stone chute into the comparative shelter of the wall, and none too soon, for at that moment a hundredweight block whistled down the gully and disappeared with a rush into the bergschrund.

Realising that to lose a footing now would spell disaster for all, we climbed down, belaying very carefully, as delicately as was possible with 50lb rucksacks, and watching with apprehension the seething mass of rocks in the gully bed.

After a considerable expenditure of energy, both nervous and physical, we reached the mouth of the gully, and a final highly technical move, which involved swinging with one arm on an 19th century piton – a sign of a previous epic descent? – brought us to the snow lip above the bergschrund.

It was by now afternoon, and although we were out of danger from the gully, we still had to cross the bergschrund by means of a rapidly thawing snow-bridge. This danger was short-lived, however, and we were soon heading across the glacier for the valley. When we finally reached our destination in the late afternoon we realised that the whole trip had taken six hours, of which more than three had been spent in the gully; but as a result of those three hours we had joined the host of others who have learned by bitter experience that alpine gullies are not to be trusted.

Our Odyssey had finished. Four years from schoolboys to alpinists. More than a dozen alpine peaks had been conquered, and many memories linger even after fifty years. What followed for the members of the RGS branch of the Austrian Alpine Club has been, or will be, recorded elsewhere. Certainly for some the mountains became part of their lives and took them to the Andes and the Himalayas, and back to the Alps many times. The journey was one of discovery: the first encounter with high mountains and their challenges, but also a discovery of inner self on the road to adulthood.

Djebel Toubkal: High Atlas, Morocco.

by Ian Ferguson

Normal Route from Neltner Hut up Djebel Toubkal (4167m)
August 6 1997
Normal Route, Adrar n'Dern (4005m)
August 2 1997

We moved through baking heat, with the air suffused by aromatic figs, cypresses, juniper, dates and other deep, oily, lingering perfumes. The countryside was arid and dusty, but never parched or barren, and veined with tinkling tiny channels, for which French *arroser* would be adequately descriptive but where 'irrigation' would be industrial, heavy-duty overstatement. There was an abundance of Martian-crimson foothills with liberal scatterings of low, deep-green bushes keeping an even, timid spacing. Cicadas sang incessantly. Shade was at a premium.

A treeline became our companion. Trees and shrubs lower in the valley overcame their shyness, crowding around the watercourse while leaving the higher slopes to little clusters of porched, cuboid dwellings distinct from their surroundings only through trapping dark squares of shade. Thistles and prickly pears had been harvested and a little washing had been hung out.

'*Stylo, M'sieu!*' '*Bon-bon!*' We had respectfully covered up, and desisted from photography as asked. Grimy children tugged and begged charmlessly.

Tomatoes, potatoes, carrots, onions, melons, oranges, dates, figs, olives; maize drying in piles on the roof; goats, sheep, chickens: this was the exotic colouring and culture of the Berbers. Tier upon tier of cultivated terrace. Plucking of prickly pears, by means of two very long poles and a piece of string. Four bullocks in harness thresh grain atop a building no bigger than a squash court; as they rotate around a post, the innermost is bent double. Dust billows.

Night *à la belle étoile*.[18] The *Voie Lactée*[19], and a handful of *étoiles filantes*[20], stretched from horizon to horizon and reached down to Earth with a clear impression of depth and dimension, more striking phenomena

---

18. *A la belle étoile:* in the open air

19. *Voie Lactée*: Milky Way

20. *Étoiles filantes:* shooting stars. There is a good case for these French expressions given the widespread use of French in Morocco, a former French colony. Ed

194

for which, in the circumstances, the delicate French words seemed better suited. The hour's low-angled morning light arrived as a welcome, precious relief from the bleaching vertical rays of daytime.

We moved higher, towards the first pass, initially a broad plateau of bleak gravel. Widespread scatter-cushions of lime and pale green proved to be false friends, formed entirely of continuous prickly spikes. Pleasant relief for the eye, but for the backside better pick a trusty anglo-saxon-style boulder. Rain threatened.

Unnoticed, our steps became lighter, as the trend of our journey switched from ascent to descent until – *hop!* – a secret valley appeared, flat-bottomed with green fields, waterfalls and a fairly substantial river, the Ourika. Chance for a refreshing swim – or, with an unlucky choice of location, water so cold that feet go numb before a minute passes or before you realise that as you can no longer feel the riverbed, you will fall over and take French leave with the current…

A six-foot pile of dried thistles approached us, supported by a hennaed girl of twelve or thirteen who appeared somehow to have contrived to borrow her skin from her grandmother. Large dark birds circled overhead.

A descending mule does not regulate its own speed. The preferred method is to hold firmly onto its tail, which allows it to concentrate on the placement of its front feet, while the *muletier* takes responsibility for direction of the aft end. An ascending mule may respond positively to pushing and shoving. The general operating instruction for a mule is 'Osht!' (bawled) and, if the mule can work out what it is you want done, it may do it. By temperament they are stolid: replacement of a shoe, for example, can be done with one man supporting the hoof on his knee while the other hits the shoe as hard as he can with a hammer, and the mule will ignore proceedings. Supporting the hoof on a rock would cause it to split. A standard local mule will carry around 100kg, but the loaded mule will take no account of the change to its own dimensions, so innocent would-be passers-by should beware of meeting one in a narrow place.

Look out too for your respiratory health. The paths are deep trenches filled with fine, powdered dust: in the villages, they contain chicken bones, strips of cloth, old batteries, straw or mule dung. A breath of wind to lift the dust, and the effect is of breathing steel wool.

Morocco, so we were told, is a cold country where the sun shines brightly.

With the sun shining brightly, the colours are strong, and the wind can be fierce. Afternoon zephyrs proved quite capable of flattening the tent under which you might be taking a wise siesta.

My hiking vocabulary was improving; others would grimace at halts as their *ampoules* or *cloches* (blisters) would be *arrachées*[21] with pointed instruments then patched up. I'd learned the sharpest lessons of personal medical admin on previous mountain excursions, and concentrated on keeping the suncream frequent and liberal – and avoiding unnecessary wading, an obvious precaution which seemed beyond the wit of the local guides.

Later, at apparently the highest village in the Atlas at 2590m, the irrigation is heavy-duty. Water gushes; trenches are deep, narrow and very fast-flowing. Temporary dams can be shifted with a triangular hoe to redirect irrigation elsewhere, to another vegetable plot or individual tree. Fast flow ensures there's water left to reach the farthest parts of the network, after losses, diversions and evaporation on the way.

Adrar n'Dern: Mountain of Mountains, 4005m. From here, there are fine views of the Anti-Atlas and the Sahara in the far distance. It is a rounded hill, reminiscent of Butser Hill[22] in its benign compound curves, but hued from ochre through dun to scarlet. *(See Plate 47)*

Good quality scree-running is as rare a treat in England as climbable ice, but we found plenty on Adrar n'Dern and formed the following rules:

When you're going really well, it doesn't do to land on a big bit that doesn't move;

Better not to get hit by any big bits;

Look out for thin patches… same logic as rule (1);

Don't think about the consequences of a mistake;

Don't wipe out.

This was as close to Alpinism as our excursion got. With ample time for acclimatisation, effects of altitude were barely noticeable amongst the other challenges to our well-being. Our chosen summits were benign in form: broad and rounded with spacious plateaux for picnics or sporting events. None of the 'Bridges of Mohamed'[23] to be found on other Islamic hills. Crampons or ice-axe would be as appropriate as a packet of pork

---

21. *arrachées*: deliberately burst, punctured

22. Butser Hill in Hampshire, on the South Downs.

23. As-Sirat, the hair-narrow bridge which every believer must cross to enter Paradise. There is one on Pic d'Aneto in the Pyrenees, for example, for which nervous ski-tourers rope up.

scratchings: there was not a snowflake to be seen. The only hints of our altitude were atmospheric: the proximity of mesmerising, fast-changing evening clouds with 'Fingers of Allah'[24] playing light and shade on the sands and browns of our surroundings, and the one or two privileged, memorable mornings on which seas of cloud lapped in the valleys below us, stretching away across the Atlas to leave us marooned upon our own islands or archipelagos with the suspicion that, yes, we were in some sense far from ground. But in general, our journey entailed no climbing; rather, travel through a barren land.

One of our guides, Khamis, is affianced to a girl hereabouts, and is teased rotten.

At one stop, a muleteer has so much sugar surreptitiously added to his tea that no more will dissolve; great hilarity ensues, but little discouragement to drinking it: a local with front teeth is a rare sight, given the habit of drinking mint tea through a lump of Morocco's greatest export.

There are party games: only quick-witted topological wisdom saves me from remaining tied to a young Frenchwoman for, well, perhaps not forever, but certainly a long time. Another has her birthday to celebrate, and is gleefully presented with a half-metre ingot of local sugar, highly phallic in form.

Further on I enjoy a fine education in the versatility of the word *putain*[25] – noun and exclamation – when the keen photographer of the group discovers that boulders have been sneaked into her rucksack during her artistic reveries.

Locals gang up, announcing that the Englishman's T-shirt is due for a clean. (And indeed, dust and sun-cream have done their worst.) I hand it over, and a twittering of excited ecologically-aware middle-class Frenchwomen anticipate displays of authentic Moroccan backwoods cleaning methods. My shirt is thrown in the nearby stream, then a plastic jerry can produced from which a few litres of liquid are liberally splashed.

There is a reek of neat bleach, and holes appear in my shirt.

At the Lac d'Ifni, we swim, while locals cavort and fish for trout. They watch us fill our bottles and, eventually, drink. Much later they tell us how ill we'll be, drinking water from that lake.

Without exception, all in the group have long passed sundry stages of digestive discomfort in any case. No arrangements in field hygiene could

---

24. Sunbeams

25. *Putain:* whore, tart (colloq). An expression of dismayed disgust. Ed.

survive the couscous: *'Ah, un bon couscous!'* was the excited cry, but the reality was a frantic spoon contest with the toothless, slobbering muleteers for choice boiled sheep components. Never mind the aesthetic difficulties: whatever ailment anyone else might have, we'd surely share it. And, of course, the little pink paper cairns were ubiquitous.

Study of French was compulsory for five years of my school career, with never a whisper of the valuable information that an Englishman signing up for a package holiday hiking trip with a French firm, choosing a difficulty grade one less than the most extreme, would find himself accompanied almost exclusively by young Frenchwomen. (I can't claim rat-like cunning: I had an invitation from one of them.)

And so, a pleasant couple of notches on my ice-axe: Adrar n'Dern and Djebel Toubkal, two '4000ers', one the highest in North Africa. Three or four years later a major clean-up operation was mounted by foreign tour companies around the squalid, bespattered popular access points to Djebel Toubkal. *Insh'allah,* the tourism will prove sustainable, but the evidence of my visit was that the 'Norafs' had not reached the enlightened state of the Nepali Minister of Tourism who was quoted as saying that they would rather welcome clean tourism than clean-ups.

The Ascent of Mount Nsunzu (2,600m), Zambia
by Alex Jackson and Oliver Garnett

For two months between April and June we stayed on a farm at the foot of Mt Nsunzu near a town called Mbala (1670m). After arriving and acquainting ourselves with our surroundings, we then waited for our hosts to return to Lusaka, leaving us in control of the house. That afternoon, glowing with a new-found sense of freedom, we enlisted Sylvester, a Zambian employee of the farm, to guide us up the mountain. *(See Plate 48)* The route began gently as we followed a small upstream branch of the Kasandika River through the bush, while staying wary of stepping on, and never directly over logs while keeping our eyes open for snakes. Southern Africa harbours many of the world's most deadly snakes, including the black mamba (growing up to three metres long), the Gaboon viper and the puff adder. One injection-filled bite in a remote location like Mbala would seriously inhibit anyone's ambitions for a life beyond a prospective fifteen to sixty minutes. Dusk is a period of high snake activity, so we were extremely vigilant because the aim of our hike was to see a sunset from the top.

After a short walk, we reached the base of the shoulder running up the side of Mt Nsunzu and started our proper ascent. Sylvester led a painfully fast climb onto the shoulder, thereby demonstrating just how unfit we were compared to any of the locals, a fact that would be depressingly drummed into our psyche for the duration of our three month trip. Once on top we walked the length of the hill then dropped down into the valley again to make a more direct route to the summit: we hacked our way down and up the steep slope, machete in hand, sticky with sweat in the African heat. Imagine the shoulder linking to the main summit as a U shape: we were walking down the valley in the middle and up the other side. After a few hours of steady uphill climb we reached a giant mushroom growing in the bush which Sylvester spotted first; we swiftly bagged it for dinner back at the base.

Despite these mushroom antics we eventually reached the summit in time to see our sunset. The sky was clear and we could see around in all directions, and even into neighbouring Tanzania as the dipping sun scored long, dark shadows across the golden *bushveld* below us. The chatter of a troop of baboons drifted up from the surrounding forest as three eagles played the updrafts while searching for prey in the evening light. Not a road or car in sight, just a few mud hut compounds barely visible in the rift valley below. It was definitely one of the more memorable moments of the trip. *(See Plate 49)*

As the sun began to fall faster and faster towards the horizon we grabbed our torches and started a fast descent along the same line we had come from. Because of the remoteness of the mountain there is absolutely no light pollution, so the stars are clear and bright enough to provide a decent amount of residual light which, on top of our torchlight was enough to navigate our return by. Entanglement in spiders' webs was a common problem in the low light and posed a potentially unknown threat as we hadn't been informed about any types of spider. Army ants were also a real hidden nuisance. These ants often make a 'transport tunnel' of their finest and bravest ants across an open gap, literally a living protection shield for other ants to pass through, defended from the outside world. Should you step on one of these densely-packed ant tunnels, suddenly your legs and shoes are covered with ants whose physiology is unfairly skewed away from thorax and abdomen towards pincers. Within a minute the particularly malicious clandestine division has made its way up inside your trousers and has entrenched itself in your groin. Suddenly these giant pincers all start biting and the only option is to remove clothes and pick the tenacious bastards off one by one. On the farm they once had a whole cow eaten by these ants; sure, it was lame and ill so couldn't move, but it is hard to imagine a worse fate.

We reached the house well after the sun had truly set, by navigating using the sound of the river, and by torchlight with the stars for general orientation. Thankfully, our snakebite kit remained unopened.

The sad fact is that Mbala, over and above Mt Nsunzu, one of the highest mountains in Zambia, has so much to offer from a tourist perspective. The locals have been blessed with the second-highest waterfall in Africa: Kalambo Falls, which you could literally walk off if you wanted to, such is the lack of regulation; and Chisimba Falls, which are potentially second in beauty only to Victoria Falls in the south. As a side note, Kalambo Falls harbours a record of human tribal existence over the past 300,000 years, the site simply lying beside the river unexplored because of a lack of government funding. The other main highlight in the tiny and seemingly irrelevant town of Mbala is marked by a modest pillar in the middle of the town's roundabout: Mbala was the last place a shot was fired in WW1. Mbala, then called Abercorn, withstood a German attack directed by General von Lettow-Vorbeck some nine days after he had agreed a ceasefire. As a result, on November 25 1918 the Germans finally surrendered and were forced to throw their weapons into the local Lake Chila, fourteen days after the official armistice.

And I won't even begin to mention the amazing variety of wildlife and the unspoilt beauty of the countryside...

Hiking in the Japanese Northern (Kita) Alps
by Mike Norris

Crammed into a cupboard-sized apartment in Tokyo, I was keen to trade the soaring skyscrapers for the towering peaks of Nagano. The Northern Japanese Alps may lack the height and breadth of the Swiss Alps, but, when it comes to scenery and serious hiking, they offer a fantastic experience in the hills.

Over seventy percent of Japan is mountainous, with characteristically steep mountain walls and deep mountain rivers. Scrambling up these rivers and waterfalls to their mountain source (*sawanobori*) is a popular and adventurous pastime in itself. The beautiful deciduous forests are celebrated for their changing beauty throughout the year. Viewing cherry blossom (*hanami*) in spring and the changing colour of the leaves (*moumijigari*) in autumn are national events. Mountains are considered sacred in Japan, with Mt Fuji (3776m) being a national symbol. Ancient wooden Shinto shrines are stumbled upon deep in the mountains, origami strips representing lightning (*hei*) dangle from the mighty pines, and little Buddha figures are planted in crevices. The flora and fauna are also diverse, with the chance of seeing monkeys, bears, snakes and a prolific variety of bird life. Best of all, natural hot springs (*onsen*) are found throughout the volcanic mountain ranges, and their health-giving and soothing properties nicely round off any mountain adventure.

The plan for this trip was the three day 'Hodaka traverse' from Mt Yarigatake (3180m) and Mt Okuhodaka (3190m) along a knife-edge ridge largely above the altitude of 3000m. The launching point was Kamikochi.

Kamikochi, the birthplace of modern mountaineering in Japan, with its astounding natural beauty, lies deep in the heart of Nagano. The Reverend Walter Weston, considered the father of Japanese mountaineering, climbed Yarigatake in the 1880s and wrote *Mountaineering and Exploration in the Japanese Alps* (coining the term 'Japanese Alps'). These ranges had, however, long previously been explored by Buddhist priests when climbing was practised as natural worship. The unspoilt beauty of Kamikochi has long been acknowledged with its establishment as a National Park in 1934. Even now, only public transport is allowed access into the resort to minimize pollution.

When leaving town by crossing the Kappa Bridge, the Azusa River is seen to have remarkably clear, sparkling waters. The banks were framed by the dappled sunlit bamboo grass and larch forest. To top off the idyllic setting, a troupe of macaques chattered playfully across the track. The bustle of city life was soon far removed as I followed the dancing torrent.

As I progressed up the mountain, a vast array of delicate white, purple, and yellow wild flowers filled the clearings, and grand mountain panoramic views started opening out. Ahead of me lay my goal for the day, Yarigatake (3180m) sometimes referred to as the Matterhorn of Japan. The peak itself is a 100m pointy pyramid of rock sitting on top of Japan's finest mountain ridge.

After uncountable zigzags, I reached the most enormous mountain hut I've ever encountered, with room for over three hundred hikers. Overcrowding is not only confined to the cities! Thankfully though, Japanese are fastidious about climbing 'in season', so now even in late August, hikers were few. Still, I was very pleased to drag out my bivvy bag and prepare for my night alone under the stars. For seven hundred yen, I even enjoyed a chilled beer, straight out of the vending machine. *(See Plate 50)*

The next day I set off for the summit after breakfast. Because of its popularity in the summer months 'Yari' is, unfortunately, covered in chains and ladders and even has a marked route for ascending and descending. This does temper the enjoyment of the climb. Nevertheless, after twenty-five minutes or so I climbed the last ladder onto the smallish table-top summit and took in the views. These were fine, with Japan's big mountains all around and in the distance Mt Fuji 'floating between heaven and earth'.

On returning to the ridge I traversed south along the ridge passing over Kitahodaka to its high point Okuhodaka (3190m). This is *the* ridge to do in Japan. It is classed as a hike but has a good deal of scrambling, again with chains and ladders on the interesting bits. There is some enjoyable exposure and it is clear to see why rock alpinists come here to test their mettle.

After another peaceful night bivvying on the ridge, I descended to Kamikochi full of anticipation. The real gem of hiking in the mountains of Japan is the indulgent pleasure of sinking into a *rotenburo* (natural outdoor hot spring bath) to soothe those weary muscles. *(See Plate 51)*

Few countries are so easy to hike in as Japan, with its fascinating natural environment, outstanding public transport, friendly hikers, and first rate tracks and maps. And let's not forget the beer-vending machines and hot spas!

Climbing Mt Fuji

by Mike Norris

Mt Fuji, at 3776m, is the highest and most famous of Japan's 'Three Holy Mountains' (*Sanreizan*) and is celebrated for its near-perfect conical shape. What's more, being visible from downtown Tokyo on a clear winter's day makes it incredibly inviting. In fact, around 300,000 people attempt to climb Mt Fuji every year. The real key therefore to the enjoyment of the climb is to make sure you avoid the other 299,999. This is actually easier than you might think and can be done by simply steering clear of the religiously followed 'climbing' season (July 1 to August 27). Keen to avoid the pocket-size oxygen-can hawkers, the queues at the mountain hut coke machines and the squeeze on the summit, Aaron and I made our dash in mid-January and came across a total of four other climbers on the entire mountain. Of course, on the downside, we had to face freezing winter winds straight off Siberia – definitely the lesser of two evils.

Setting off from my snug apartment at midnight after a day's work, we reached the lower slopes of Mt Fuji at 3am. We had been prepared to sacrifice our ethics and follow the road to its end, half way up the mountain at the *go-gome* (fifth station: every Japanese mountain is divided into ten stations). Unfortunately, a closed road barrier forced us to toughen up and walk from the bottom. Abandoning the car, we followed the marked walking trail.

Despite the snow-covered track and dense snow-hung pine trees, route finding seemed surprisingly straightforward. The 'station' huts confirmed our course and we were able to count our way up the mountain. As the day dawned, these hut markers still proved the best way of assuring us we were making any progress. The summit appeared so foreshortened, and never came any closer. Mt Fuji is one of those curious mountains that look beautiful from afar, but once on their flanks, come across as a featureless lump of rock. There was little to distract us and the rise from sea level to over 3000m had the surprisingly acute effect of gluing our feet to the ground.

From about the seventh station, the route became very icy; we stopped to crampon up. The day was fine, but the sun did little to warm us against the icy winds that severely cut the temperature. *(See Plate 52)*

We reached the summit at around 11am and stared down into the impressive deep volcanic crater. Once on the top, we appreciated the climb and took in the expansive view, unobscured by any other mountain, because Mt Fuji stands alone.

The chill soon encouraged us to descend at full speed, bum-sliding and rock-hopping where possible. We reached the car at 3pm, were back home for dinner at six and ready for work the next day!

Tramping Trips in the New Zealand Alps
by Dr Mike Floate, QSM

My love of the mountains was first aroused on a Youth Hostelling and hill-walking trip to the Lake District with Brian Court in the 1950s while we were still at school. I well remember sitting atop Castle Crag in Borrowdale waiting for our map to dry out in the sun. I had dropped it in the River Derwent, and still have it among my treasured possessions. As we sat there I gazed in awe at the fells and crags around us, and realized that I had 'discovered' something special.

First tramping[26] trip in New Zealand

It has only been since coming to New Zealand in 1984 that I have returned to more serious hill and mountain activities. My first experience came in June 1984 (having arrived in January of that year), when I was invited to go on a winter trip in Fiordland with some new-found friends who happened to be members of the Otago Tramping and Mountaineering Club (OTMC). This was a three-day trip to Lake Hauroko and a traverse of the Hump Range. I had to use mainly borrowed gear, as mine was still in transit from Scotland. The first day should have lasted eight hours to Teal Bay Hut but it actually lasted for eleven hours of up and down in the bush with the final two hours in darkness: I was buggered! It was the seizing up of my knees (having not carried a big pack for nearly twenty years) that caused the delay. The next day I was permitted to trudge alone up to The Hump (3502ft/1067m) on the strict understanding that I must follow markers and not get lost. In the meantime the other members of the party went to explore the Wairaurahiri River, to give me a head's start. That worked well because it was almost midday before they caught me up, and I was happier not holding up everyone else. From there on it was a case of me following where others had been plugging steps in deep snow to help me make progress. It was still hard to pull my stiff knees out of each and every footstep in the snow. We did reach the Hump Hut before dark that day: imagine my surprise when the 'girls' made cheesecake for desert, putting it out in the snow to cool down! The next day was occupied with the descent to the South Coast, to come out at Port Craig. I learned a lot that weekend about the great help, encouragement and comradeship

---

26. Local term for hill-walking.

I received from a group mostly half my age, and the supportive rather than competitive nature of tramping in New Zealand.

Later, those experiences inspired me to get involved with the New Zealand Mountain Safety Council, Bushcraft Instructing and Search and Rescue and spend thirteen years on the national executive of the Federated Mountain Clubs of NZ (FMC). This I recalled recently when asked about the background to my award of QSM *'for services to conservation and mountaineering'* in the New Zealand 2009 New Year Honours List.

The two excursions described here represent the highs and lows of tramping in New Zealand: one over the Copland Pass between Mount Cook and the West Coast, and a seriously wet, five-day trip through the Pyke and Hollyford Valleys in Fiordland.

Copland Pass in Mt Cook National Park, New Zealand, 1985

The early New Zealand experience of crossing the Southern Alps via the Copland Pass in 1985 was something I will never forget. The old Hooker Hut was, late at night, full of people, cooking tea nearly at midnight, then again early in the morning as we prepared for an 'alpine start' at 4am. We headed up the hill at first light and made good progress to the Copland (Nissen Hut) Shelter (at about 6,000ft/1829m) for a wee rest before roping up for the steep pitches to follow across the ice and around 'the slots'. We reached the pass (7,050ft/ 2148m) by crossing a narrow snow-bridge at about 11.30am in fine warm sunny conditions, and then enjoyed absolutely magnificent views all around the pass and across the Hooker valley to Mt Cook. We said farewell to our guide, a very unassuming but very competent mountaineer and regular great guy, the late Paul Scaife, and sat around for a long time soaking up the wonders of this special place. That meant we had a long way to go down to Douglas Rock in the afternoon, but that did not matter after the exhilaration of the climb and the spectacular views from the pass itself. Down to the hut about 6.30pm. A bit buggered but my diary records this as, *'one of the best days, if not the best day of my life.'* At that time I was just a few days short of my fiftieth birthday.

A wet trip in the Pyke Valley in Fiordland, NZ, 1987

This story is about a seriously wet trip in Fiordland in February 1987. It had a delayed start because bad weather had held up our light plane transport from Gunn's Camp in the Hollyford to Martins Bay on the West Coast. We actually got there about mid-morning and had a pleasant wander round the coast to Big Bay. The afternoon trip through the 'Dry Awarua' was uneventful but the night ahead of us was far from that. We camped on a seldom-used airstrip in the Pyke River Valley, fortunately on relatively high ground. Listening to the evening weather forecast on the radio was not easy because of crackling due to a distant thunderstorm. The forecast said nothing about rain; the rain started about 9pm and rapidly got heavier. About 1am someone called out from the other tent, *'This tent feels like a water-bed!'* After checking, I replied, *'Our tent is a water-bed!'* We quickly went out to investigate and found the river all around us, about four inches deep and rising. Dick and Mary seemed comfy in their tent and were reluctant to come out but I told everyone to grab their sleeping-bags and head for a disused freezer box, occasionally used by deer hunters, about 6ft by 6ft by 6ft: just big enough for our party of five. The water had risen to an inch or two below the door sill, so it was still dry inside. We sat there all night cramped in our freezer box where fortunately the water level outside never quite exceeded the sill height. When it got light we unwound ourselves and tried to make the best of the situation. There was little we could do except wait for the water to recede which it began to do about mid-morning. Fortunately it was not cold and we had got some of our gear, including food, under a rough lean-to structure the night before. Gradually we got packed up and ready to move as the water went down. Most of our gear was wet and weighed a ton!

As the day wore on we followed the receding waters down the valley, but it took a lot of searching in the bush to find places where it was just possible to cross side-streams, except one. Here, there was a guidewire which went under water into a deep channel filled with surging muddy water. By now it was quite late in the day so there was no choice but to camp nearby on the nearest thing we could find to a dry spot.

Next day showed us that the guidewire actually served as a hand rail to help you across a narrow fallen log 'bridge' which was now only a few feet below the surface of the water which had dropped significantly and cleared greatly. It was now about chest deep but crossable. During this day we spent a lot of time in and out of water, sometimes waist deep, but our greatest challenge was crossing the well-named Barrier River, and then the Olivine. We could see the welcoming Olivine Hut just yards away, across a surging brown torrent. Mary couldn't help herself from weeping at the sight, and the thought of a warm dry bed on the other side. Again, mutual support and encouragement came to the fore, and we spent an hour or so bush-bashing upstream looking for a crossing place. Imagine our relief when we found a place where the river was wide but much shallower. Using our mutual support skills and battling waist-deep water we made our way diagonally downstream and across, now less than an hour down to that hut.

It was mid-afternoon when we reached the hut, which was empty, but was soon festooned with wet gear drying out, thanks to a great fire. What really reflected our feelings was the sight of Mary doing a *haka* in her bra and pants in the middle of the hut, yelling at the top of her Cumbrian voice!

The rest of the trip was uneventful even if we did have to struggle through the 'Black Swamp' before reaching the road end. We all learned lessons from this trip, and Mary has dined out on her story for years, but more than anything else it emphasized the importance of mutual support and encouragement, working as a team, and keeping level heads in the face of adversity. When you look back it is always the good bits of the experience that you remember, if you have the right attitude, and if you really have that love of the mountains that I 'discovered' all those years ago in Borrowdale.

MUNRO AND BELOW

Munro[27] and Below: Introduction

Back on home territory, this section encompasses a sense of 'how it all started'. Tales of obvious ascents, because they can be read about anywhere, have been avoided. Instead, editorial choice has centred on some unusual, very personal accounts involving an interesting mix of pleasure and pain.

The *Anthology*'s youngest contributor, James Moulang, briefly describes the fudge-orientated distractions of a family day out on Skye's most 'Himalayan' peak, Blaven, the view from the summit of which, over the rises and indentations of the Scottish coastline, the spiky Cuillin nearby and the patchwork of Hebridean islands beyond, provides what for some is the finest panorama in the world. Back on the mainland, with some sharp ironies and an acute eye for both companions and scenery, Alison Raeside, representing the OG parents, tells of a much-enjoyed traverse of the rocks and ridges of that outstanding Applecross Corbett, Beinn Bhan. Keith Browning, meanwhile, reminisces about formative experiences, getting to grips with various Welsh hills in that famous summer of 1966.

Several articles provide a more serious dimension. David Dunmur's real-life adventure on the North Face of Ben Nevis describes the considerable mental, emotional and physical demands required to rescue a hang-glider from the dizzy heights of the North Face. By contrast, the apparently extreme suffering of an American student in a blizzard on the Cairngorm Plateau, just six months before the Lochan Buidhe disaster, descends from danger into the comic bathos of a failed attempt to cure his ensuing blisters with home-made lager.

The section would not be complete, however, without recognising that the UK offers such excellent technical climbing opportunities. The editors are much indebted to the *Anthology*'s most prolific contributor, Ian Ferguson, for his unusual and technically complex accounts of a night-time

---

27. The Munros are Scottish summits above 3000ft (914.4m), but not all of them have drops greater than the generally-accepted guideline rule of 250ft (76.2m) on all sides of a summit. A Corbett is a Scottish mountain with a height lying between 2500ft (762m) to 3000ft (914.4m) with a drop of at least 500ft (152.4m) on all sides of any summit and any adjacent listed hill. The definition is thus more precise than that of the Munros. Perhaps rather surprisingly, there are at present 221 Corbetts and 283 Munros. Ed.

climb on The Ben and a more than eventful, sea-lashed pull up the Old Man of Stoer.

Following a lecture on one of the Himalayan giants, Menlungtse, Sir Chris Bonington went on to show some exciting pictures of St Kilda, with the message that, whatever the gigantic and extreme wonders which the rest of the world has to offer, the UK could offer every bit as good a range of experiences. We hope that our selection in this part of the *Anthology* reinforces that point.

Rescue on the Ben

by David Dunmur

I arrived at university with two Austrian alpine seasons under my belt, but no rock-climbing experience apart from abseiling practice in one of the chalk quarries dotted around Guildford. It was inevitable that I would join the mountaineering club (OUMC) during the Freshers' Fair, and there began a lifetime involvement with mountains.

The climbing scene in Oxford during the late '50s and early '60s has been well described by the popular mountaineering author, Richard Gilbert. Our equipment was poor, and climbing to a high standard was also very high risk. The challenging climbs had long unprotected leads, and even if there was protection it couldn't be counted on; there were more than a few fatalities. Still, I survived, not as a hard man, but as a reasonably competent average climber-cum-mountaineer.

After nearly six years, and having encountered my future wife on Commando Ridge during a club meet at Bosigran, Cornwall, I was soon married and ready for pastures new, ie a job. Bristol, with a flat overlooking the Avon Gorge, wasn't too bad, and the local climbing kept me in touch with former like-minded friends from university. It was through these contacts that a remarkable opportunity came up. I was invited to join four other ex-OUMC members (the club at the time only had male members: girls had to join the OUWMC) in a consortium to buy an almost derelict cottage in the heart of the West Highland climbing area. The building overlooked Loch Leven just outside the village of Glencoe. It would cost £180 each, and since our now small family of wife and baby didn't even own a house for ourselves, it took some delicate home negotiations to secure the share. What an investment!

It was The Cottage, variously known as No.3 Tighphuirst or the Glencoe Hilton, that provided a Scottish base for all the families of the shareholders, later expanded by the purchase of No.4 with the help of two further ex-Oxford mountaineers. Over subsequent decades of expanding and maturing families, the cottage became a frequent, sometimes exclusive, holiday destination, summer and winter. Not surprisingly, growing up with the cottage inspired many of the children, now continuing into the third generation, to take up mountain activities in later life.

During a week in June 1995, my son Alan called from Edinburgh to say that he and some mates were planning a trip to the cottage at the weekend to do a classic route on the North Face of Ben Nevis, Tower Ridge. Would I like to join them? Nothing could have stopped me. With the weather set fair we gathered in Glen Nevis at the Visitor Centre. We were off. *(See Plate 53)*

After an hour or so, one leaves the summit tourist track to head north and then into the Allt a' Mhuilinn glen, which leads up under the impressive North Face of the Ben towering 2000ft above the valley floor. I had been there before: winter climbing on the North Face of the Ben was an Oxford climber's rite of passage, rivalled only by surviving the threat of dysentery and the other horrors of the CIC hut during a winter meet.

But this was summer. Hours of daylight, not a cloud or breath of wind to disturb the day, just 1500ft of Diff/VDiff climbing in fantastic situations, and me safeguarded by my son and his friends. The route has been described in many places. It starts at the Douglas Boulder, a huge lump of rock that terminates the main ridge, and which can be turned to the left by the East Gully. Once we had gained it, our party of two ropes of two made easy progress along the ridge crest. The holds are good, at least in dry conditions, and the airy situations added to the sheer pleasure of the climb. All around were spectacular views: to the north, the Great Glen carves its route towards Loch Ness and beyond. To the west, the hills of Morar and Knoydart provide an enticement towards the mountains of Skye. As we gained height, more of the great North Face came into view: Observatory Ridge and the deep gullies that provide so much sport for winter climbers.

Tower Ridge takes its name from the Great Tower which stands like a sentinel towards the top of the ridge, and this must be traversed to complete the climb. But it is not quite over as the notch beyond, Tower Gap, must also be negotiated: a bold step over space onto good holds is the fair weather solution. Once past, one can relax and look around – only an easy pitch or two remains before the summit plateau. *(See Plate 54)*

On such a summer day we knew we would not be alone on the summit, and indeed from our vantage point we could see a hang-glider poised above the cliffs of the face. His wings were strapped to his back and he was ready to fly. There was a certain amount of trepidation in his 'take-off' approach, and he made a number of false attempts – getting the feel of the thermals perhaps. The scene diverted us a little from the climbing, but we had a route to finish, and after a few minutes the hang-glider disappeared from view.

I was first to reach the summit – I must have led on the final pitch, but I'm not certain. What I do remember vividly was the overwhelming sense of joy, achievement and sheer pleasure at having completed such a classic climb. It was an emotional moment: tears welled up in my eyes and my throat swelled; I could scarcely articulate my greetings to the others as they appeared.

The euphoric moment was short-lived: from across the plateau came an anguished cry, 'Are there any rock climbers here?' It came from the group of hang-gliders clustered at the edge a few hundred yards away. The panic in the cry indicated an urgent problem. Alan, Jerry and Mark grabbed a rope and ran over as fast as possible. I gathered the rest of our gear and followed. *(See Plate 55)*

From the summit nothing untoward could be seen. The group of would-be aviators were peering over the cliffs of the face. The hang-glider had indeed launched himself into space but, far from catching the thermals, he had dropped like a stone and become lodged on the face about 50ft below the top. His position was precarious, like a fly on not very sticky flypaper. His torso was lying in a narrow, steep, but open gully with his feet dangling over 1500ft of open space. The wings of the aerial contraption, strapped to his body, were projecting from the vertical rock, ready to catch any breeze. The slightest movement or breath of wind would dislodge the unfortunate and he would plunge to his death on the rocks hundreds of feet below. *(See Plate 56)*

Having run the hundred yards or so across the summit plateau, Jerry, Mark and Alan fixed a belay, and got a rope down to the crash-site. By some miracle they reached the hang-glider before he slid from the face. It was not clear if he was injured, but at least he wouldn't die. He was conscious, though in a state of shock. The weight of the wings was considerable, and it was necessary to attach both the wings and the flyer to the cliff, to prevent the wings dragging the victim off the rock. This was quickly done. The dazed flyer was able to clip onto the rescue rope and detach himself from the cumbersome wings. Then it was possible, with a great deal of verbal encouragement, to ease him up into a position of safety. Quite a crowd had now gathered, and help was at hand. The Mountain Rescue had been alerted and a helicopter was on its way to take the crash victim off the mountain.

The unfortunate flyer would not die that day on the North Face of The Ben; there was nothing more that we could do. After our triumph on

Tower Ridge we were all desperate for the pints of beer awaiting us in Fort William, a two hour downhill jog away. A few words were exchanged with the Hampshire hang-gliders – yes, they were a southern bunch – and we were on our way.

But this was not the end of the story. One evening, many months later, channel-hopping on TV, I happened on a docudrama, 'Michael Buerk's 999'. And there was a dramatised account of the rescue of a hang-glider on the North Face of Ben Nevis. Was there a mention of the quiet lads from the Glencoe Hilton who saved the guy? No way! If anyone reading this recalls the incident or those involved, then I will be happy to direct them to the rescuers. Somebody out there owes their life to a mid-life-crisis ascent of Tower Ridge.

A Blizz on MacDhui
or, How Not to use Home-Brewed Lager
by Catherine Moorehead

Poor Ken! All the way from sybaritic Berkeley, where (at the time: 1971) student riots were organised in daily rotation in different places across the campus. The cold, grey Calvinist vennels[28] of Edinburgh proved all a bit trying for the young man from the sunny softness of California. But after a time, American grit surfaced. My hyperbolic burblings about the beauties of the Cairngorms were answered with genuine interest. Could he see what the Cairngorm Plateau was really like? After all, rising to only 1300m above sea level, they weren't exactly Denali, were they?

Having practised the now almost-defunct art of hitching up the A9, we arrived lateish on a fresh-feeling May day at Loch Morlich. The intention was to traverse Bynack More (1090m/3576ft), a substantial Munro, drop down to the Fords of Avon then pootle up the Lairig an Laoigh for a bit before swinging right to the Etchachan Memorial Hut. From there, we would tackle Ben MacDhui which, at 1309m/4300ft, a surprising (?) number of people do not know is the UK's second-highest peak.

I wasn't long out of school. My Geography teacher had warned me about the ecological incorrectness and aesthetic disregard inherent in Munro-bashing, a piece of excellent advice flagrantly disregarded for the next twenty-five years until thirty-seven friends saw me to the top of the final one, Meall na Teanga, above Loch Lochy, in late July 1996. Being in those days young, slim and fit, and Ken being wiry and determined, we made short work of a trackless Bynack More (which now resembles an angled version of Spaghetti Junction) then bumbled down over A'Choinneach to the Fords of Avon. Two or three Marines were occupying the shelter, the scene of a singularly unpleasant event seven years later when a friend dropped her contact lens into the heather; they fed us dry biscuits, jam and tea. Then I noticed that Ken seemed a little reluctant to go on. Blisters had already appeared. With the cruel insouciance of youth I declared that he was actually fine but as a concession, we would make for the Shelter Stone that evening rather than the Etchachan Hut. A short walk along the Loch Avon-side, now with white ponies beginning to stir across it, took much longer than

---

28. Vennel: local word for alleyways. Ed.

expected: Ken's pain was obvious. We reached the Shelter Stone as dark was falling.

A dry night, a hearty meal and some hefty bandaging – I don't think the theory about leaving blisters out to dry had come in by that time – took some of Ken's misery away. In the morning, he seemed, despite the fact that Loch Avon's ponies had become fully-grown shire horses overnight, to be ready to continue.

We scrambled up the broken clifflets and over the slabs and boiler-plates next to the Feith Buidhe to reach the bouldery Plateau. I revelled in it: with the possible exception of Loch Coruisk, there is surely no more impressive place in the British Isles: there is a tremendous sense of the mills of God (?) grinding 'slowly but exceeding strong'. Ken's feet, however, on such irregular ground, really were giving him hell. I could see that the summit of MacDhui was out, especially since a strong north wind was now ripping across the Plateau and bearing some very ominous clouds with it. The sensible course (bit late for that) seemed to be to head for the Lochan Buidhe Shelter and sit out the approaching storm.

We staggered up the gravelly sludge of the Feith Buidhe drainage area, bashed by the wind which knew that the smooth plateau provided no serious resistance to it and took full opportunity to try to move across it, unlike us, as fast and as directly as it could.

The trouble (one of several) with the Shelter was that it was built in a gentle dip next to Britain's highest lochan (only pedants count the pool near the top of Ben Alder as being higher), an excellent spot for snow to accumulate. By the time we approached the bothy, the wind was positively screaming and ice snowflakes stuck darts in us. Only the ventilation chimney was visible. We hacked away at the snow covering the bothy, only to find the door frozen (the Shelter was no more than a metal cuboid covered in turf and boulders). More hacking. (Of course, we did not have ice-axes or crampons, nor head-torches or even very good gloves.)

The interior resembled the guts of a crevasse. Ice covered the walls; little light came through the one small window which in any case was thoroughly iced up. As the wind hammered away, the noise became quite hard to live with. We couldn't light the stove: all my matches were soaked. Ken was shivering, and I didn't feel too good, despite (!) my sodden, ice-encrusted, double-layered gaberdine anorak. The only food which we had left and which could be eaten was a pathetic little tin of tuna and a tin of some loathsome form of reconstituted chicken.

Ken could, in any case, hardly eat, or indeed speak because of the pain in his feet.

We were in a sticky situation. The snow was building up on the outside of the bothy. The speed of the flakes was bad enough in itself but made worse by the wind coming from the north, the direction we were heading into: to go south towards Braemar was unthinkable. What had to be done had to be done. After half an hour or so, the bothy became intolerably cold. Despite Ken's still restrained moans at every step, we clambered out of the tunnel-cum-chute leading up from the door and back out onto the Plateau. The speed of the wind was such that we could hardly breathe. Lashed by flying ice and spindrift we forced our way over the shoulder of Cairn Lochan then on down to Lurcher's Meadow, normally a pleasant spot for a break, before traversing Lurcher's Crag with the intention of descending to Windy Gap (Creag a'Chalamain) then further down to the Rothiemurchus Forest.

As we tackled Lurcher's Crag (1083m/3448ft), little more than a jagged pyramid of granite boulders about 100m high, with a fearsome drop into the Lairig Ghru just off the summit, I tried to think ahead about how Ken might later respond to the misery into which I had so blithely led him. More immediately, we had to cross the boulders where our feet more often than not slipped through gaps covered by snow between them. This must have been for Ken the most refined form of torture, and yet he never directed a cross word towards me. One remark was perhaps a little terse, but I was glad to get away with only that.

Descent was in some respects even worse for Ken as his scraped feet rubbed against ill-fitting and inadequate toe-caps. Even getting below the snow-line and onto the boggy ground leading down to the Lairig path constituted no improvement as boots sank into the mire, each time to be extracted with painful effort from the peaty black gloop. And on the path, as we passed that gnarled old wonder of a pine tree, the first in Rothiemurchus, at about 2100ft, the signal that safety is now almost assured, the tree-roots provided their final twist to Ken's misery.

I had a strong sensation of gradually coming out of a dream as we lumbered along, to reach Aviemore at a snail's pace by late afternoon. Hitching proved a slow business. We had only made Perth by midnight and were obliged to beg for a few hours' rest in a lorry-drivers' dormitory somewhere just off the North Inch. At 5am we left and, although I think we couldn't afford it, we caught the earliest train back to Edinburgh.

Oh yes, the home-brewed lager... In one of the university halls of residence some friends (Brian and Min, he who kept a family of ducklings in a drawer in his room) had acquired a dustbin and brewing kit and were busy producing their home brew for one shilling a pint, a hefty profit as the manufacturing costs were a mere threepence a pint[29]. The lager tasted strongly of rotting apples, but it got you drunk and therefore did its job.

On returning to our halls of residence, Ken, on examining his suppurating, lacerated extremities, declared that he was incapable of walking to the university Health Centre. Not to worry: his cure was in front of us. At a specially reduced low rate 'for humanitarian reasons' from Min, we acquired pints of the home brew and soaked Ken's feet in them in a vain attempt at sterilisation. Although clearly effective at slaughtering many a microbe, unaccountably the brew proved ineffective at healing Ken's wounds. We pretty well carried him to the Health Centre a few days later. A very unimpressed medic (Edinburgh medics have always fancied themselves) declared that the infection had got so out of control that Ken was required to attend the clinic every day for the next three working weeks in order to get the wounds re-bound.

Brave Ken! He never said a word against me, though heaven knows what he must have thought.[30]

---

29. For younger readers unfamiliar with pre-decimal currency, a 'shilling' now equals 5p, and 'threepence' equals 1.25p. Min's profit on each pint was therefore a healthy 300%!

30. The unhappy postscript to this tale is that the greatest single disaster in the Cairngorms occurred only a few months later, in November 1971, very close to the Lochan Buidhe Shelter. Five teenagers and their instructress lost their lives in an extended blizzard which prevented them reaching the relative security of the Shelter.

'It has every attribute of Hell except its warmth':
a traverse of Beinn Bhan

by Alison Raeside (with technical and other assistance from Mark Raeside)

L et's get something straight: I am not a climber, I am a gentle walker who has been led astray by dodgy company. The decision to tackle Beinn Bhan therefore must have been made when I was out of the room; the mountain looks like a hillside which has been attacked by a ravenous giant, leaving a series of ghastly gaps and teeth marks. When I protested, I was told it would be 'fine', I was not to worry, and that we were driving to the top and would just enjoy the gentle walk along the ridge.

My wedding anniversary has, in recent years, been spent enjoying a pleasant walk in the Scottish hills as a build-up to the most important part of the day: Dinner. This year was our twenty-fourth wedding anniversary and I was surrounded by delightful friends and family. I was sure that they would look after me and ensure that I was back in time to have tea by the fire, a warm bath and change into something floaty for a romantic evening. The walk was to be with four others: my husband, Mark, and Catherine Moorehead (both owners of short, functional, Scottish legs which are ideal for stomping up mountains and destroying everything that gets in the way) and two brothers who rejoice in the surname Twentyman: both over 6 foot 5 inches, with strides as long as their names suggest.

Beinn Bhan means 'white mountain'. It measures 2939 feet (896m) and is therefore classified as a Corbett. It is in the Applecross range of Wester Ross, surely some of the most dramatic and unspoilt scenery in Europe. You cannot picture this peak as a triangular mountain; instead, picture a long ridge stretching from north to south; and on the eastern side imagine a series of vast indentations which are its famous dramatic corries. The description 'It has every attribute of Hell except its warmth' was given in an 1892 account of the climb and is a fair summary of how the mountain looks from below.

Reader, we cheated. We did indeed drive up the notorious Bealach nam Ba (the Pass of the Cattle: Applecross's link to the outside world) and parked at the top. Remember, we were under huge time pressure: the champagne was on ice, the red wine was by the aga and the venison was in the oven. On this day, the 'white' of the mountain was provided by murky cloud and low mist. The beginning of the walk was marked by Catherine and my husband disagreeing (good naturedly) about the route; I diplomatically followed my husband, thinking that this was probably wise on our anniversary. It didn't stop Catherine muttering sotto voce throughout the beginning hours of the walk that 'had we taken her route we would have been here two hours ago...'

The start of the walk was bizarre: vast slabs of rock littered the landscape as if spat out; too close to walk between, the only option was to leap from rock to rock, pretty treacherous stuff. The three chaps got way out in front while arguing about the pronunciation of 'Bhan' (the answer, I am told is something like 'Varn'); Catherine and I were playing 'snog/marry/avoid' (or some equally intellectual game) to keep up our spirits at the back of the expedition. The next phase was no picnic either: we had to walk steeply uphill along a narrow ridge where the rock on the east fell sharply into Loch Kishorn and the west sloped towards the Atlantic; we had wonderful views towards Red Point and the Outer Hebrides. At this point, I am delighted to say, one of the fierce Twentymen lost his nerve and had to be nursed gently along.

After forty-five minutes of steep climbing, we reached the top of the ridge; expecting sharp rocks, it was bizarre to find the mountain topped with gently rolling swards of grass; also at the highest point there are the ruins of a shieling (walled sheep shelter); indeed, the 1892 Scottish Mountaineering Club account of the ascent reports a meeting with two shepherds gathering their sheep at the top; neither spoke English and were sheltering in that same spot while waiting for the mist to clear. *(See Plate 57)*

We sheltered there also, enjoying our modest lunch before exploring the summit ridge; there are dizzying views from the top into the corries, each one almost encircled by steep rocks and with a shimmering black loch at its base.

We walked off the hill at the south-east point. It was a very, very long way down. I was exhausted, and kept lying down in the heather; when asked what I was doing I said I was 'examining the wild orchids'; the truth was that I had found a bar of chocolate in my rucksack, and I was lying down to scoff it privately. Catherine went bombing ahead and practically skipped down the hill; could it by chance have been the sniff of the open claret waiting at home that energised her? Hours and hours later we walked through the front door; I had just enough time to drag myself into a bath and into a clean pair of jeans before I heard the dulcet screams of the bagpipes; as a surprise our daughter had organised a piper to play while the first of the champagne was drunk; she clearly recognised that in order to keep me awake some desperate remedy was called for. Not perhaps the ideal wedding anniversary for most people: but it was certainly mine.

Family in the Mist: a Day Out on Blaven

by James Moulang

My family and I had arrived on the Isle of Skye, and while a day indoors working on a thousand-piece jigsaw seemed appealing, we decided to brave the lousy weather and attempt a mountain.

I found it hard to see how it got its name, literally meaning 'blue mountain'. Smothered by mist, the grey mass loomed over our group and, smothered by midgies, we swatted ineffectually. A dose of courage in cube form, fudge, and we began our ascent.

As we followed a brimming river to the base of the mountain, it was easy to see the appeal of Blaven. In the summer, maybe. With good weather. And no midgies. Playing in the river resulted in a shoe full of water, which I learned to regret. Reaching the base, I felt a renewed sense of the challenge that lay ahead, but another cube of fudge set me right.

Roughly half way up the mountain, we reached a loch, where we enjoyed another of our mountaineering staples: hard-boiled eggs. Reinvigorated, we continued on our ascent. Soon, we reached a scramble, my first time despite being a frequent walker. I relished the opportunity, if only to worry my parents, and climbed up with glee: despite my eagerness, we completed the scramble without any unfortunate consequences. *(See Plate 58)*

The final stretch leading to the twin peaks of Blaven is littered with boulders, which we hopped between, occasionally losing our balance and experiencing the moment of panic, weightlessness and helplessness just before grabbing onto the nearest fellow hiker instinctively. A bit of friendly competitive spirit kept our motivation up, as we passive-aggressively overtook then fell behind another group of walkers.

Reaching the summit was made no less satisfying by the mist. We eagerly left our bags behind and ran to the second peak in a shameless act of trophy collecting. Then, too gradually to be noticeable, the mist began to clear. First in patches, then spreading out as strips were dragged away by the wind, until a great expanse of Skye's landscape was viewable. This day had made me put away the camera, and focus on other aspects of walking that I enjoyed, but had not realised: collecting trophies, pushing boundaries, meeting other walkers, and most importantly, clotted cream fudge.

The Reluctant Mountaineer, or One Damn Thing after Another[31]
by Keith Browning

The Scouts had been stuck with a 'Sixties attitude to adventure and risk that is not acceptable to society in 2000.' (Report into the death of a Scout Leader on Cader Idris, 2000.)

I had spent my primary school years in Cardiff, living not far from Caerphilly Mountain. It wasn't really a mountain, more like a large hill, but it was a wild open space, and in those innocent days of the post-war years children were allowed to play freely away from home. No adult ever supervised us. I was just one of many kids from Rhiwbina who learned a bit about life in the outdoors as we roamed the neighbouring countryside. I had been a Cub Scout in Cardiff, so when the family moved to Surrey it seemed natural to rejoin the Scouts, at the RGS.

I was a fourteen year old patrol leader in the RGS Scout Troop when I took part in my first summer camp, back in the country of my youth, Wales. This was the end of my third year at Guildford and my second year in the School Scout troop. The RGS Scouts were used to half-day hikes along the North Downs, to Shere and Newlands Corner, but those Surrey hills were very different from tackling real Welsh mountains. I was fit and strong and pretty well up for any challenge thrown at me. I was also a keen geographer, and my map-reading skills were good, so I was as prepared as anyone for this trip into the unknown. I had, however, never done anything like this before, and didn't quite know what I was letting myself in for. I was also responsible for leading my patrol of six other boys, most of whom had even less experience of mountains than I. At least I had climbed a Welsh mountain several times before, if only a small one.

A few weeks before summer camp, I realised that it coincided with the final stages of the Football World Cup being held in England in 1966. As an avid football supporter, I began to regret having to be in Snowdonia for the last ten days of the tournament. This was made worse when one of my friends said his father could get tickets for all the England games and the Final. I did manage to be at Wembley to watch England's opening

---

31. One Damn Thing After Another: a novel by John Masefield OM (1878–1967), Poet Laureate

game, but that was all. I had signed up for camp, and as a patrol leader I was expected to be in Snowdonia.

The Summer Camp ran from Wednesday 20 to Saturday July 30 with the first and last day being for travel. An advance guard of two Scout Leaders and two patrol leaders travelled by Land Rover a couple of days before. When the full contingent arrived, the campsite had already been prepared by our advance guard at a farm two miles from the town. We all slept well that night after the long train journey from Guildford, and woke early for breakfast and briefing about the coming week's events. Our camp was in a large field, which I remember being a very lush green and full of thistles. Green because it rains a lot in that part of Wales, although apart from one memorable day the weather stayed dry for us the entire time. Behind the campsite, and it was difficult to judge how far away, was a rather large dark looking mountain. Now, I would probably call the scene beautiful, but fourteen year old boys in 1966 didn't use words like that. This was Cader Idris.

During the next ten days we were to take part in expeditions to climb both Snowdon and Cader Idris, visit the Talyllyn narrow gauge railway and a working slate quarry. There were also to be several smaller scouting exercises, based closer to the campsite, including a patrol exercise at night. My deputy patrol leader and best friend, Brendan Chaplin, and I had also to complete our senior hiking badge, which involved a night away from the main camp and a hike of at least fourteen miles. This was to be an action-packed ten days which I would never forget.

We were to be introduced to the mountains with an acclimatisation session, a gentle walk up Cader Idris (The Chair of Idris). Patrol leaders were briefed about the route up Cader, and the mountain was there for all to see in full view from our campsite. There were a couple of checkpoints en route, and we were told we would be met at the summit. The route would be circular, starting from the campsite and taking us right round the 'armchair' profile of this dark, imposing mountain in an anti-clockwise direction.

It was a fine day when we left the campsite, and it was anticipated the round trip of about eight miles would take four to five hours to complete. The walking was easy and the scenery spectacular. Each patrol set off fifteen minutes apart; we were third of the six to start. The path was clear and the map-reading straightforward. We met one of our leaders at the base of the climb and we could see another patrol ahead. As the path ascended, the scale of Cader Idris became more apparent: we could see the vertical inner sides of the 'armchair'. From the summit, the rocky face plunges over 1000 feet to the lake below: a tarn and cirque carved out by a glacier some 10,000 years ago during the last Ice Age. There are few better examples in the UK. *(See Plate 59)*

The top was more of a narrow plateau than a sharp point so we took a little while to find the checkpoint and report to another of our scout leaders. The weather had remained clear till the summit, and although the path followed the edge of the 'chair', we never seemed to get too close. Until just before our rendezvous the weather had remained good, but quite quickly visibility deteriorated and a swirling mist descended. We headed off to look for the path that would take us round the far edge of the 'armchair' and down the mountain. As we started the return journey, I could see another patrol in the distance but they quickly disappeared into the mist, as visibility reduced to only a few yards. The mist was also making the rocks slippery and so we knew we would have to take more care on the descent than we had on the relatively easy walk up the mountain.

It was clear from the map that the footpath passed close to the edge of the precipice, but it was a well-trodden path and I had confidence all would be fine. We kept closely together and continued to walk in file in the swirling mist. At one point we had to take great care as the path, with its large boulders and loose rocks, became more challenging and increasingly slippery. I turned round to my left to check everyone else was fine behind me and at that moment a hole in the mist appeared for just a few seconds. To my horror I could see the ground to the left was a precipice and disappeared to the tarn, some thousand feet below. My heart seemed to miss a beat and I stopped dead. We still seemed to be on the path, but the edge was less than five yards away. I called back for everyone to take care and just follow me closely. A couple of minutes later we were back on easier ground; the mist cleared and the sunshine returned.

The return to camp was uneventful but as we continued down the far arm of the 'chair' I kept looking back to the summit, imagining how easy it would have been for any one of us to have taken a quicker route down. Brendan, who was acting as 'rear gunner' for the patrol, said he never saw the drop, and I didn't ask the others. I was more concerned that we keep everyone motivated for the climb to the summit of Snowdon.

The above account was written from my recollections of an experience over forty years ago. The memory can often plays tricks and amplify how dangerous the situation might have been. After reading a whole series of newspaper reports and climbers' guides, however, I realise that my recollections were accurate. Cader Idris is indeed a very dangerous mountain, and there have been many fatalities, including a Scout Leader in 2000. Despite being easy to ascend, the mists arrive so quickly, and the path takes the hiker only a few feet from disaster.

After a rest day and excursion, the following Saturday night was the only available time when Brendan and I could undertake our fourteen mile hike and so complete one of the most prestigious Scouting badges. As the weather forecast seemed unpredictable, it was decided our route should stick to well-established paths and minor roads and not venture onto the open mountains. The overnight camp was arranged to be in a field behind a public house. Not a very exciting expedition, but it would qualify us for our badge. The plan was to complete most of the hike on the first day and be back at RGS camp HQ early on the Sunday morning, so that we could take part in the day's planned activities.

We set off with fully loaded rucksacks containing provisions, tent and cooking stove (not so light in those days), and reached the halfway point at around five o'clock. Our rendezvous with one of the leaders was on time; he wished us well as we headed to our overnight campsite. Conditions were good and the whole hike looked as if it was going to be rather a non-event.

The inn, near Llanelltyd, where we were aiming to make overnight camp, was now only three miles away. Quite suddenly the sun disappeared and the skies became dark and menacing. We had expected it to be light until past nine o'clock, but at six it was almost black. The rain started and the water just kept coming and coming. There was nowhere to shelter as we plodded along an unlit road, with our worldly goods strapped to our backs. A car stopped to offer us a lift but, after a little debate, and in good Boy Scout and RGS tradition, we refused. We weren't going to cheat: we were going to complete the task as set and as planned.

Three miles should have taken us no more than an hour, but it was nearly nine o'clock before we finally saw the lights of our small tavern. They were expecting us and offered to put us up in the house. Yet again we refused and somehow, despite the wind and rain, managed to pitch our tent on the grass behind the car park. We had had nothing to eat, and it was too wet to cook our rather unsuitable rations of raw meat, potatoes and tinned peas. Exhaustion took over, however, and we just fell asleep, the rain continuing to pour from the skies.

I knew that England was playing Argentina in the World Cup that afternoon, and we were keen to know the result. Our teacher/leader at the rendezvous didn't know and neither did the publican at our inn. This was Wales in the 1960s, although it could easily have been mistaken for the 1860s!

The next thing I remember was waking in sunny daylight. Brendan was still asleep and it felt like it was early morning, maybe 6am. I eventually found my watch in the mound of clothes and couldn't believe it. Half past one, what a strange time! Had my watch stopped? No, it seemed to be ticking all right. Totally exhausted, we had slept for over sixteen hours, and we were already well overdue at the campsite. The bad weather had cleared and we packed quickly, but still with nothing in our stomachs. On the way back we did manage to find a small shop attached to a petrol station where we bought a couple of Mars Bars. They also had a Sunday paper. *England 1 Argies 0* was the headline.

We arrived back in mid-afternoon. We hadn't been missed and nobody had come to look for us. The campsite was almost deserted as everyone else was out on a navigation exercise, and when they returned no-one seemed very interested in our adventure. They were, however, glad to hear the football result.

Before the main event we had another 'visit', this time to the slate quarries at Blaenau Ffestiniog, and we also underwent a 'night' exercise, an orienteering trial, in the woods surrounding the campsite. Everyone, however, was looking forward with anticipation (and some, trepidation) to the RGS assault on Snowdon.

The culmination of our North Wales experience was to be an ascent of Snowdon. Three groups, selected on the basis of experience and physical ability, would take three different routes. A small group of those with some previous climbing experience was to ascend via Crib Goch, a difficult route. I opted for the medium group which was to take the Watkin Path, and the third was to go up the Pyg track, a relatively easy walking route. The most experienced Scout Leader would usher the more adventurous over Crib Goch, another would escort us up the Watkin Path, and the other two leaders, with less climbing experience, would oversee the others up the 'easy' route.

My group had an uneventful walk and made it to the summit soon after one o'clock, in less than three hours. The weather was glorious with no sign of a cloud. The small group that had come via Crib Goch arrived soon afterwards and we all expected to see the small group of 'ramblers' appear at any minute. After an hour there was still no sign of them. It was decided to send the two groups that had made the summit back down to wait at the coach. The leaders stayed and waited at the top.

It was another two hours before the final group arrived at the summit. They had been through, for some of them, a living hell. They had started up the Pyg track as planned, but due to some poor map-reading they ended up on Crib Goch. For some time they hadn't realised they had taken the wrong route and became, not knowing whether to turn back or carry on, virtually marooned on this jagged razor of rock. Despite their lack of experience, the two leaders coped well with the trauma; slowly everyone made it along the ridge then on to the summit. *(See Plate 60)*

At one point they were going to turn back, but the group voted to continue, if very slowly. The weather was good and they completed the Crib Goch route without further problem. When they returned to the coach the 'ramblers' were all rather proud of their achievement and after all the excitement my group felt rather cheated, as we were the only ones not to ascend Snowdon the difficult way. Having now seen many photos of this rocky precipitous ridge I'm glad I took the easier route.

I thought at the time that this was a strange thing to happen, but now know it is quite common as both routes start together and then diverge. The guidebooks now make a particular point of emphasising the potential problem.

The traverse of Snowdon was the final adventure of the summer camp. All had been achieved without serious incident, though each had poten- tial for disaster: a missed step in the mist on Cader Idris, two scouts half-drowned and missing in rural Wales, an inexperienced group with inexperienced leaders stranded on Crib Goch. The incident rate among Scout-related activities has always been extremely low, but when an incident occurs, particularly a fatality, there is always a call to close everything down or legislate the activity out of existence.

Later, as a teacher, I organised or accompanied many school trips to destinations all over Europe: there was always the possibility that something could go wrong. My time in the teaching profession was spent during the massive expansion in extra-curricular activities which happened in the 1970s, when innovation and excitement was part of the outdoor experience. I left teaching before the restrictions of the late 1990s made it impractical to organise these trips: the paperwork was so laborious, and the regulations so onerous that the whole operation became a thankless task.

The question has to be: how many of the millions of children who have been denied outdoor activities because of health and safety regulations have instead ended up a victim of domestic accidents at home? How many have also found themselves in trouble in other ways, particularly in the inner cities? They would probably have been much safer at the top of a misty mountain in Snowdonia.

The unpredictability of even the most docile activities was put into sharp focus by another event during the Snowdonia summer camp, which I have so far neglected to relate. During one of our rest days, we visited the restored narrow-gauge railway at Talyllyn. This was one of the first tourist attractions of its type in the country: my 'trainspotter' tendencies were fully satisfied. We travelled by coach in a circular route taking the coast road past Penmaenpool on our way to Towyn and returning inland via the Talyllyn Lake. If we had returned by the same route we would have come across a great tragedy.

Breakfast briefing on the Saturday morning following the trip to Talyllyn was interrupted by the news of a dreadful disaster that had occurred near Dolgellau only a short time after we had passed through the town the day before. A pleasure boat on the river had hit the wooden toll bridge at Penmaenpool and had capsized with many fatalities, including children. We were told it was the major news item on the TV and radio news programmes, and was headlined on all the newspapers. This was, however, one of those major tragedies which seems to have been very quickly erased from the nation's consciousness.

Four children and eleven adults had drowned when their five shilling pleasure trip from Barmouth ended in tragedy as the boat, 'The Prince of Wales', was swept into the wooden bridge at Penmaenpool. The boat was making a regular excursion, with an experienced crew, but the tide that day in the Mawddach estuary was exceptionally strong. As the ferryboat turned to moor at the George III Hotel for lunch, it struck the bridge. Thirty-nine people were on board and many of the survivors were hauled out of the water by onlookers at the public house. Four people from one family were among the casualties.

Strangely there was no formal enquiry into the tragedy and despite several of the staff from the inn risking their lives to save the passengers, no one was recommended for bravery awards. It was treated by the authorities as though it had never happened. Perhaps the horrific Aberfan disaster, which occurred a few weeks later, killing 144 people, including 114 children, caused the memory of Penmaenpool to be lost so quickly.

The summer camp ended with the long train journey back to London, on Saturday July 30 1966, one of the most famous days in the history of twentieth-century England. On the train in Birmingham, I was listening to a crackling radio when the Germans equalised and sent the World Cup final into extra time. And we were somewhere near Stratford-on-Avon when Geoff Hurst scored his hat trick goal to win the trophy for England.

Although I survived many more field trips, both as a student and later a school teacher, I never ascended a decent sized peak again. By contrast, my companion Brendan seemed to be inspired by the experience as he became a serious rock climber, and later took to the air as one of the pioneers in the sport of hang-gliding. In many ways I was a very reluctant mountaineer, and would have much rather been at Wembley than camping in North Wales. My duties as Scout Patrol Leader had prevailed over football, and that ten day summer camp was probably one of the most formative experiences of my life.

Northern Sandstone at a Silly Time of Year
by Ian Ferguson

The Old Man of Stoer: Original Route
(First Ascent 1966: Patey, Robertson, Henderson, Nunn)

They must have seen it all, on the petrol station forecourts of Aldershot. Not an eyebrow was raised at the purchase (in mid-October) of a diminutive inflatable boat with single collapsible paddle, suitable for the entertainment of an undernourished toddler in a flat calm.

On the other hand, it was for the best that we finished Tyrolean Traverse practice before drinking-up time. It is hard to imagine that the clientele of 'The Drummond' would have exhibited their most gentlemanly traits had they had the opportunity of finding a lady airline pilot suspended in the rainy dark ten feet above the car park of my Stoke Road flat. (A suitable venue, with a telegraph pole less than a rope's length from the flat's external staircase and banister.)

Preparations had been meticulous and prolonged. Sunrise and sunset times, tides, a test inflation, assembly of the required gear and loan of extra ropes, route planning and timing and rucksack loads. Clear male and female role expectations (key to the success of any expedition) had been delineated: I would undertake the Maritime Assault while Kirsti would sort out the knitting.

The best-laid schemes o' mice an' men gang aft agley. British Airways got Kirsti and me to Inverness but our baggage only to Edinburgh. The best part of a day's climbing was lost to Inverness Lassitude...

...Saturday dawned unpromising, although the relentless strobe of the lighthouse made the actual time of dawn quite hard to determine from within the tent. It was decided, therefore, to go and clap eyes on the objective and, sea-state permitting, to establish the bridgehead. There was brief excitement as the tip of Cirean Geardail hove into view after 'tabbing'[32] considerable quantities of kit across the cliff-top bog, but it was a false peak. The Old Man himself appeared about fifteen minutes later, an imposingly dour pillar reaching up from the white horses of the Minch towards the murky November clouds. A seal, or just possibly a dolphin, was basking near its foot and having fun at the expense of the

---

32. Tabbing: Tactical Approach to Battle: carrying a heavy rucksack a long way.

cormorants by surfacing underneath them, causing them to start up and flap away to try to dry their wings.

The descent from the clifftop was damp and frightening, and the platform of stone which forms the 'beach' from which to conduct bridging activities was not only remarkably slick, but seemed at first to provide precious little in the way of anchors to the specification required for a Tyrolean traverse: 'six of them, each fit for a large elephant'. On the far side of the water, three pitons and some orange string looked promising. *(See Plate 61)*

The Appointed Mariner had run out of excuses, and gingerly descended towards the water, clutching (and tied to) his craft and a large bag of dry clothes. The channel itself is too sheltered to permit surfing, but even without breaking crests the amplitude of the waves exceeded the victim's inside leg measurement by around nine inches: he was soaked to the waist before embarkation could be completed. Once aboard, confusion and despair, with monstrous pilot-induced oscillations, terrible scraping of the 'hull' against the harbour wall, and big green seas rinsing the decks. Ashore, the hysterical giggling was eventually broken by the instruction, 'Small movements! Don't leap around so much!' Calm returned, and things started to go more or less swimmingly, depending on one's point of view. With Stability and Control more or less established, Propulsion was the next challenge. No doubt the ancient Celtic Fergusons were good with coracles: the modern Ferguson eventually worked out his technique and the far bank was gained without ever quite succumbing to a complete rotation on any axis. Moby Dick thankfully took no interest but kept to his cormorant-bothering. Breathless and damp, the crew struggled onto relatively dry land, while clutching the vital bight of rope. He was grateful to hand responsibilities over to Kirsti. *(See Plate 62)*

Masterful heaving and entanglement then proceeded on the mainland, the fruit of many hours of pleasurable practice with pulleys, prussiks and unwary cabin crew in the hotel rooms of Tel Aviv not ten days before. Eventually a strum on the main filament determined the Horrible Engine to be fit for use, and the Mariner attached himself, cleared to cruise the return leg at a mean altitude of eighteen inches above sea level. The tension had been finely judged, and the low point was passed with only partial immersion, but a breaking wave scored final revenge by completely soaking the suspendee. By this time it was clear that a rainwater soaking was also inevitable, and pausing only to slacken the tension in the ropes, a contented pair bogtrotted back to its tent while admiring the distant Hebridean street-lamps.

Despite the produce of Lochinver's off-licence and a dismal weather forecast, Sunday morning's relatively small and dark hours saw two optimistic climbers standing once again in clifftop rain, three kilometres north of their tent. Kirsti's Geordie imprecations were interpreted to mean that the rain could be expected to continue, but given that we were going to get cold and wet in whichever direction we headed, we ignored the pursuing cumuli and descended the waterfall to our rope bridge. Where possible, this gentleman defers to a lady, and Kirsti was first to set off across the lapping brine. She seemed to learn a lot for the return journey. I deployed some of my most helpful and encouraging shrugs and smiles, and decided that in contrast to her, I would clip my harness directly to the traverse rope, rather than dangling any further beneath it than necessary. Soon two damp climbers stood shivering at the foot of the stack and, resplendent in full waterproofs, old school socks (mushroom grey, Kinch and Lack circa 1986) and a pungent reek of overnight-soaked rock-boot, the leader addressed himself to the route.

The first pitch comprises a very steep east-facing wall with two horizontal breaks which are to be traversed for several metres to gain a ledge on the pillar's south face. A tentative first attempt was rebuffed, but a couple of juggy holds let things get under way at last. Protection was provided by a pair of cams and what seemed to be a loop of aged clothesline looped through a hole in a balsawood block jammed in the upper break. It seemed churlish not to clip into that as well, but happily the fixed gear of the first belay was more substantial.

Twenty feet above the angry ocean, the traverse could fairly be described as 'full value' for a grade of VS 4c, and a tall order for Kirsti, a leader with two V Diffs and a Severe to her name. Worse, the initial holds also demanded a taller climber than South Shields had supplied, and so for both members of the party to get around to the sunny side was a time- and energy-consuming business. Matters were nearly made worse when I got cramp up one side. By my arm movements, I seemed to be signalling that I thought my partner was 'chicken'. She wasn't, and she did well to get herself to the belay.

If the chocolate hadn't boosted morale, the weather and climbing at this point certainly did. Seventy feet of dry, slabby Torridonian sandstone rising from crashing foam that glowed golden in the low-angled autumn sunshine out of a relatively clear sky. Punctuated by horizontal breaks for hands and feet and just enough protection to keep things comfortable, the second belay was gained in something under ten minutes. At last we were having fun, and with nearly four hours left before dark, thoughts could even dare to flicker towards 'summit' success. No daydreaming though, with Kirsti arriving very soon afterwards and grinning from ear to ear. A glance along the landward side of the ledge was comforting, as pitons a few metres along would allow a direct retreat by abseil if needed. The crux pitch was postponed briefly for photography.

Once again, a false start was rebuffed, but a careful re-reading of the guide showed that a bleak-looking slab should be preferred to the more evident line of weakness. It was not trivial. A falling climber would hit the ledge before loading the belay direct. This rock seems to have relatively few narrow or tapered vertical cracks, but plenty of wide horizontal breaks with a scaly, limescale-like surface and a cup-shaped profile. I found no way to protect this section, or even imagine any gear that would really have helped. With caution very much in mind, I started to puzzle out the moves. It was intricate and eventually undignified, but neither desperate nor strenuous, and when I was finally able to disentangle head and an arm to find a welcome nut all ready to clip, I had no argument with VS 5a as the published grade. A psychological challenge of Stoer is that the steepness of the climb restricts any view of when or whether difficulties might let up, but thankfully the subsequent 'delicate tiptoe across slabs' led easily to the 'cave with thread belay' which appeared glowing golden above the now distant waves. *(See Plate 63)*

The worst was over; we had less than half the climbing left to handle, and that on easier ground. But the exposure and situation were dizzying, and fatigue was beginning to tell. The view of waves between my feet was occasionally obstructed by a lurid green helmet which would appear, and eventually, with a jerk on the rope, vanish again. Hours seemed to pass. My forearms burned.

With less than two hours' light left, and the excitements and exertions of three days taking their toll, the thought of calling it a day was easy to share and the decision not difficult to take. So, a few photos; an abseil back to the landwards ledge, and then a nervous shuffle along to precarious perches alongside the fixed gear and some cautious snipping and tying. A single rope reached comfortably, and down we went. I took the first Tyrolean, this time running out a safety rope so as to avoid the helpless feeling as Kirsti struggled up from the low point. Soon, we and the vast majority of our gear were back to the mainland.

We even got to the clifftop before the legal end of twilight – just! We'd had high hopes, but limits to our strength and the speed of our ropework to get it all done in a short November day, and perhaps Kirsti's phrase sums it up, 'I looked at where we were, and I thought, this is the sort of thing Chris Bonington does! I'm not Chris Bonington!'

Luckily the bar in Lochinver sells carry-outs on Sundays, or the night could have been miserably dry.

Many thanks to Porn-Star Pete (for the rope and cams), Mark (for the boat idea), Anna (for the ride home) and all my climbing partners of 2003 for inspiration. For those interested in making their own attempt, Tom Patey's *One Man's Mountains* offers an excellent description of the first ascent: but note should be taken that at least one person has died of exhaustion and drowning through failing to escape from the low point of the Tyrolean traverse, a fact of which the author was not aware at the time of the attempt described above.

The author possesses a sturdy, capacious and tractable inflatable craft complete with short paddle suitable for the oceangoing aspect of the climb, and would consider sale, rental or leasing arrangements…

VS 4c 70', 5a 70' completed; [4a 40', 4b 50' unclimbed, orderly retreat]. Access by very small boat and Tyrolean Traverse. Leader Ian Ferguson, second Kirsti Samson, Sunday November 30 2003.

Half a Gully by Moonlight

by Ian Ferguson

Point Five Gully, Ben Nevis

Ian Ferguson and Garry Walters
March 30 2007

Pitches: Ian, Garry, Ian, Garry, Ian, Ian, Garry.

The weather said go for it. But 'it' was 'The Ben'; I had only two routes there I wanted to fight through the crowds for. I'd just got the better of a cold, and climbed nothing stretching for months. Garry? We knew precious little about each other: stronger, fitter than me, but limited mountain experience and less than a pitch on ice.

Friday dawns: SAIS and MWIS[33] are unequivocal. The Ben is in perfect condition: there's nothing else left in Scotland this late in the season. A big stable anticyclone: wind and temperature dropping, skies clearing, and a full moon. The mountain will be completely, surreally full. Tickets at the CIC Hut: 'Zero Gully: party number seventeen, please!' But what's the alternative?

Garry turned up, full of apologies, at 10am. He'd remembered everything except his waterproof. So he took my old one, and off we went.

I grumbled my doubts at him. Then I told him my really stupid idea so that he could laugh and we could choose something sensible. We'd get to the Fort about 6pm. We could walk in and take a look at the routes by last light. We could go really lightweight – just sleeping-bags – and crash out at the foot of the route, or, if the sky was clear and there was some moonlight, we could just carry on up and climb it...

6.15: North Face Car Park, and a minor kit explosion. By half past we were off.

8.00: CIC hut, to my surprise, as I didn't know I could match guidebook time! The mountain was looking exquisite, palette by Roerich[34], and the dark horizon of cloud behind Carn Dearg was clearing rapidly. A large, tent-bearing population was heading up the Allt a'Mhuilinn path...

---

33. SAIS: Sports Scotland Avalanche Information Service. See: *www.sais.gov.uk*. MWIS: the excellent Mountain Weather Information Service. See: *www.mwis.org.uk*. Ed.

34. Nicholas Roerich, (1874–1947), was a Russian mystic, painter, philosopher, scientist, writer, traveller, and public figure.

9.00: well-established in Observatory Gully, and accompanying a solid-trudging pair who were looking like bedding down at the foot of the route. The route itself was looking super, a real clean, well-defined line. The moon, while well-risen, was tucked behind Observatory Buttress, leaving the route in deep shadow, an unforeseen weakness in the plan. The other party greeted us. Sure enough, they were headed for Point Five too, and shared my gloomy forecast of crowds. Would we be pushing our grade? A little, perhaps. They didn't want stuff dropped on them: one of the leader's clients had had a hand broken last week. They'd have a couple of hours' kip and then push on up.

Nice to have a Guide behind us, just in case. Or, more likely, to rapidly overtake us.

By 10pm, we had dug our sleeping-bags into a smear at the foot of the ice. The sky was clear; the route was clear; the first pitch looked juicy. No reasons to retreat were appearing, so we geared up.

The first pitch *was* juicy. The belay was comforting; a little hex and a good nut, out of the line of any falling debris. The main difficulties, which were significant, were psychological. 'I'm starting 300m of classic steep gully. It's pitch black. I've been out of the game for six months. My partner's new to this. I want to look pretty for my wedding photos in two weeks' time. They don't let you fly with broken bones and Heidi and I have just booked expensive honeymoon flights to Peru. Hell, I want to be at my own wedding!'

Beautiful névé. Beautiful axes: light as a feather, and solid as my old Predators. Stick, pull, kick. Heidi's axes, she'd love this climbing. Garry's got mine with the finger-guards, so I'll mash my knuckles as I always do when I'm nervous... Every axe placement was a quiet joy, but hard to get weight on your feet: 1) because you climb like a Wendy and don't place your feet properly; 2) it's actually quite difficult to see where to put your feet in the dark unless you point your head-torch downwards and stick your arse out and oh Mamma Mia look at that drop.... Concentrate on the task in hand. Things are getting steeper: névé's nice, but it won't hold a fall. Get a nut in the gully wall. Make sure of the route-finding. This pitch has a complicated description, and to drift off route would be disastrous. Keep the head-torch swivelling.

Over the bulge: hard, but only in the head, and make certain we're in the right place. 45m is a long pitch, but surely I can have little more rope left? Keep the climbing tidy...Yes! a tangle of old nylon appears in my lonely pool of light: the belay, exactly where it's supposed to be.

Jacket on to keep warm, shout safe, and start to belay Garry.

What is this? Oceans of time are passing. Well, the responses were clear and he knows what we're about. Fair enough, he hasn't done a lot of this sort of thing, and he doesn't know my axes. Give him a minute or two. Admire the moonlight creeping down Tower Ridge (bright enough to see in colour if we were climbing it!) and the Plough fitting into the shape of the skyline; Lochaber glowing orange beyond Carn Dearg.

Garry struggles to the belay looking shell-shocked. Mmm, he'll get his eye in. 'Mate, I think we're going fantastically. But it's you that's driven six hours today, not me. If you really want to tell me you're right out of your depth and you've had it, we'll go down. We set up the harnesses so we can swap leads out of sequence easily – I can't lead every pitch, I need you to do some of them, but I'm still going strong. Whaddyou think ?'

He spoke with actions. 'Follow the ice-choked chimney. Forty metres.' More time passes, and some bits clatter down and give me a fat lip. I huddle under my rucksack and pretend to be asleep while feeding the rope out. Eventually, there are shouts and apologies. I take the belay apart and set off with an eye out for an axe-leash Garry's dropped.

Dear God, where did he pull this lead out of? This is heinous! Chimney: steep, head-on, some gear would have been a nice bonus... No matter, beautiful, dancing moves on trustworthy ice. Stick your butt and back into the wall, axes planted high and parallel across your body and back-and-foot your way up. Tremendous. Well, he certainly changed personality once he left the belay, all credit to him. I wouldn't have fancied this, so what will I face on the crux pitch? No route-finding, just pure quality climbing. Right to the belay, and due congratulations to Garry.

Brown, dirty, steep, bulging, complex organic shapes of rimed, frosted, shaggy, broken icicles and twisted ice appeared. They were otherwordly, compelling, horridly fascinating. Yes, this is the start of the 'Rogue Pitch'. Steep, sure, but not mad-desperate steep – perhaps this is just the start and the tough bit comes later? Garry won't be leading it, that's clear from his face. OK, let's get ourselves together and push on. It's a thirty metre pitch, so the difficulties can only keep coming for so long.

1.15am: up and at it. From the base on the left or up the ramp and then traverse to the bulge? Up and traverse. I take Garry's advice and throw one precious screw into the thick ice out right, under the overhang, to save me lobbing full-blooded onto the belay if I fall. Now, I teeter out and start to 'assume the position'. My hands were swapping axes to let feet work their way around. The bulge at head height was very much 'in your face'. High axes to get tucked in under the bulge. Encouraging words from Garry, that's kind. Right, let's get one high axe above the bulge. Beautiful stick: that's in something solid. Now the other? Nice – same again, you could pull on these until Monday – which is lucky, because my arse is fairly hung out in space. Garry seems to think so too. Work the feet up; can't get the head-torch to point under the overhang so go by feel and really throw weight on the axes. Keep scampering the feet up, front points skittering tentatively, too shyly into the ice. Hands placed well up the axe shafts. Feet firmly, fiercely over the bulge and nearly up to the axes, climber doubled over. Time to get an axe out. Jiggle, jiggle and pull: a little resistance, but the proper filing of the picks really pays off and out comes the axe, without such a jerk as to tumble the climber from his footing. Another solid high placement and shuffle feet and axes to get more or less secure – if widely bridged. Time for protection: a hasty screw goes into soft material; time to use the screamer, and time to leave this awkward tiring posture before my forearms pump out. More soothing words from Garry but now only a steep section to push on through, nothing we haven't seen before. Stick, pull, put faith in the feet. *(See Plate 64)*

Stick, pull and up; repeat, repeat, and keep the head together because we don't know what's going to face us in a minute.

Head over the top and all that's left is just a long, narrow, low-angled gully. That was the 'Rogue Pitch' on Point Five Gully[35] on the Ben, led by moonlight, no drama, no rests on gear, in fine style.

Twenty metres up the gully and I start looking around. Directly, in the right wall, a historical-looking piton in a tiny crack. Nothing else. That'll do nicely. Clip, get another screw in, exhale, and call, 'Safe!' Three pitches up, all the difficulties are done; weather, temperature and moonlight just fine. *We could do this!*

Rockfall clatters and echoes from way, way over in one of the other corries. Let's keep it tight and careful, it's the small hours when accidents

---

35. Point Five Gully: 'The most famous ice gully in the world' states the Scottish Mountaineering Club guide, as the first winter ascent was carried out in six days in January 1959; and the second ascent by the unstoppable Robin Smith and Jimmy Marshall took a few hours in February that year.

happen. Five pitches to go; only two more for me to lead. Up comes Garry, eyes on stalks – about as wide as mine were following his pitch. Retreat from here would be a pity. Off he goes.

Oceans of time pass, and some unhappy shouts reach me about absence of gear for a belay. 'Drive your axe in, clip it and sit on it!' Eventually a call of, 'Safe, but don't fall off!' Up we go, easy ground, on all fours, hands half way up the axe handles. Pitches 4–8: 'follow the gully to the top; the cornice is usually passed on the right.' Will the cornice force us to abseil back down the whole route? Surely the recent ascents will have left us an easy breach? We focus on staying on the route: most of the variations noted in the guidebook seem designed to add interest and difficulty to the standard route. We want neither; we want to finish before the gods look down and see what we've been up to before taking against us.

Garry wants food and water, but not at this 'belay'. I'm parched too. My belay is fine: two screws in good ice in a steep little chimney section. So we refuel and I volunteer for the next lead, and therefore the dreaded cornice... Again, easy scampering on plunged axe-shafts, with one or two screws in the icy wall on the right, just in case. A little *nunatak*[36] on the left has a nut stuck in it, and a pinnacle I can reach on rope stretch, so I belay. The woolly mittens are awkward with the axe-leashes. Garry is still apologetic for dropping one, and has fashioned an alternative out of a four-foot sling. He heads on up.

Still not cold, but I endure an occasional thirst. I take the chance of a bit of one-handed photography, and feel suddenly very exposed, sitting in the spine of a vast open book as lights crawl up the Allt a'Mhuilinn. And the little headlamp is much nearer, probably only a pitch below us. The orange lights beyond Carn Dearg have been constant companions. In fact, the sky over there is beginning to brighten and hopes of topping out in full darkness are long gone. We look like setting my usual slovenly standard of over an hour per pitch, and Gary seems to have decided to burrow rather than climb.

An *absolutely enormous* cornice glares down from every aspect of the top of the gully, and it looks as if I'll be lucky to get through it even if Garry runs out the full fifty-metre rope on this pitch to get me near the foot of it. No chance of that: he seems set on chipping and sculpting and the rope surely hasn't moved this month.

---

36. *Nunataks* are small areas of rock emerging above ice sheets and glaciers.

Come on man, I want to finish this and go.

Ten metres – five metres – what's the difference? I've got the hard job of tunnelling through the cornice and you aren't even going to get me near it; we'll be here until midday and overtaken by half a dozen parties...

Enough. He's belaying – I've lost my patience, stripped my belay and headed on up even before his shouts. By who-knows-what illusion when close up the cornice magically shrinks to a benign little three-foot affair. The ropes go through a gap; *Garry has topped out through the cornice and we've finished the climb in seven pitches!* No gear at all: he must have been having a brave moment. One axe into the top of Ben Nevis, then the other, and pull, and crawl, undignified, over the top into the sunlight.

There's Garry, and handshakes, and amazement, and relief and laughter, and we've beaten the sunrise. It's 6.15am and sunrise isn't for seven minutes yet. And all of Scotland's hills are in pastel colours, vapour and frost. *(See Plate 65)*

Steak pie is enjoyed at the door of the rescue hut. Twenty minutes of fitful kip with freezing legs and head on a coiled rope follows. We stagger from the hut. Some teenagers arrive in baggy khaki on a charity walk. They didn't see us on the way up: 'You must be hardcore,' when they hear what we've done. Laughter when we find that Kingston is home ground for me too. They brandish our axes while we take their picture. They head for the Lakes and we for Carn Dearg, while taking a moment to admire Tower Ridge. The steep snow slopes are now in the sun, beware balled-up[37] crampons. Two abseils: past the avalanche debris, then crampons off for the boulderfield and our corrie appears soon enough. Garry offers to fetch the bivvy kit. I stretch out for a snooze in the shade. I count fifteen people in Zero Gully: there are shouts of, 'You'll have to wait, there isn't room on the belay!' A belay device falls from high on the mountain and narrowly misses Garry. To late-coming climbers, our early descent and past-our-best appearance give away what we've been doing: 'We saw lights high on the mountain last night. It must

---

37. Balling-up: describes the phenomenon in which snow in particular conditions forms large lumps underfoot, sometimes in less than a single footstep, thereby raising crampon points away from the surface of the slope so that they provide no grip. A sharp tap with an ice-axe shaft removes the snow; otherwise, fatal falls are not uncommon.

have been beautiful,' and, 'Full moon! What a great idea! So you had it all to yourself!'

1.15pm: pausing only to break Garry's Krooklock off his car (the key being back in Nottingham, probably along with his waterproof), we set off for bacon sandwiches in Fort William, followed by scratchy catnaps and service stations, to get home by midnight.

My mashed knuckles will show in the photos, but I'll get a ring on my finger without wincing.

ECLECTIC ADVENTURES

Eclectic Adventures: Introduction

Not all adventures lead to the summit of a mountain, and in this section we have collected tales of a slightly off-beat nature. Some would say that climbing crumbly limestone on vertical ladders bolted to a thousand foot cliff-face was off-beat. Not for an intrepid RGS team exploring the *Via Ferrata* of the Dolomites, one of whose members, James Slater, gives a blow-by-blow account of the expedition. Charles Vivian's cross-country race across the sands of the Sahara might not be everyone's idea of adventure, but for sheer endurance it ranks with the toughest mountain challenges.

Our contributors to Eclectic Adventures have found all manner of challenges. Facing up to them brings sometimes pain, invariably hardship, but ultimately satisfaction. Even the complexities of history and literature come alive through a search for evidence of Hannibal's elephants (David Dunmur) or a mystical moment on seeing the real Dracula's castle (Jeff Rawson). But Miriam Manook's archaeological find at c3900m on the China-Kazakhstan border could not have been planned, and indeed remains unexplained.

There are cautionary tales also. David Benest's expected exploration of the mountains of South Georgia ended in the bloody conflict of the Falkland Islands. Our military do not choose their adventures, but are expected to respond as heroically as explorers and adventurers pursuing their own eccentric quests. Military exercises come in all shapes and sizes; it is best to start modestly, and an account by Ian Barker and David Dunmur of a night exercise by the RGS CCF and Scouts to capture Leith Hill may awaken memories.

An irresistible attraction, at least in anticipation, is often for physical discomfort. A number of our contributors in this and other sections opted to experience such an attraction in the extreme cold of the polar regions. Tom Fulda in his account of climbing in Greenland tells of escaping the cold, and eating whale, while Colin Carmichael, on a school trip to Iceland, mostly recalls the girls. Reality when it bites, often bites hard, but, as reported by Richard Payne, our younger adventurers always seem to rise to the difficulties and dangers, even opting to bivouac in the frozen wastes of Svalbard, in appropriately named 'snow graves'. Perhaps an overheard comment after that experience provides an epigrammatic conclusion to this anthology, *'Right, now I feel about as personally developed as I will ever be!'*

The World's Toughest Footrace
Le Marathon des Sables (Sahara)

by Charles Vivian

It is not the critic who counts, not the man who points out how the strong man stumbled, or where the doer of deeds could have done better. The credit belongs to the man who is actually in the arena, whose face is marred by dust and sweat and blood; who strives valiantly; who errs and comes short again and again; who knows great enthusiasm, the great devotions; who spends himself in a worthy cause; and who, at the worst, if he fails, at least fails while daring greatly.

Theodore Roosevelt

Recalling these words of greatness temporarily made the pain in my feet subside and ease the worry in my mind about what lay ahead. I had just completed the first day of the *Marathon des Sables,* a one hundred and fifty-three mile, six-day race across the Sahara Desert, commonly known as the world's toughest footrace. Day One had been far tougher than expected: the fifty-degree heat, the fifteen-kilo pack, the dunes, the rocks, the pace...

...I was lying on my back in our Bedouin tent, a sandstorm blowing furiously and my legs raised in the air in a futile attempt to reduce the swelling in my feet, while desperately trying to rationalise what I had got myself into and how I was going to get through it. Little did I know at this stage that what had started as the biggest shock to my system since birth would become the greatest and most rewarding adventure of my life.

In October 2003, a family accident gave me the impetus to do a fund-raising event for Stoke Mandeville Hospital. Bungee jumps, half marathons and marathons were commonplace and donor fatigue was rife. A colleague from work had run the *Marathon des Sables* the year before and, although he had had a horrendous time, he said it really caught the attention of sponsors and was a great way of raising money. My mind was made up: I was going to tackle the big one. It seemed too much of a challenge to undertake on my own, so I sent a speculative email to some friends to see if they wanted to join me and, incredibly, five replied saying 'yes'. A week later the 'Adventure Racing for Charity' Team (ARC) was born; we were set for our first major adventure.

In October we received confirmation that our entries had been accepted. With the event scheduled for early April, this gave us about six months to go from slightly overweight and 'overpartied' mid-thirties year-olds to fine-tuned racing machines. Training was tough: my abiding memories are of collapsing with cramp two miles into my first training-run in Richmond Park, completing the epic fifty-five mile 'Thames Meander' on Valentine's Day as my running partner collapsed with hypothermia, and my spending hours and hours on the physio's table having knots worked out of my legs. The other key part of preparation was buying kit: the *Marathon des Sables* is a self-sufficiency race, so you have to carry everything, apart from water, that you need for six days in the desert. Many an evening was spent in internet chat rooms talking to fellow adventure racers on the other side of the world, or ordering the latest blister treatment from Peru. The week before was spent packing and unpacking our packs to see how light and streamlined we could make them. In the end we got them down to fifteen kilos for the start, two kilos of which was the emergency flare that the French organisers kindly gave us on arrival in the desert!

In 2004 there were six hundred and fifty competitors in the *Marathon*, two hundred of whom were British. The first time we got to eyeball the competition was at Gatwick Airport. It was easy to spot them: among the groups of package-holiday travellers were scattered lean, mean-looking athletes, many sporting military insignia and all carrying the latest in adventure racing kit. Just the sight of them made us wonder if we were going to be able to succeed. Tucking into our fried breakfasts before flying felt like our last supper, particularly when we were joined by Karl from Kent, who told us he had spent two years training on a treadmill in his greenhouse packed with electric heaters!

On arriving in Morocco, we had an acclimatisation day before travelling into the Sahara. The trip to the start-line resembled a scene from Mad Max[38]: we, the British contingent, were herded on board fifteen old army trucks and, standing in the back like prisoners of war, hammered on into the desert. We descended on the camp in a cloud of dust, noise and diesel fumes, announcing in style our arrival to the other four hundred and fifty competitors.

---

38. A 1979 Australian dystopian action film. (Source: Wikipedia.)

I had never before seen a desert and my first impressions of the Sahara were how beautiful and varied the terrain was. Much of my training had been done on bridleways in the UK but the camp at the start of the *Marathon* was set between two rocky mountains while the ground underfoot was more Snowdon than sandpit. It also amazed me how windy it was and how cold it got at night. Having kept clothing to a minimum, it meant that every night we had to put on every article of clothing we possessed just to stay warm. By morning we were frozen.

I will never forget the start of the race. It is run by a legendary Frenchman who spends the fifteen minutes before the start standing on top of a Land Rover, psyching up the competitors. Tradition has it that you also sing a song together before starting. This was to become a morning ritual with Patrick (the starter) reading the names of those who had withdrawn the day before, like comrades lost in battle. The countdown to the start was accompanied by a helicopter sweeping over the competitors and beaming the pictures all round the world. We were off...

Day One: Sunday April 11 2004
Oued Amsailikh – Oued El Khait; 18 miles; 41°C
After months of training and preparation, the competitors were eager to get going; there was a tremendous buzz on the start-line. We had been warned that as a result, many competitors set off too quickly and end up with tremendous blisters or very tired legs. We had therefore decided to walk Day One, to acclimatise and preserve ourselves for the heart of the race. Working as a team and taking things very steadily, we completed the first day successfully, without incident, finishing just ahead of the camels who sweep the route at the back to pick up any stray or injured competitors.

Day Two: Monday April 12 2004
Oued El Khait – Lac Iriqui; 21 miles; 43°C
Day Two was a day worth forgetting, with the prospect of Days Three and Four looming. Having broken ourselves in gently, however, we began to find our rhythm on the long, flat plains that the route covered and made up a hundred places in the field.

On arriving in camp, blisters had started to appear. Several team members paid their first trip to 'Doc Trotters', the medical support team. Contrary to expectation, they felt much better on their return to the tent after forty-five minutes of attention from a very attractive French nurse armed only with a scalpel and iodine!

Day Three: Tuesday April 13 2004
Lac Iriqui – Dayet Chegaga; 24 miles; 40°C

The dreaded dune day! Competitors are required to cover the majority of the thirty-seven kilometres across the legendary (indeed mythical) dunes of Erg El Ghoual. The event organisers had also set an aggressive completion time in order to weed out weaker competitors before the double marathon leg the following day. *(See Plate 66)*

Despite worsening blisters, we performed strongly in the dunes and very much enjoyed the beautiful scenery. We all made it home within twenty minutes of each other. In camp that night, however, stories abounded of competitors getting lost in the dunes and missing checkpoints, or of people running out of water, and of cases of delirium with several competitors requiring medical evacuation and rehydration drips on the course.

Days Four and Five: Wednesday April 14 and Thursday April 15 2004
Dayet Chegaga – Jebel Megag; 49 miles; 42.7°C

The double marathon sector! Following the previous day, there was general reluctance throughout the camp to get out of sleeping-bags in the morning. Having prepared for this distance we felt relatively confident. This challenge, however, turned out to be incredibly tough. The terrain varied between more dunes, sandy tracks and rocky plateaux; we also encountered our first sandstorms. Competitors are given the option to split the distance and camp overnight. Feeling the effects of their blisters, some team members decided to do this, completing the seventy-six kilometres in a very gutsy twenty-six hours. One other team member and I, however, decided to blast on through the night and completed the leg in a very creditable sixteen hours and twenty-two minutes. Regrettably, in the process, my companion suffered a ruptured Achilles tendon which was to hamper him for the rest of the event. The highlight of our overnight run was passing through a kasbah long after dark then contending with the attentions of curious local inhabitants, whose usual nocturnal activities we had disturbed.

Day Six: Friday April 16 2004
Jebel Megag – Jebel Bou Debgane; 26 miles; 43°C

It is bizarre to recall that we all woke on the morning of Day Six thinking of the day's marathon race as a short and easy sector, following the exertions of the previous days. It fulfilled our expectations, however, and we all completed this sector in under five hours. To this day I cannot believe how straightforward it was!

Day Seven: Saturday April 17 2004
Jebel Bou Debgane – Tagounite; 12 miles

The final day mixed elation that the event was almost over with sadness that the adventure that we had been focusing on for so long was soon going to end. We also felt sorry to be leaving the Sahara to which we had become accustomed, but for which we had developed an awesome respect.

The route took us through several villages with the locals applauding us all the way. We finished in Tagounite with an army escort to ensure that the local kids did not steal the kit from some very weary competitors. *(See Plate 67)*

We had done it! It had taken us between forty-five and sixty hours and there had been much blood, sweat and tears along the way. The talk, however, on the finishing line was of what a fantastic event it was, how wonderful the Sahara is and most frighteningly, what was next!

Our fundraising efforts had also gone well: we raised over £10,000 for our selected charities.

Hannibal's Trek across the Alps

by David Dunmur, from the papers of John Foster and Michael Hetherington

The quest for Hannibal's route over the Alps from France to Italy in 218BC has motivated scholars, eccentrics and adventurers for more than two millennia. The classical sources for the story stem from Polybius (b.202 BC) and the better-known Livy (b.59 BC). Only Polybius had any real connection with the events, and his account claims to have retraced the route some seventy years after Hannibal's epic journey. And epic it was: 20,000 infantry, 12,000 cavalry, 10,000 pack animals, 10,000 porters and camp followers and 37 elephants. All these found a route over the Alps in the autumn of 218BC to begin the conquest of the Roman homeland.

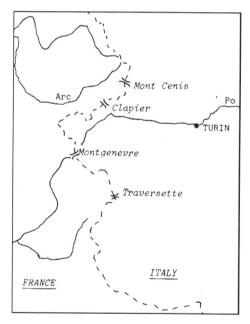

Sketch map of possible crossing points of the Alps for Hannibal

The route of this mighty invasion, one of the greatest ever in military history, has been the subject of intense investigation, mostly, it has to be said, by armchair historians who read the literature and through diligent analysis of texts arrive at their erudite conclusions. A few intrepid adventurers have explored the valleys and passes that separate south-east France and Italy

255

in the hope that Hannibal's route would be revealed by the local terrain or perhaps even abandoned artefacts. Despite two thousand years of enquiry, even today the search goes on, using modern techniques of geomorphology and geoarchaeology.

In 1957 a group of RGS scouts led by Latin teacher Jack Lauder journeyed to eastern Austria to learn the basics of alpinism and climb a few of the less-challenging peaks. Among them was classics scholar John Foster. The consequences of this school trip echo down the decades, but for John they had an immediate effect, as he relates in laconic style in the school magazine for the following year.

NIHIL SINE SOLE SINE SIGNO

All expeditions have mottos, and we were no exception; the first three words we purloined from a French sundial, the last two we added with more regard for alliteration and English commonsense than for Latin syntax. Our expedition was not only pre-eminent in its motto; it rivalled all others in its thirst for truth and adventure. We were going, if not to conquer the Alps, at least to cross them; if not to find Hannibal, at least to look for his route. We had composed dissertations on the method of search, had read through articles, books and libraries and even made notes; we avowed with scholastic modesty that we were going, not to discover the undoubted route of Hannibal, but to eliminate a few of the many unworthy candidates for that honour. We were truly a scientific expedition.

The expedition by John Foster and his co-investigators from the RGS Sixth Form was by no means the first since Polybius, but in 1958 it was something of a trail-blazer. The first modern sourcebook for Hannibal's crossing of the Alps was published in 1955, entitled *Alps and Elephants: Hannibal's March* by Sir Gavin de Beer, Director of the Natural History Museum. Then in 1956 a group from Cambridge, including John Hoyte, of whom more later, explored three possible routes: the southern route via the Col de la Traversette (2947m), the northern route via the Col du Clapier (2497m) or Mont Cenis, and an intermediate route via the Col de Mont Genèvre (1830m). Of these, the Col de la Traversette was favoured by Sir Gavin de Beer, while John Hoyte and his colleagues had concluded that the Col de Mont Genèvre (1830m) was the most likely. There were many other possibilities, and so plenty of scope for our original explorers from the RGS. The story continues,

Arrived in France and placed by the SNCF before the lower bastions of the Alps, our science faded: our expedition began to resemble the trio Don Quixote, Sancho and Rosinante and our exploits their adventures. The expedition left civilisation, Briançon and the railway station on the 16th August: five days later we discovered, thumbing our texts of Livy, that we had not only failed to find Hannibal, but had lost ourselves. Remembering that well-famed expeditions are always lost, however, we were given much encouragement and, perusing the map to find ourselves at 8000ft (2438m) and in close proximity to Italy, we were even triumphant until enveloped in the cloud of sleety snow that caused us to adopt the first three words of our motto. Thus damped and dismayed, we took refuge in a barbarian hut where we were revived by varied Gallic impotations and by recounting to ourselves the tales we would take back to England. We returned to lower heights, having assured ourselves that Hannibal did not go over that pass, the Col de la Traversette.

Wishing for no more adventures, we then crossed to Italy by the Col de Malaure with no greater inconvenience than exertion. After a day of descent we made our first valuable criticism of Livy, for of this region he observes, 'the character of the inhabitants is less wild than those above.' But it was here in a coffee house that the Expedition clashed with the Italian Army. The latter was there regaling itself when we entered and, in spite of our permit from the Prefecture de Police at Briançon, was disposed at first to treat us as Carthaginians: it was here we added the last two words to our motto. At last, when we had concluded a peace and come to a suitable arrangement with the Italian commander, we were allowed two days to retire our forces to France.

Having hurriedly recrossed the ridge of the Alps by another most desolate pass, the Col de la Croix, and after numerous other lapidary excursions, we returned to England busily converting the ramblings of Don Quixote into a scientific theory. We made much of our attempt to melt rock with vinegar and fire, and tried to deduce Hannibal's route by the position of the forests from which he would have gained fuel to satisfy his own rock-splitting caprice. With geological precision we labelled the stones stuck in the soles of our boots and attempted to imagine the wishes and whims that would have led Hannibal to use any particular pass.

By such scientific methods we audaciously claim to have eliminated at least three passes from the galaxy of pretenders to a position on the route of the greatest march in History.

Our apology for these wanderings is that of an eminent Victorian pursuer of Hannibal, William Law: 'The value of the thing pursued is not alone a test of the merit of the pursuit.'

J.C.F.

Hannibal's route over the Alps continues to attract attention: see *The Times*, 17 February 2010, *Hannibal's real Alpine trunk road to Rome is revealed* by Norman Hammond, Archaeology Correspondent. The favoured pass now seems to be the Col de la Traversette, discounted by the RGS team, though until excavations uncover the detritus of an army of 50,000, there will always be room for speculation. A comprehensive review of the Hannibal story is given by one of the current authorities, William C Mahaney, and fifteen collaborators in *Mediterranean Archaeology and Archaeometry*, Vol. 8, No.2, pp.39–54, (2008). The conclusions of the RGS Expedition never reached contemporary journals, but the study was ahead of its time.

In 1959, a Cambridge group which had carried out a reconnaissance in 1956 reconvened under the leadership of John Hoyte as the British Alpine Hannibal Expedition, and took an elephant, Jumbo, over the Col du Clapier, one of the northern routes. A member of that expedition team was Michael Hetherington. More recently Michael had joined the Old Guildfordians' Bhutan Expedition of 2008, which also included David Dunmur. Sadly, Michael Hetherington did not live to travel to Bhutan. Early in 2008 he disappeared without trace while walking in the Drakensberg Mountains.

The RGS on the Dolomites' *Via Ferrata*:
a Sixth Form CCF Expedition, Summer 2005
by James Slater

Tours and excursions at the RGS Guildford have, for me, always been full of new experiences, tough challenges and special memories. The Sixth Form Combined Cadet Force Expedition to the Dolomite Mountains in Italy was no different, and was a highlight of my school career.

Proudly dressed in our royal blue *Princess of Wales Dolomites Expedition 2005*[39] polo shirts, the team of twelve left on the last day of the academic year; for some, the last day of their school lives and to the delight of many, an absence from Swimming Sports and Final Assembly. A short flight and a minibus transfer meant that it was not long before we were seated in a pizzeria close to our campsite with our feet up and, beer in hand, seemingly unaware of how hard we were going to be pushed physically over the next ten days.

Small tents and interesting sleeping patterns meant that some were awake and ready to go by 6am the following morning. They were joined by everyone else at 7.30. There was no time to be wasted: a quick breakfast and we were off to our first *Via Ferrata*, Strobel up Punta Fiames. My first new experience was not climbing the beautiful mountains, or even clipping onto a wire, but was instead the Italian roads, or more precisely, the Italian drivers. It seems that in Italy the road lanes are only recommendations: we often found cars overtaking other cars which were overtaking other cars themselves, before ducking in at the last minute to avoid a head-on collision. It seemed I was going to fear for my life more on the road than hanging two thousand feet in the air from a wire!

First day 'blues' – learning the basic skills and becoming familiar with the surroundings – leading to slightly wayward navigating, meant that we soon found ourselves walking straight up a narrow scree slope. It was at this point that I began to wonder what I had let myself in for. Long walking days were not what I thought I had signed up to. Nevertheless, my mood brightened when we put on all our gear and started scrambling up a rock face. In an endeavour to spice up the descent, three other brave explorers and I dared to cross an immense ravine filled with dangerous beasts and complex obstacles, all requiring a combination of brains and brawn that

---

39. The CCF is attached to the Princess of Wales' Regiment.

only an RGS army cadet can muster! Meanwhile, the others took the path. After our refusal to listen to Mr Usher's desire not to go to the summit, he decided to leave us in a nearby village, some even without boots. We had to find our way back to the campsite with only a sketch-map to hand. I learned fast that the teachers were here to put us through our paces. They wanted men, not boys!

By the second day my views were confirmed that this holiday was anything but a holiday. Another early morning and another long and arduous ascent; the horrible feeling of exhaustion at the base of the climb was enough to spark a few disagreements in camp but not enough to stop us battling on. Now on the rockface of the Col Rosa, we negotiated several unprotected (no wires) obstacles, two requiring the aid of the safety rope, before reaching the first wire. The *Via Ferrata* Ettore Bovero on Col Rosa was a much more nearly vertical route than that of the previous day. Normally, climbing *Via Ferrata* is little more than a tough scramble. But on this occasion we found ourselves without footholds or handholds while climbing up a sheer face with the use of the wire in both hands and our feet flat against the rock face. Despite having thick leather gloves I began to feel the heat of the friction between my hands and the burning wire as blisters started to appear. The sense of achievement at the end of this day was immense. The mix of tiredness, cuts and bruises coupled with the view from the summit of the route we had just climbed left me with an ecstatic peace about me.

Each day it became clear that the descent brought far more joy and at times silliness than the ascent. Admittedly the descent was much quicker than the long walks up to the base of each climb, but it was more the concept of throwing myself off a mountainside, running down it out of control, and yet not hurting myself that thrilled me. Now the most popular part of our day, the idea behind scree-running was to trundle as fast as possible down a slope covered in shingle to allow your feet to sink into the scree in order to cushion your fall and just about remain under control. Scree-running, described by Mr Usher as 'my favourite bit', brought out our childish side; like little children who had just been given a new toy we charged down the mountainside. It wasn't until Mr Usher injured himself that everyone began to take things a little more slowly.

Trips like this are never the same without their mishaps and dramas; this expedition was no different. Highlights include Jono Frost falling five metres onto the wire bolt below him, narrowly missing Stuart Jackson as he fell; Gordie losing the valve for his water platypus, forcing him to drink one and a half litres while clinging to an open rock face; me proving that Motorola walkie-talkies can survive a 25ft fall onto solid rock; and more mundane matters like lost minibus keys.

Barbara was a beauty! She was striking, gentle and yet still a challenge. Her reputation went before her and we weren't going to miss out on the opportunity to climb her. Reaching the climbing spots of *Via Ferrata* Barbara well before other climbers, we had her to ourselves. The group of daring RGS explorers at the base of this climb was for once quiet as they stood in awe at the breathtaking scenery of picturesque ravines, gorges and cascading waterfalls contrasted with more gentle streams and waterholes. This beautiful place in front of me and the experiences I had had thus far meant that a moment of reflection allowed me to appreciate all that God had given to me. Barbara provided me with some of my guiding memories as well as some of our most beautiful photos from the ten days.

Our toughest climb: Tomaselli was not for the faint-hearted and certainly not for those who suffered from vertigo: a grade F *Via Ferrata*. Taking a cablecar, we started the ascent of this beast at 2800m. The guide book described the route as 'immediately airy and strenuous'. This route demanded a lot of vertical climbing and exposed traversing while offering few handholds or footholds. In many ways I found this route quite insane, perhaps because of mid-climb cable changes to exposed ledges offering 2000m drops; my heart was in my mouth on a number of occasions. We reached the summit, particularly striking in this case, and we were confronted with a breathtaking 360° panorama of the scenery. At the top I found myself standing next to a large cross, while survey-ing our beautiful world, being afforded another moment of peace and tranquillity away from the normality of Guildford, its pace of life, and exams so recently finished. It was an opportunity to reflect and ponder life's great riches once again. Having had our highest packed lunch of the week and having signed our name in the book of passing mountaineers who had made it to the top of Tomaselli, we found our way back down again. *(See Plate 68)*

These ten days afforded us the opportunity to learn many other things besides scrambling up rock faces and map-reading. Although not to my delight initially, I soon realised that, as a student soon to be embarking on life at university, it probably was a good idea and to my benefit that the teachers showed me a few culinary skills. There are only two related matters I roughly remember from the trip, however: one was how to cut an onion so that you do not end up crying; second, although still a little woozy from the dizzying heights of Tomaselli, we tucked into the nicest dinner we ate all trip, cooked and put together by our very own teachers!

After our rest day, including a history lesson about a local, collapsed dam, a bit of sunbathing and a pedalo war that resulted in a twenty euro fine for a half-sunken boat, we went in search of our next adrenaline fix: extreme mountain-biking. I am a thrill-seeker at heart, so this day's activity suited me perfectly and was certainly an appreciated change from stamina-busting ascents up the Dolomites. This day, however, saw more drama than was first expected. Everyone scrambled to reserve the best bikes while not realising that a better bike might require more skill to ride. The short tarmac route between the bike shop and the cablecar provided a chance to get accustomed to the bikes and lured many of the unsuspecting riders into a false sense of security. The first small but steep descent made us realise that the day might be slightly more difficult than expected. Braving the terrain, it soon became apparent that the teachers were getting more and more nervous, even worried, about the lack of control that we had over our bikes, particularly myself, often overconfident and quite cocky when it came to such things as extreme mountain-biking. It was again up to the teachers to temper my rather bullish approach to the slopes and varied terrain. It was amazing that I didn't have a crash! A high speed adrenaline rush, however, was what everyone was aiming for and others were not so lucky. Kieran and Gordie fell foul of a few falls, one serious enough to land Kieran in hospital, though thankfully he only needed some bandaging. *(See Plate 69)*

We managed to squeeze in another day's scrambling and on the final night, in the pizzeria where we spent so much time with beer in hand reminiscing about our incredible days, it was appropriate that both student and teachers thanked one another for a special trip and an unforgettable expedition. The trip was a huge success: new experiences enjoyed; new skills learnt and great memories forged. My thanks to Mr Usher, Mr Kerr, Mr Yetman and the team for what was for me a remarkable voyage.

The Great Find at Musk Ox Col
by Miriam Manook

The first European expedition to the Dzhungarian Alatau range of mountains in north-east Kazakhstan in the summer of 1998 had, it is fair to say, been dogged by difficulties of terrain and access to the intended unclimbed peaks. So the findings at Musk Ox Col were a spectacular, and unexpected, highlight.

Organised and led by Catherine Moorehead, with the climbing phase led by Alpine Guide Nick Parks, our illustrious party of eight sixth formers was joined by our expedition doctor and legendary mountaineer, Barney Rosedale, climber and inimitable expeditioner Sally Westmacott, veteran Central Asian explorer John Turner (now a stalwart of *Mountain Kingdoms*) and expedition artist Mark Hancock.

The aims were to explore and ascend the previously unclimbed peaks within the Dzhungarian Alatau range of mountains which form the border with the Xinjiang (Uighur) Autonomous Region of China. Having successfully arrived in Almaty, the former capital of the ninth-largest country in the world, and sampled the local delights of open-air karaoke in Panfilov Park, we loaded up with sufficient supplies (and vodka) to see us through three weeks in the mountains, the highest of which rises to Semeonov-TienShansky (4622m). We set off by bus across the steppe with our motley Kazakh back-up team.

Unknown to us, our route to Base Camp in the Baskan Valley involved the combined dramas of crossing a raging glacial meltwater river in army trucks (one of which got stuck mid-river, requiring nocturnal rescue by bulldozer); eliciting the services of the local Forestry Commission for their six-wheel-drive lorry and a night's shelter, and then, having met our Kazakh ponymen, subsequently finding our gear dumped on a hillside on the 'wrong' side of an enormous unstable boulderfield at the lower end of the valley's upper glacial lake. (The ponymen suffered their own traumas: a ring of poison round the pack-ponies to prevent attacks by bears resulted in the self-defeating death of a pony from poisoning.) Meanwhile our Heroic Leader Moorehead had narrowly avoided death by drowning during a precarious solo river crossing. Our expedition could hardly have found itself in less optimistic mood at the start of play, having established Base Camp at 2750m in the Baskan Valley.

Still, onwards and upwards. The following several days of excursions, surveying, practising our snow skills and engineering a formidable Base Camp Lavatory, not to mention the inception of entrepreneurial Kazakh-Anglo-Chinese laundry services (laundry opening times from 2.42pm onwards every day, the moment the upper glaciers' meltwater reached Base Camp), allowed us to regain hopes of high peak success.

Advance Base Camp was established after reconnaissance on the central moraines of the Baskan Glacier where climbing parties were decided upon in order to make our summit attempts. After a fantastic first ascent of Dzhambula (4292m), the spectacular snowy peak at the head of the valley, a second team set their sights on climbing Peak Semeonov-TienShansky (the highest of the range), while a further team tackled the expedition-named Peak Spudnik(4012m) on the headwall of the main glacier coming off Semeonov-TienShansky. Since the ascent of Spudnik involved crossing a fore-summit, Torrance's Top, a couple of the party had elected not to thrutch (Rosedale's word)[40] onwards to the summit but instead, having noticed some apparently wooden objects poking through the ice on the col, occupied themselves with a high-level glacial archeological dig while the remainder of the party cramponed their way up Spudnik.

This find, at what was later to be named Musk Ox Col, proved to be most extraordinary. Situated at c3900m, the col forms the China-Kazakhstan border. Indeed, expedition members who were themselves part of the dig reported that a long tongue of glacier 'like a motorway' stretched down into Xinjiang. Initially, expeditionary interest had been piqued by a piece of horn being noticed in the ice and, while the summit party went on to climb Peak Spudnik, the remainder of the team spent a couple of hours digging into the ice to a depth of approximately two metres, to reveal a hoard of animal bones, and some human artefacts. *(See Plate 70)*

Little knowing what these specimens represented, the find was brought back to the UK where they were sent for identification to the Natural History and British Museums.

The animal bone specimens were identified by Richard C Sabin, Curator of Mammal Group Division of Tetrapods and Fish at the Department of Zoology of the Natural History Museum, South Kensington. He reported that the partial mammalian mandible found on Musk Ox Col was likely that of *Equus caballus* (domestic horse) and that if it could be proven that

---

40. An obscure portmanteau term probably deriving from 'thrash' and 'clutch'(?), implying the action of progressing laboriously over difficult terrain.

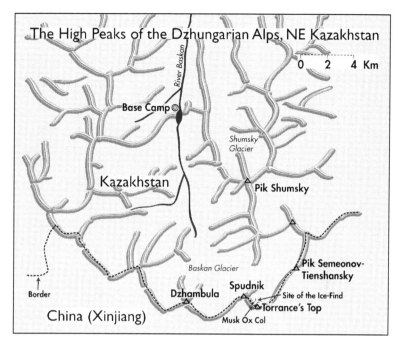

Map of the Kazakhstan-China border area and Musk Ox Col
(Redrawn by Mike Caunt, graphic designer, from an original map by Mark Hancock)

this was 'associated with other (human) remains' then it seems 'likely that a domestic horse was either being employed as a pack animal or was being ridden across the mountains (as is still the case with indigenous peoples in this region).' Meanwhile, identification of the 'single large bovid tooth' was more problematical, since it was larger than both comparable teeth from domestic cattle and domestic yak. Sabin reported that, 'Comparison with wild yak *(Bos grunniens)* dentition was far more favourable, and a closer match in terms of overall morphology.'

Unfortunately the human artefacts have yet to find themselves the object of such erudite study. They consisted of two fragments of a bow, a catapult, some pegs, an embroidered belt (left in Kazakhstan), an animal goad and two small shards of orange-coloured pottery. After initially being given to the Department of Pre-History at the British Museum, and then passed on to the Department of Western Asiatic Antiquities, they were unhelpfully proclaimed to be 'definitely Asiatic' and since wood identification as promised did not occur, they were passed on to Paul Sharphouse, a technical consultant and expert in wood. He examined the specimens visually and established that the section of bow was buckthorn *(Rhamnus spp)*; the animal goad and catapult were willow (*Salix spp*) and the second section of bow was birch (*Betula spp*). He made no assumptions about the country of origin, but all of the genera identified are found widely distributed across Europe and Asia. Interestingly, Mr Sharphouse suggested that, since the specimens all included the pith, and since the 'central region around the pith contains juvenile wood which is weaker than the outer wood…the items may have been cut for the convenience of their shape or availability rather than their strength properties.'

Truly the ice find at Musk Ox Col does represent a fascinating and unfinished story. One theory proposed by Catherine Moorehead is that a refugee from the Chinese side in a Dzhungarian war believed to have been fought about 300 years ago died with his pack-animals when trying to find a shortcut into safety in Kazakhstan. The descent from Musk Ox Col (which should now of course be re-named Wild Yak Col) would be difficult, perhaps impossible, for animals, assuming the ice and snow were roughly in the same condition as at present. The ascent from the Chinese side would be laborious but rather more feasible. Certainly, the glacier expeditioners agreed that the approach from the Chinese side constituted a 'motorway' of a route. Since there is an easier valley route into Kazakhstan, however, one which could be seen from our higher summits if one continued westwards, the traveller crossing Musk Ox Col must have at the very least been unfamiliar with the geography of the area, and therefore possibly fleeing from civil unrest. And he might have been caught out in a storm, to die of exposure and hypothermia with his animals as he was unable to flee any further.

Unfortunately, more accurate carbon dating of the find required more resources than the end of the expedition could muster and although valiant fundraising efforts were made by the late Rev Hereward Cooke, father of expedition member Frances Cooke, it has never been possible to write the final chapter of this curious story.

What is, however, clear is that the scope of mountaineering expeditions is not confined merely to the ascent of surrounding physical peaks, but also to an exploration of the geography and history of an area and the lingering sense that, however exciting our opening-up of the Baskan Valley was, and however fraught with difficulty our journey to get there seemed, at some point centuries ago on a windswept icy col, another traveller, caught out by the all too frequent squalls we could attest to, looked down onto that selfsame valley.

Scouting for Girls?

by Colin Carmichael

Iceland (1970)

The RGS Scouts became adventurous in 1970. That summer, a small group went on a two week trip to Iceland. Unfortunately, the memory plays funny tricks. I remember very little about the trip, apart from the name Kirsten Portstendóttir. She was one of a small group of local girls whom we chatted to outside the Youth Hostel in Reykjavik. She must have seemed like a rare and exotic creature to a hormonal sixteen-year old for me to have remembered her name after so many years.

The trip was mainly about hiking, staying in tents and mountain huts, around remote parts of Iceland. At weekends the huts were visited by locals on their traditional 'benders', arriving in beaten-up 4x4s under the pretext of herding sheep back to the city and providing excellent role models for the impressionable RGS Scouts. We also did some sightseeing, including the impressive waterfall at Gullfoss; I remember being very surprised at the lack of barriers and health and safety equipment.

The trip gave me a life-long love of Iceland; I have been back several times. On the first trip I walked through the remote interior, through glacial meltwater streams and past hot water bubbling from the ground, the atmosphere permeated by the smell of sulphurous gases. On another occasion, I drove in a 4x4 from south to north, through a desert of black volcanic dust, following posts in the ground rather than roads, and fording rivers. Iceland is a great place for getting away from it all. The mountain huts are still pretty basic, although many have spectacular views and natural hot pools outside, where you bathe in warm water while staring up at the stars and drinking cold beer. Drunken Icelanders with their strange habits, including eating dried cod with margarine and supporting Burnley FC (I recall a passionate conversation during a recent trip about where it all went wrong for the mighty Clarets in the 1970s) still visit at the weekends.

North Cape (1972): Are we nearly there yet?

A trend had been started. Two years later the Scouts travelled to the North Cape, near enough the northernmost point of Europe. The Scout Group had raised enough money to buy a 'people carrier' – what was then called a 'van'. It was green and very uncomfortable, loaded to the gunnels and with a rather rickety roof-rack covered in groundsheets. The trip involved taking the ferry from Newcastle to Gothenburg and then driving up through Sweden, a bit of Finland and then Norway (over 1000 miles of straight roads and pine trees). The trip was led by 'Dickie' Dawkes, our senior PE teacher.

Yet again the memory plays tricks but several vignettes will hopefully capture the essence of the trip.

I was the 'quartermaster' and had to buy the expedition food. I remember it being bagged up into individual portions lined up on the floor at home. This would now be called 'work experience' and would probably be the ideal preparation for a career in logistics or fast food.

We collected mosquitoes on behalf of the Ministry of Agriculture and Fisheries in Guildford. Why? Because they gave us a small amount of sponsorship money. Apparently, Sweden and Norway had plenty of the little blighters, because of the continuous melting and re-freezing of the layer above the permafrost. I remember sucking 'mozzies' up a plastic tube into a bottle in the dim glow of the van headlights. I never discovered what happened to those I didn't swallow.

We drove like madmen to get to the North Cape to see the midnight sun, only to be defeated by the weather. When we got there, the sun was obscured by clouds. It was another thirty years before I saw the midnight sun.

Finally, I was very disappointed by my first sight of reindeer. They were rather mangy specimens, who were obviously struggling to survive on a diet of lichen, being minded by disconsolate looking Lapps. The romance of the wild?

The trip was fantastic fun. The Scouts had once again enthused me with a love of travel and of messing about in the great outdoors.

A Day Out on Lyngmarksfjeld (Western Greenland)
by Tom Fulda

At a latitude of 69° 15′ and with a population of about eight hundred, Godhavn is the largest settlement on the island of Disko, just off the west coast of Greenland. Both island and settlement are now correctly known as Qeqertarsuaq, literally translated as 'the large island'. The island itself covers approximately eight thousand square kilometres and is characterised by basalt mountains rising steeply from sea level to plateau with permanent ice-cap, reaching altitudes of 1500m.

I visited a Danish cousin there in July 1983. For the first few days the weather was variable, with plenty of low cloud but also some sunny intervals. We familiarised ourselves, often late into the evening or overnight, with the locality. At this latitude the midnight sun continues until July 24: it was commonplace to come across groups of young adults chatting and socialising in the surrounding countryside at 2 or 3am. Even at that time of day it never felt cold when there was a clear sky. Despite an overnight ground-frost in shaded areas it was comfortable to walk around in just a T-shirt because of the dryness of the air.

On July 18, the weather was glorious. We seized the opportunity to climb Lyngmarksfjeld, which rises directly from sea level and looms above the settlement. The lower reaches are covered with a rich variety of tundra vegetation that thrives in the microclimate of the south-facing slope. Higher up, however, this vegetation rapidly diminishes to reveal bare scree beneath towering cliffs of crumbling red basalt. There are no paths, marked or otherwise: clearly this was not the route for us. Instead, a route was found up a small steep valley between the cliff face of Lyngmarksfjeld and the adjacent Apostelfjeld. *(See Plate 71)*

Though steep, the going was good, initially. Underfoot was dry because of the porous nature of the rock. We skirted round the remaining snowfields and after a couple of hours rested at about 600m. By now we were well inland but looking down the valley between the two mountains we could see the sea, dotted with an assortment of icebergs glistening in the distance. From here the going was harder. It became more exposed and involved scrambling up steep, loose and friable rock. There was nothing solid to hold on to so we angled our way slowly upwards, back towards the cliff edge overlooking the settlement. After twenty to thirty minutes the going eased

269

off as we approached the plateau. A short distance behind the cliff-face the plateau has a permanent icecap which rises gradually to over 1000m, but we had neither the desire nor the equipment for tackling this. At the cliff edge, however, the height is only about 700m. This was our target.

From here the view was simply breathtaking in all directions. To the north, the gently ascending slopes of the icecap were a dazzling white. East of us, the glacier valley of Blæsedalen stretched northward into the distance. Beyond Blæsedalen is the nearby mounded peak of Skarvefjeld. But the air was clear and looking further beyond could be seen Illulissat Ice Fjord far away on the horizon, a distance of sixty miles. This massive glacier drains seven per cent of the entire Greenland ice-sheet and, moving at an average of twenty miles each day, calves enormous icebergs into Disko Bay. Turning to the south, we could see the expanse of Disko Bay with icebergs dispersing westwards. Beneath us the settlement stretched out, houses dotted among the barren rocks in a disorderly fashion. Out to the west, icebergs disappeared into the distant expanse of the Davis Strait, towards Baffin Island three hundred and fifty miles away. In the calm warmth of that sunny afternoon, with barely a breath of wind, we sat down and absorbed every detail from this panoramic viewpoint. *(See Plate 72)*

And then it was time to go. In our exhilaration we virtually ran down the mountainside, retracing our ascent route until we reached the lower slopes. There was obviously no rush to descend before sunset so we took a longer route, finishing at the base of the mountain by some springs surrounded by bright green moss and a great variety of flowering plants blooming in the short summer season. I don't remember exactly how long it took us to return: it seemed like a fraction of our ascent, but I do clearly remember what we had for supper that night. Whale curry using meat from an animal the locals had caught a couple of days earlier was on the menu. We tucked in heartily.

Certainly not the hardest climb I have ever made but without question one of the most memorable.

Pulking on Svalbard[41]

by Richard Payne

Our aim was to climb Newtontoppen during the summer holidays. At 1717m it is one of Svalbard's highest peaks. It lies on the main island just 500km from the North Pole. We all realised that it would be an ambitious undertaking in the time available.

We were transported by inflatable boats to Skottehytte with enough food, fuel and equipment to last for twenty days. Then, carrying heavy awkward loads, we set off up Ebbadalen towards the Ebbabreen glacier to stack a series of food dumps.

It took three days to get all our equipment above the snowline. The going was generally good but with heavy loads it was taken slow and easy. The snowline lay at about 450m on the southern side of Bastionfjellet; we resisted using the new pulks[42] until past the 500m contour to preserve their lives at the cost of constantly asking, 'When will we start pulling them instead of carrying them?' *(See Plate 73)*

After a morning spent with the final load carry we started 'pulking'. An hour later, we made camp, having proved to ourselves that all the kit worked. We also explored a crevasse with some fantastic ice formations.

We spent the next morning practising ice-axe arrest training on the west flank of Bastionfjellet, and that evening set off with all fourteen of us pulling pulks around its north-west shoulder, and then contouring as much as possible in a north-east direction for about four hours. The snow conditions were not good and the pulks had to be dragged through soggy wet snow. This was particularly tough on the students, as they began to realise how difficult the journey was possibly going to be. To their credit we did cover 9kms, but at the expense of our collective sense of humour! *(See Plate 74)*

We camped about 3km south of Slatertoppane at 900m and slept through the rest of the night. Conditions next day were poor and, after making a food dump for our return, we set off in very limited visibility. This deteriorated to the point where we were following a bearing in high winds, barely able to see more than 100 metres ahead. After only 3kms we had to stop and put up tents at the 1000m contour.

---

41. Formerly Spitsbergen.

42. Pulks: sledges suited to Arctic travel.

Thirty-six hours later the storm cleared at about 2am and we found ourselves in bright sunshine, with all the tents and equipment covered in verglas. We were wandering about after going 'tent crazy', taking photos and then returning to sleeping-bags for a few more hours' sleep! By now we had started to lose track of time and days but the rest had done the trick. We headed due north, making excellent time in perfect conditions over newly frozen snow, across the high ridge of Lomonosovfonna to 1255m. The descents were a nightmare, however, as we had to tow the pulks with rope instead of metal traces: we were dragged left, right and centre; there was also disappointment at not being allowed to sledge downhill on them! After some 11kms we camped at 1100m, 2kms south of Saturnfjellet. More perfect weather and snow conditions helped us continue next day between Titan- and Tethysfjellets to another awkward descent. *(See Plate 75)*

The views, in clear blue skies, were incredible as we travelled north-east down Keplerbreen, with 360° views of untouched snow peaks. We headed for our next camp, an oasis of rock called Elpet where we stayed for twenty-four hours. There we were fortunate to be able to watch a partial eclipse of the sun, and also made meteorological observations and recorded snow samples before breaking camp to get a little closer to Newtontoppen.

We covered about 5kms that evening, then camped at approximately 79° latitude close to Hookfjellet. Next day was 'summit day': we left early in glorious sunshine with just day-packs. Roped up, we snowshoed up a series of gentle snow ramps to a rocky viewpoint at 1500m where we had lunch. The final 200m of ascent was steeper but we made good time to the summit under perfect blue skies and with limitless views stretching from the island's northern shores to the south and to Longyearbyen.

The descent back to camp gave us some further amazing views. On the way, some Young Explorers asked to 'bivvy out', which we all (some very reluctantly) did having dug 'snow graves' on one of the coldest nights! Next morning some YEs were amazed that we were all still alive; others were just unimpressed and miserable about their 'experience from hell': for others, it was 'the best thing so far!' *(See Plate 76)*

As we retraced out route up Keplerbreen we noticed two sets of baby polar bear tracks, which broke the monotony of the journey especially as we kept looking around for the mother bear! We turned south around Tethysfjellet and returned to the food dump near Saturnfjellet.

Next day we tried to find a new route past Uranusfjellet and in the afternoon in poor visibility entered the 'crevasse field from hell'. We zigzagged over flat ground until Clare, who was second on her rope, disappeared out of sight into a crevasse: in fact only her pulk was visible above ground!

As the second rope moved to assist, Alison also partially disappeared and then Dave went up to his waist on the third rope! We spent three hours going nowhere and eventually in very poor visibility turned round and retreated back past Uranusfjellet; but at least our initial crevasse rescue training had paid off!

We were exhausted, and slept late; in fact very late, into the next day, then dragged the pulks at 'night' with the temperature dropping and weather coming in behind us, while heading for our next food dump. We moved quickly up onto a high ridge: once at 1100m with a bitter wind behind us we averaged 5.5kms per hour until visibility dropped to a few metres and the temperature without wind-chill fell to -5°C. We made it to the dump just before the storm hit and then spent another thirty-six hours in the tents, this time as veterans of doing nothing but sleeping and eating! (Paddy ate 9000 calories in one go and then, while others slept, watched it all come up again!)

Next day, we had to dig the tents out and deal with the substantial drifts covering our equipment. We then headed off south-east towards Base Camp, while still trying to keep to the flatter high ground. The visibility worsened again and the temperature dropped as we witnessed 'diamond dust' and other optical effects created by the sun over Flemmingfjellet. We were now well-versed in rapid tent deployment and again, having arrived just in time, we had to sit out another stormy night.

On the following morning half the group took weather and snow recordings while the 'boys' built an excellent traditional four-person igloo with properly cut and shaped snow blocks. Yet again it was overheard that, 'this was the best day so far!'

As we set off on a bearing in yet another day of poor visibility, we entered a period of 'navigational embarrassment' which led us down the wrong side of the Terrierfjellet *nunatak*; two hours later we had returned to the correct point! Here we saw foreign footprints for the first time in over two weeks and so we knew that we were nearing the end. Our descent onto the lower glacier was slowed as Cecily vomited her porridge onto the snow. Having just packed up the tents, we put them up again so she could sleep until she felt better. As we had only one day's food left we eventually had to push on and towed her pulk behind another (which was both interesting and challenging over some rough ice ridges and streams).

We managed to continue dragging the pulks (having changed out of snowshoes and into crampons) all the way to the end of the ice, where we made our last camp just before the moraine. The site was less than ideal but many were tired and we needed to rest before carrying everything over the terminal moraine and down to the shore.

Next morning, we hauled everything onto our backs and made for the beach where we left everything except our personal kit and tents, to be collected by the boat team. The final few kilometres were an easy stroll compared to the last three weeks of pulling, pushing, dragging, lifting and generally tortuous manhandling at times, for over 160kms!

The expedition had been a challenge for the whole group, the leaders included. Many had said it was 'too ambitious' but this just fired up the students to prove them wrong. Never underestimate what teenagers are capable of doing if they set their minds on it! They have to be pushed, sometimes pushed very hard and often deliberately placed in difficult circumstances, beyond the point of mental comfort, in order to achieve the most gratifying results. At the end, one student was overheard saying, 'Right, now I feel about as personally developed as I will ever be!'

A Sojourn in the Falkland Islands
by David Benest

Until March 1982 I cannot say that I knew very much about the South Atlantic. I recall an article in *The Guardian* suggesting that the Falkland Islands might soon be invaded by Argentine troops and mentioned it to a close friend, whose response was dismissive. I rejoined my Battalion and set off to Central America where the independent country of Belize was under threat from Guatemala. We were to remain there for six months to prevent such an occurrence.

The invasion of the Falklands duly took place on 1 April and we were soon summoned home. I received a call asking if I could train the Battalion on the new radio – I was Signals Officer – and I said we could, not realising at the time that not a single set was allowed to be switched on until we landed in East Falkland. I did not think that a war was very likely, made my own appreciation that we would be sitting on South Georgia for some time and thus packed all my snow- and ice-climbing kit in anticipation of some interesting times, having already spent two seasons in the Alps. How wrong!

The Falklands are topographically rather similar to the Western Isles. I only managed to get to East Falkland. From landing at San Carlos, I walked to Goose Green, flew to Bluff Cove and Fitzroy, flew again up to Bluff Cove Peak and then walked into Stanley. The terrain varies considerably between the hills around San Carlos: in our case, Sussex Mountain, the billiard ball flatness of the Goose Green isthmus and then the ridge of peaks all the way to Stanley, dominated by Argentine-held features such as Mount Kent, Sapper Hill, Twin Sisters, Mount Longdon, Tumbledown and Wireless Ridge. All of these had been held by Argentine conscripts since early April as the South Atlantic winter worsened. Poor administration and the cold gave rise to a steady number of corpses piled up at Sapper Hill beside the track, to be disposed of either by being dumped at sea or as target practice for napalm attack by the pilots of the Pucara, a slow flying but very effective counterinsurgency aeroplane.

Landing at San Carlos on the night of 21 May was a fiasco. My landing craft (LCU) was meant to have been third ashore after the lead assault companies. In fact it went in first as we alone had on board radar that could locate the kelp, or seaweed. Thus did war begin, back to front and with a fuming Commanding Officer, Lieutenant-Colonel H Jones, who to my own consternation, had broken radio silence to let everyone know how he felt about the matter.

The approach to Sussex Mountain was hard work as we all carried everything that we could in bergens[43] weighing well over 100 pounds. We were all soaked to the waist during the landings, and casualties were already mounting from exposure. Dawn on Sussex Mountain was beautifully clear, as had been the night sky in the southern hemisphere, with low pass satellites overhead, to which I waved, rather optimistically. As I looked down the valley I could see our first enemy aircraft, a Pucara, on its way to recce the landings. It soon was no longer, as the first operational use of STINGER by the SAS patrol ahead took effect by downing the aircraft while the pilot landed safely by parachute. But we were to experience almost incessant air attacks for the next twenty-five days.

Sussex Mountain was something of a misnomer, more like part of Dartmoor and with climate and terrain to match. It was largely boggy, with a high water-table which ensured that digging in was like digging a pond for one's feet. I shared a trench (I dug in about six times altogether) with the adjutant, David Wood, later to be killed at Goose Green. We were lucky in that our ''ole' was dry, and sheltered us from the incessant wind, sleet, snow and rain. I still have the photograph to prove that I was not born bald and that one could survive a wash and shave stripped to the waist, Swedish style.

Marching south towards Goose Green was tough on the ankles, given the tussocks and darkness. More casualties arose, especially among those with heavier loads, my signallers included. We piled into the farm buildings at Camilla Creek House to get out of the wind and cold: I recall about twelve of us trying to stay warm in a tiny shed. The BBC World Service announcement that come the dawn we were about to attack Goose Green led to a rapid evacuation into the stubbly grass around the abandoned settlement. In the meantime, patrols, both of which were seen and fired on, had been sent forward so as to recce Goose Green itself, forcing them to withdraw in haste.

The night battle was to be in our favour as the Argentine conscripts were reluctant to offer any real resistance on a completely dark night. But the time allowed to capture the settlements was hopelessly optimistic. Dawn changed everything: now the enemy had all the cards in his favour;

---

43. A type of military rucksack. Ed.

he was able to pin our two lead companies down for several hours, during which time the CO attempted his own charge and was mortally wounded. I briefed a helicopter pilot to go and get him out after the vital ground, Darwin Hill, had eventually been taken (nobody tasked to do so initially) but the helicopter was shot down and the pilot killed in front of me, by which time H Jones was dead as well. Movement in such an open and exposed landscape would be met with lethal force; the only answer was to remain in cover and use any available firepower to best effect. But with high crosswinds, and given the closeness of the enemy, most indirect supporting fire was out of the question. Direct fire support weapons ultimately prevailed and the billiard table battles moved on apace.

It was fortunate that the enemy had been convinced by now that they were facing a brigade attack and that Goose Green was on the main axis of the British breakout from San Carlos, when in fact it was but a diversion, revved up by 2 PARA. The capitulation and occupation of Goose Green soon followed, with questions remaining to this day as to how and why so many lives were lost for an objective that was militarily of no significance. Goose Green's only role was as a base for a flight of Pucaras, all of which had been destroyed by Harriers before the landings. Now 1200 prisoners of war were in need of reception, feeding, medical treatment and evacuation to Argentina.

In the meantime, on the day of the battle, 3 Commando Brigade was on the move towards Stanley on the northern route, the two divided by a ridge line that was more or less impenetrable. We quickly realised that on the south side, the enemy had kindly left and that the route to Stanley was thus open. Brigadier Tony Wilson was persuaded that an advance on foot with 2 PARA picketing the heights was something of a waste of time. Options for moving forward to Bluff Cove and Fitzroy were: go in the only surviving Chinook, call sign 'BN', (eighty men at a time, standing room only, just like the rush hour in London); by landing craft, as did the Scots Guards; or by logistic landing ship (LSL) into Fitzroy Harbour, as did the Welsh Guards. Fortunately, the locals at Goose Green had sabotaged their coastal freighter, but were quickly able to restore it to use. They offered to bring all our supplies forward at night on condition that the vessel would not remain in Fitzroy harbour in daylight, given that it was overlooked by enemy positions on Mount Harriet to the north-east. For reasons that remain unexplained, the LSLs *Tristram* and *Galahad* remained in the harbour in daylight. We watched as Skyhawks attacked very low and fast, with direct hits on the vessels, leading to the deaths of around fifty Welsh Guardsmen and many more seriously wounded. We did our best to assist with the casualty evacuation but the Guards were finished as a fighting force.

Being ordered to return under command of the Commando Brigade was something of a relief after the bombing of the ships in the harbour. We were most grateful to find ourselves in reserve behind 3 PARA, destined to take Mount Longdon that night. The terrain had completely altered, with granite peaks all around which, when combined with harassing fire from the Argentine 155mm artillery, provided a lethal cocktail of artillery and rock fragments. We had been treated to some fresh lamb while at Bluff Cove and this in turn had its effect on the digestive system, resulting in soldiers dropping out of the line of march in the darkness to attend to nature's call, white arctic underwear dropped in the process. How undignified an end to be 'caught with your trousers down'!

But the terrain also provided safety from the shelling and an adroit company commander steered us into a 'safe zone' at Furze Bush Pass, where we were able to rest for about twenty-four hours before our next battle, though without sleeping-bags. With our useless barrack boots, nearly all those ashore were later diagnosed with permanent cold injuries to toes and fingers, myself included.

Our second battle was for Wireless Ridge, a featureless morass of ponds, bogs and peat hags, the latter fortunately providing much welcome safety from 'incomers', but not the bombs from aircraft, which were still being dropped right up until the final moments of the war.

By dawn, Stanley was in sight and we hastened thither, wishing to claim that we were not only first ashore but first into Stanley. We were ordered to halt at what turned out to be the Argentine Air Force Officers Mess, now the Stanley Museum, which was the perfect location for Battalion HQ, not least in that it was well-stocked with brandy!

So ends the story of how not to go climbing on South Georgia. I fell in love with the terrain of the Falklands and 'enjoyed' my return in 2008, many years later, although it became a very strong emotional experience. The weather is just like Northern Ireland or Scotland: four seasons in a day. The people are as friendly as one could wish for. I never saw my snow- and ice-gear again: I suspect it is now many fathoms below the South Atlantic. I have never returned to snow- and ice-climbing, much preferring ski-mountaineering in lieu – but that's another story!

Camlough Mountain (Northern Ireland)
by David Benest

I began my exploration of Irish hills at the age of sixteen, while still at the RGS. I took the ferry from Holyhead to Dun Laoghaire, then hitched through southern Ireland to the Macgillycuddy's Reeks, climbed its highest mountain, Carrantuohill, and subsequently rested in a youth hostel below in Silent Valley. I recall walking back over a pass and meeting horse-drawn jaunting cars, usually occupied by overweight American tourists in search of their 'roots' and Irish identity. I did not then realise just how many US citizens were actively supporting a campaign of terrorism against the British further north.

I first visited Northern Ireland as a nineteen-year old subaltern in The Parachute Regiment, having completed my A levels at the RGS before moving on to Sandhurst, my place at Queen's University Belfast to read Geography having been denied for domestic reasons: these were the days when eighteen-year olds were deemed fit to fight but not to live financially independent from their elders.

South Armagh is a beautiful place, dominated by the twin hilltops of Slieve Gullion and Camlough Mountain. As a 'new' subaltern I was under command of my sergeant, Bob Holmes, whose opinion of me was rarely flattering, until he lost his way on a mobile patrol near Newry. Map-reading and orienteering in the CCF at the RGS paid off at last.

We patrolled the local area so as to deter terrorism, which in South Armagh had been rife for decades. For me, the ascent of Slieve Gullion and Camlough Mountain was the icing on the cake, a sheer joy, although the locals were unable to speak with us for fear of PIRA retribution.

I returned to this part of Northern Ireland on several occasions, in 1979, 1980, 1996 and 1997. Numerous patrols and ambushes were par for the course on each occasion, the death toll from terrorist attack a constant, most notably at Warrenpoint on 27 August 1979 when we lost more soldiers to PIRA in a two phase attack than we were to lose in the Falklands War at Goose Green and Wireless Ridge. In addition, I was technical sponsor for Counter Terrorism in the MOD from 1986–9, 1993–4 and 1999–2002, so visits to South Armagh were a regular feature of my life.

In South Armagh we carried out a programme of technical measures that would both deny the use of Improvised Explosive Devices (IEDs) as well as overt and covert surveillance in our attempt to outmanoeuvre the terrorist Active Service Units (ASUs). Both worked, and I think our contribution to the ending of this longest of all British counterinsurgency campaigns – it lasted from 1969 to 2007 – was a vital ingredient. There were amusing aspects to all this, not least the brigadier who summoned me to his office demanding to know what we had done to his regimental yacht, holed and sunk by a Royal Navy submarine periscope, I think – not me guv! Obtaining 'kit' was relatively easy, most senior officers being not too keen on knowing what we were up to and thus giving a free hand to a young major prepared to spend taxpayers' money very quickly in reaction to immediate operational requirements.

My final tour of duty in South Armagh was based at Bessbrook Mill, precisely where I had begun in 1973. I embarked upon '3D' operations, something I had perfected in West Belfast as a company commander. In essence, the aim was to deploy in such a manner that foot patrols, mobiles, static Observation Posts (OPs) and heliborne 'top cover' worked in synchronisation, thus creating a security 'bubble' within which PIRA could not operate with impunity.

It worked, up to a point. After nearly six months of no attacks, and in the knowledge that PIRA was 'losing', they realised our weakness. Camlough Mountain dominated Bessbrook, around which we had a ring of vehicle check points (VCPs). On top of Camlough Mountain was one of my MOD projects, SALIENT, a manned OP equipped with some very powerful surveillance devices, overlooking Bessbrook and providing vital safety over-watch. But there was an evergreen tree between the OP and the check point which PIRA exploited by parking its sniper vehicle in its lee, thus obscured from R13, as the OP was configured.

Lance Bombardier Stephen Restorick was on duty on the evening of 12 February 1997, politely checking vehicles through, when the sniper opened fire, using a Barratt 0.5 inch sniper rifle, imported from the USA, at a range of about 200 metres, fatally wounding Restorick as he was dealing with a local female resident's driving licence. Restorick died soon after, the last soldier to have been murdered in Northern Ireland until the Good Friday Agreement.

The Secretary of State, Sir Patrick Mayhew, arrived the following morning and I showed him the scene. I demanded of the police that they, not the British Army, should be involved in the checking of civilians, allowing us to do what we were good at, patrolling the rural areas in depth around

Camlough Mountain, so as to prevent further action from the sniper team. I also demanded that the tree be felled, thus allowing direct vantage form R13. All these requests were denied, much to my frustration. The news on Ulster Television that tragic evening that it was thought that Restorick had accidentally shot himself led to a rapid conversation between myself and the Director of Programmes, Allan Bremner, a personal friend, who stated that UTV was merely repeating the statement issued by the police. The police in turn denied that they had ever given such a false statement to UTV. I had no reason to disbelieve Allan on the matter, every reason not to trust the RUC, whose record of misinformation was by then legendary.

Camlough Mountain is now at peace, the OP removed, as have all OPs that dominated South Armagh since the late 1980s and served a real purpose in minimising loss of life. Yet the threat of terrorist violence continues to this day to haunt South Armagh, regardless of the Good Friday Agreement and with no deterrent in the form of the OP on Camlough Mountain.

The Real Dracula's Castle[44]

by Jeff Rawson

They say that good things come to those who wait, and perhaps this should be the hill-walker's most consoling maxim. The climb in our case had been a hard one, frequently lacking any proper path as we moved through the stifling heat and high grasses, and only exacerbated by our wholly inadequate stock of equipment or supplies. Apparently boating shoes are no substitute for hiking boots, nor wine for water. Still, we consoled ourselves, with about another one hundred metres to go, that the summit really was in sight, and that food and shelter had been left only a couple of hours behind us. Yet, it had been approaching three weeks since we set out from home, and we had travelled well over a thousand miles – the width of a continent – in order to arrive at this point in time and place.

The time had been the glorious July after completing our A Levels, and the place was none other than the Carpathian Mountains, deep in the heart of Transylvania. Yes, we had paid homage to Dracula's Castle, contemplated the presence of wolves and bears, albeit briefly, and even entertained the fantasy of dark, windswept peaks brooding beneath the pale glow of a full moon. The reality however, unsurprisingly, could not have been farther from the cliché as the ground finally levelled out and we drank in our surroundings. The three of us had watched together as entire countries slipped past the windows of railway carriages; had gazed from out the tops of cathedrals over the capitals of Europe; had sat and watched the sun rise behind the Brandenburg Gate, and seen it slowly set over the blue Danube; yet nothing could compare with the truly breathtaking sight before us now.

Below were green undulating hills of farmland, scored by small villages and the single ribbon of dusty road which ran between them. Rising from these, through densely wooded forests, were the majestic mountains which lay about the horizon, quiet and slumbering in the blue afternoon heat. Indeed, at this height the only sense of energy or movement came from the wisps of cloud that flowed, trailed and silently caught the crest of a nearby ridge. Perhaps the only thing harder than climbing hills or mountains

---

44. The castle in question is a ruin lying at the end of a narrow ridge high above a forested and craggy gorge deep in the Romanian Carpathians. It is not Bran Castle, near Brasov, which is where all the tourist coaches end up. Ed.

is ultimately, however, attempting to relate that invariably intimate and astonishing experience to anyone else. All I will say is that after all the talking, all the joking, all the debating, and even all the arguing of our long European adventure, all three of us fell largely silent for the first time; perhaps sensing that this was the truly special moment we would all remember, and had shared together.

We obviously were not the only ones who thought the place touching and memorable either, testified to by a wrought-iron cross which had been erected on a particular outcrop, quietly facing the sun and all that unfenced existence for an unknowable number of years now. Indeed, perhaps it is precisely the freedom of the indefinite vistas, of the sense of infinite earth meeting an infinite sky, at once so humbling and so sublime, which is the appeal that lies at the heart of all hill-walking. Certainly, it was one that was brought home to me by the experiences of a RumDoodle Society expedition to Torridon, in the more familiar Scottish Highlands, and has only continued to grow. It also might explain why this year the three of us will be travelling to Europe again – but this time to leave behind all the stifling culture it has to offer, and to head straight to the Pyrenees, and straight to the freedom of the mountain passes.

The Leith Hill Adventure
by Ian Barker and David Dunmur

'Oscar Charlie-one, to control, over.'
'Come in, Oscar Charlie-one.'
'Oscar Charlie-one to control, where are we?'
'Control to OC1: we have no idea, get a torch and look at the map.'
'OC1 to control: the torch battery has failed; we are surrounded by trees and have lost the track.'
'Control to OC1: walk in a straight line until you hit a road. Then find a signpost and call again.'
'OC1 to control: message received and understood, over and out.'

There was a sort of apartheid between the Scouts and the CCF: the Scouts wore short trousers and the CCF had guns. But many in the CCF, though despising the Scouts at school, were in fact secret members of the Scouts in their home towns and villages. Apart from the shooting, most activities of the Scouts and CCF were directed towards common aims: self-confidence, self-reliance, basic survival skills and the ability to navigate across open country. These skills were picked up from various training sessions, ranging from the benign weekly meetings to the variously tedious, challenging or downright dangerous Field Days, Wide Games and Night Manoeuvres. Very occasionally the Scouts and the CCF would combine in joint operations which always involved the capture by stealth of some enemy outpost. One such was the Leith Hill Adventure.

The event was a night hike, well-practised within the separate organizations, but unusual as a combined exercise. The plan was to hike in pairs from Guildford and capture the highest point in Surrey, Leith Hill (294m, almost a mountain!), a distance as the crow flies of about ten miles, but more like fifteen miles following paths and tracks over the Surrey Hills. Each team consisted of a senior scout and an experienced signaller. Between them they carried essentials for their nutrition and warmth, and a bulky and temperamental ex-WWII radio. This object, weighing at least twenty pounds, was carried like a rucksack on the back of one of the team while operated by the other, both people being connected by wired headphones and microphone. The darkness and rough ground during the hike posed significant challenges to the operators because of the precarious aerial reception and transmission.

Memory, vague that it is at this distance in time, recalls a quiet chilly night for the operation, but absolutely pitch black – it must have been a new moon. David was the leader of the expedition and Ian the leader of the signallers. As darkness fell, ten or so teams set off up to Pewley Down and east over Newlands Corner, then followed separate routes across the Surrey hills of Hurtwood Common before passing the hamlets of Abinger and Holmbury St Mary. The boys supposedly kept in touch by radio.

The countryside between Guildford and Leith Hill is largely wooded, but with stretches of open country covered with bracken and scrub. There are plenty of footpaths, but in the days before trail markers it was very easy to be diverted from the intended route. In daylight this was not usually a problem, and a compass bearing would keep one on the straight and narrow, or winding, track. At night things were not so easy, especially if there was no moon. Have you ever tried taking a compass bearing in the dark? Not only is it hard to identify an objective: even if you get a bearing it is almost impossible for a team of two to follow the bearing. Walking by torchlight was not an option, and in any case the operation was meant to be covert. GPS and night vision glasses had still to be invented.

Local knowledge was invaluable in route-finding across the rough terrain. It was a fortunate pair that included a member of the cross-country team, since training runs of up to fifteen miles over the North Downs and Surrey Hills were part of the team's preparation for competitive events. Both David and Ian were members of the cross country team, from which probably derived the perverse inspiration for the night hike. Except that places and tracks looked very unfamiliar at night.

With twenty-plus young men distributed over about twenty square miles of wild Surrey countryside in the dark, it was recognized that people would almost certainly get lost, hence the need for radio communication. The range and effectiveness of the radios were limited. As leaders of the operation, Ian and David, following their own route, tried to keep in touch with the various teams, so there was at least some chance of returning to Guildford with the same number of boys who had set out.

The radio crackled into life….

'Oscar Charlie-one to control, over.'
'Control to Oscar Charlie-one, come in.'
'Oscar Charlie-one to control. We have reached a road and found a signpost at a three-way junction. It says: Peaslake 3, Forest Green 5 and Holmbury St Mary 1, over.'

285

'Control to OC1. You are at the foot of Holmbury Hill about two miles due west of your objective. Can you see your map? Over.'

'OC1 to control. No – the torch battery failed and then we dropped the torch in a stream. We have just been able to read the signpost by climbing up it and lighting matches, over.'

'Control to OC1. Listen very carefully. Take the road pointing to Holmbury St Mary; after about 400 yards there will be an entrance on the right past some buildings. Take this track and follow the path east for about 500 yards going downhill. You should come to another road. Turn left or north on the road and take the continuation footpath to the east, which leaves the road after about 200 yards. Follow this uphill, cross one further road, and your objective looms above you. Best of luck; it will be getting light in an hour. Over and out.'

It goes without saying that all participants demonstrated their own resourcefulness, and indeed many had come prepared for the challenges with extra aids for the operation. Ian's contribution to the night's success was marrow rum! Ian had spent several months collecting the drops of amber liquid that slowly emerged from a hole in the base of a vertically supported marrow from which the seeds and central pith had been removed and replaced with brown sugar and a little water. The addition of more sugar was a frequent ritual and the precariously supported marrow occupied an inconveniently prominent place in the small pantry of his home kitchen. Parents tolerated this, but only just! The resulting liquid, no more than a few ounces, was carried by Ian in his grandfather's First World War hipflask, and provided fortification and sustenance throughout the long night.

The overnight struggle took its toll. Tiredness and poor route-finding meant that not all the teams reached the Leith Hill objective. Despite, or perhaps because of the marrow rum, Ian and David did reach the summit in the early hours of the morning just before light. As dawn broke it was necessary to round up all the participants from their final resting places: Ian was found sleeping in a field in the nearby village of Coldharbour.

Details of the termination of the operation have become lost in the mistiness of time: no doubt only the first of many alcoholic amnesias to come. It is certain that Scout Leader and Latin teacher, Jack Lauder, and Captain Charles Grogan, Head of Signals and legendary chemistry teacher, would have made sure that all was well. Eventually, all returned to Guildford, once the buses started running.

The Contributors

Ian Barker was at the RGS Guildford from 1951 to 1959. He graduated from Charing Cross Hospital Medical School in 1964 and was a GP from 1968 to 2000, the last twenty-two years having been spent in the West Country. He has always walked rather than climbed but does know most of the Lake District Fells and still can walk ten miles a day in the Lakeland Valley hinterland.

School adventures in CCF and Scouting instilled in him a love of open air exploration now partially satisfied on Coastal Paths and Dartmoor Tors, with a regular January fix in the Dee Valley in the eastern Cairngorms.

David Benest was at the RGS from 1965 to 1972. He served in the British Army from then until 2009. David took up rock climbing while at the RGS, through the CCF, and progressed to Alpine mountaineering while in the Army. He started ski-mountaineering at the age of forty, in 1994 – and is still going strong. A run a day – plus fifty-seven press ups or sit ups – keeps his doctor away!

Keith Browning was at the RGS Guildford from January 1964 to June 1970. He gained a teaching qualification at Loughborough College and taught Physical Education in London, Leicestershire and Sussex for several years. He later joined the pharmaceutical industry as a salesman and, after that, as a training manager. He took early retirement in 2008 and is now living in North Portugal. As a school teacher, Keith became involved with many outdoor activity events, including trips to hilly parts of Wales, Yorkshire and France. He still enjoys walking, but now he keeps well away from the hills and prefers the seashore.

Colin Carmichael attended the RGS between 1965 and 1972 (Nettles House). He went on to study economics at the City of Birmingham Polytechnic before obtaining an MSc and a PhD from the London School of Economics. After a short time in the Civil Service he became a management consultant, first with Peat Marwick/ KPMG and then with a small specialist firm; he is still working as a consultant. He has two grown-up children; he and his wife live locally, in East Horsley. He still enjoys the 'great outdoors' and was a member of the RGS former pupils' expedition to Bhutan in 2008.

Dai Cowx arrived at the RGS Guildford in April 1984 on a one term part-time contract to cover maternity leave, and is still waiting to hear of the baby's arrival! He was soon appointed to a full-time position and has remained, teaching Geography at the RGS, ever since. He has been a Housemaster, has led the Scouts and has contributed over the years to the Duke of Edinburgh's Award and of course to X-country. Dai continues to be active in the mountains though now does fewer long and serious trips due to family commitments and trying to stop his knees falling apart from years of abuse. He is still very keen on off-road running, especially in the mountains when the opportunity arises.

Rupert Dix was at the RGS Guildford from 1983 to 1989. He is now Head of Sales Campaigns & Customer Support Business Management at AgustaWestland and still climbs regularly, mainly in North Wales and Scotland. He is also a keen target rifle shooter, regularly shooting with the Old Guildfordians Rifle Club.

David Dunmur was at the RGS from 1951 to 1959. His school experiences started a lifetime involvement with mountains, which still continues despite the physical constraints of aging. Retired for more than five years, he enjoyed the OGs' trek in Bhutan in 2008, but now is focused on remaining fit enough to ski. He still has hopes of scaling all the Pyrenean peaks visible from his house in Spain.

Malcolm Eldridge was at the RGS Guildford from 1954 to 1961. He is now retired and still intends to climb mainly in Wales and Europe when back and hip problems are resolved.

Ian Ferguson was at the RGS Guildford from 1983 to 1990. His current position in Management Consulting dealing with Russian aerospace arose from an adventurous approach to his profession, matched by his mountaineering cv with its esoteric, distinctive character. Ian's capacity for adventure will hopefully be rewarded for a long while yet with his marriage to Heidi and fatherhood of Robert (December 2009), both of whom tolerated some Hardangervidda by ski and pulk in April 2010.

Mike Floate was a student at the RGS Guildford from 1946 to 1953. He is now working as a private consultant in the field of Agricultural Science (Soils) in New Zealand, having spent thirty-two good years in academic research in Canada, Scotland and New Zealand. Mike is still active in the great outdoors, mainly tramping (ie hill-walking or hiking, for European and North American readers) in New Zealand. In the 2009 New Zealand New Years Honours List, Mike was awarded the Queen's Service Medal (QSM) for 'Services to Conservation and Mountaineering'. He does not believe that he deserves this as an individual but as part of a dedicated band of conservation-minded people in New Zealand.

Tom Fulda was at the RGS from 1971 to 1978 and is now a business consultant. He still enjoys hill-walking and trekking, both at home and abroad, as well as long-distance walking events.

Alex Jackson and Oliver Garnett were both at RGS Guildford (where Alex was Secretary of the RumDoodle Society) from 2004–2008. They are now both students at Cambridge and Imperial London Universities respectively, and currently just about find enough time to travel during the university vacations.

Miriam Manook was a Scholar at Marlborough College from 1997–1999. She is currently in London as a trainee surgeon and has a young son; her climbing at present is therefore limited to the views from Parliament Hill.

Bruno Marques studied at the RGS Guildford between 1995 and 2000, where he was involved in Cadets, Drama and Young Scientists. After two years at Godalming Sixth Form College, and a gap year spent learning to skydive, Bruno read Physics and Philosophy at University College, Oxford. While there, he juggled his academic subjects with extracurricular activities, including some obligatory rowing for the University College Rowing Team. During his second year, Bruno joined the Officers' Training Corps and completed the prestigious Cambrian Patrol, a long range exercise in Wales, before going on to pass out of Sandhurst as a Territorial Army Officer. After a second gap year spent travelling to Brazil, Bhutan and Hong Kong, where his fiancée worked for six months, Bruno joined the Metropolitan Police and is now working in the Criminal Investigation Department in East London.

Catherine Moorehead was brought up just north of the Cairngorms. She has been an English teacher at the RGS since 2001. As well as being an English literature enthusiast, she shares with Godwin-Austen a passion for adventure in high and remote places. An accomplished mountaineer, she has an enviable record of ascents (first and other), mainly in very obscure corners of Central Asia, and is a Compleat (*sic*) Munroist. She also has a desire to share her passion and expertise with others, particularly through school and other expeditions, and by writing about them.

James Moulang is currently studying at RGS Guildford and is about to enter the Upper Sixth. He climbs mainly in Skye and the Lake District.

Mike Norris was at the Royal Grammar School, Guildford from 1988 to 1993. He is now a Secondary School teacher and still climbs mainly in New Zealand.

Richard Payne was at Seaford College from 1980–1985. In 1985 he became a Young Explorer with the British Schools Exploration Society on an expedition to south-east Iceland. Since then, he has been a leader on trekking expeditions to India, Nepal and Tibet, Greenland and Svalbard. Richard is a qualified freelance International Mountain Leader and is currently assisting with Outdoor Education, Scouts, CCF and Duke of Edinburgh's Award expeditions at the Royal Grammar School Guildford.

Alison Raeside was at Godolphin & Latymer from 1969 to 1977. Her eldest son, James, was at the RGS Guildford from 2002–7. She is now a Circuit Judge in Surrey and Sussex. Alison walks (when family commitments allow) in Wester Ross, particularly the Applecross, Kintail and Torridon areas.

Mark Raeside was educated in Sheen and at the Universities of Canterbury and Cambridge. He is a Barrister and Arbitratror, and took Silk in 2002. He is a keen walker in Wester Ross and has, rather late in life, started to bag Munros.

Jeffrey Rawson was at the RGS Guildford from 2001–08. He took his Oxford degree in English from 2008–11, and is hoping to go to Guildford Law College from 2011–13. Jeff hasn't been climbing since some Pyrenees trekking in 2009, but will be heading off to Scotland again this summer as part of the Land's End to John O'Groats cycle route. Having thought that reconstructing the Ascent of RumDoodle was a bit too precarious, he is therefore aiming for a Three Men on the Bummel style adventure instead.

Richard Seymour is still a teacher at the Royal Grammar School Guildford, having started there in 1972; before this, he was at Leeds University. He continues to teach Geography and Rugby and is involved in running the Explorer Scout Unit which includes helping with mountaineering expeditions to such places as Snowdonia.

James Slater was at the RGS Guildford from 1999 to 2006. He is now a business consultant and still enjoys excursions to the mountains when the opportunity arises.

Mike Smith was at the RGS Guildford from 1951 to 1958. After a varied career in agriculture and software engineering, he now cultivates simple IT solutions for the family business while continuing to enjoy climbing – with friends or just solo – most often in Snowdonia, the French Alps and the Pyrenees.

Gareth Stewart was at the Royal Grammar School, Guildford from 1993 to 1995. He is now a project surveyor and when time permits still enjoys striding out in the UK. His mountaineering, however, is now generally limited to the French Alps, more often than not with skis on his back while trying to find untouched valleys through which to descend.

Jonathan Stuart was at RGS Guildford from 1982 to 1989. He is now Managed Services Director at Claremont and lives with his family near the Dorset coast where he enjoys walking and sailing.

Charles Vivian was at the Royal Grammar School Guildford from 1983–1989. He is now an IT consultant and entrepreneur and still climbs mainly in the Alps.

Alex Way was at the Royal Grammar School Guildford from 1999 to 2004. He is now a consultant in European public affairs in Brussels but still enjoys using his free time for hiking and running out in the wilds.

Steve Yetman was educated at Epsom College from 1990–1995 before going on to read Geography at University College London. During this time, and for several years afterwards, he also taught sailing and power-boating, finishing as the Senior Instructor of a large commercial watersports school. Following a brief spell in accountancy he joined the staff of the RGS Guildford in 2001. Today, as well as teaching Geography, he runs the CCF, Duke of Edinburgh's Award Scheme and coordinates the Period 8 activity programme. He still climbs throughout the UK and Europe.

Index